The Meaning of Rivers

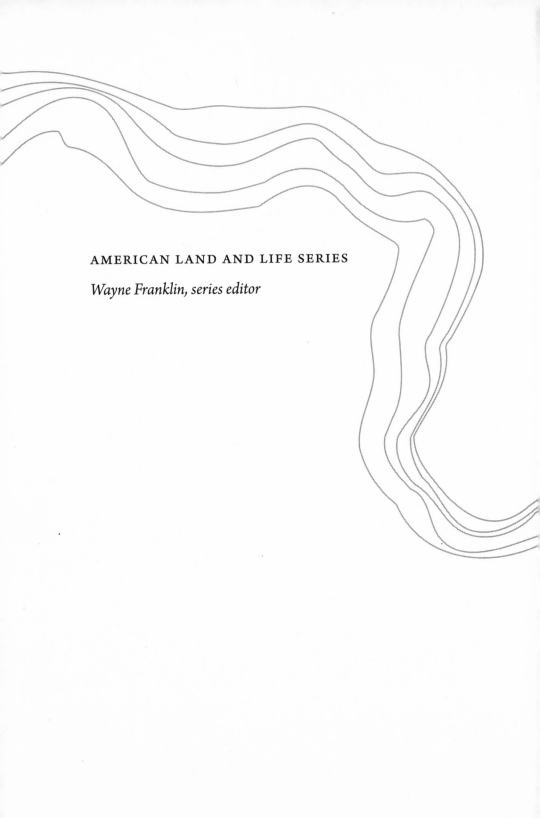

AMERICAN LAND AND LIFE SERIES

Wayne Franklin, series editor

The Meaning of Rivers

Flow and Reflection in American Literature

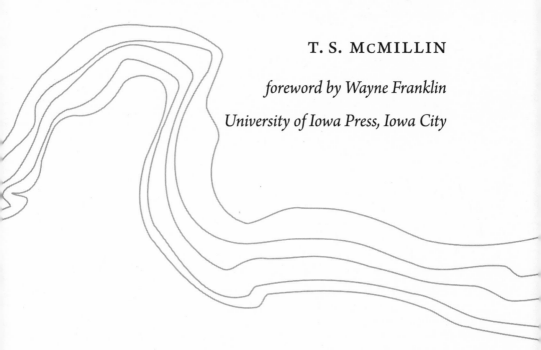

T. S. McMILLIN

foreword by Wayne Franklin

University of Iowa Press, Iowa City

University of Iowa Press, Iowa City 52242

Copyright © 2011 by the University of Iowa Press

www.uiowapress.org

Printed in the United States of America

Design by Ashley Muehlbauer

The University of Iowa Press is a member of Green
Press Initiative and is committed to preserving
natural resources.

Printed on acid-free paper

Library of Congress Cataloging-in-Publication Data

McMillin, T. S. (Tracy Scott)

The meaning of rivers: flow and reflection in
American literature / by T. S. McMillin; foreword
by Wayne Franklin.

p.   cm.

Includes bibliographical references and index.

ISBN-13: 978-1-58729-977-3 (pbk.)

ISBN-10: 1-58729-977-1 (pbk.)

ISBN-13: 978-1-58729-978-0 (e-book)

ISBN-10: 1-58729-978-X (e-book)

1. American literature—History and criticism.
2. Rivers in literature.   3. Philosophy of nature in
literature.   I. Title.

PS169.R58M38 2011

810.9'36—dc22   2010033132

Contents

Foreword | *Wayne Franklin*

Water floats memories. Think of any phase in your experience and soon you will find some stream twisting through your thoughts.

I remember very well, for example, the first time I saw the Grand Canyon. It was in June 1970, forty years ago now. I had driven north from Phoenix in a crippled VW bus and, after managing to locate a repair shop in Flagstaff, got back on the road and headed north again for the last few miles.

The landscape most of the way from California had been bleak and dry, with the sort of razor-edge beauty that only the early summer desert can attain. I had visited Sequoia National Park, but the drive since then had dried out my damp, green impressions of that place. Once past Barstow, I was launched on the real desert, and water was only a memory.

So when I got up the first morning at the Grand Canyon, left the camp-ground, and drove to the South Rim, the idea that I could hike down to confront the Colorado River was irresistibly enticing. With a full canteen and a little food, a snakebite kit, and a few other essentials, I found Bright Angel Trail and began descending. After a long period of zigzagging wonderment, with fresh views at every turn, the trail straightened, stretching out over the hot plateau. By lunchtime, I had arrived at Indian Garden, situated where a little mirage of cottonwoods had been growing and growing like a green spot in my sweaty eyes for some time. There actually was water there, and shade.

After that pause I went on my way, not out to Plateau Point, where I could have looked down at the still distant river and returned to the rim in good time, but rather farther and farther on. I went along the mule trail, which follows the route of Garden Creek before it passes into the channel that flows from Pipe Spring down to the Colorado. There was plenty of evidence of water along this route: in the greenery that, sparse as it was, nonetheless outdid anything I had been seeing for days; in the rock forma- tions themselves, which bespoke the force with which both wind and rain had been at work for longer than I cared to think; and then in the trickling flow from Pipe Spring. Soon, I discerned water's presence in an even more dramatic way, for the sound of thunder rumbled among the pagan temple forms that the Euro-American imagination, seeking some way to name and control the sheer energy of this place, has conjured up in the inner canyon. As I came around a bend, the sound became more than sound, for I was looking down on a thunderstorm as it made its way eastward above the still-invisible Colorado. Lightning flashed; thunder roared and rumbled, dying away amid rocks older by many millennia than Rome or Egypt or China. Perhaps I had looked down into a thunderstorm while airborne at some earlier time in my life, but seeing this one far below me in the canyon while my feet rested on the dusty earth and rocks towered above me created a rich feeling for the improbable structure of this desert world. Before too long, I was down at the edge of the Colorado, where I was struck by the force and size of the deep green river as it cut its way through the dark, hard gneiss and schist of the canyon walls. Everything here seemed to wear the color of the deep earth. As to the river: I could not cross it or even safely wade into it. So I stood and then sat, staring as its sound flooded my brain and the daylight, lost far above in the canyon, retreated into the sky. I had learned lessons, deep lessons, in the ponderous reality of water. For a time, the silly pretentiousness of those canyon temples disappeared and I thought only about the spiritual actuality of the river.

Memories such as these have continued to flow in my mind long after the outer images that they refer to have faded and then disappeared. Scott McMillin revives them for me in *The Meaning of Rivers*. His effort is both ambitious and disarmingly simple. He wants, as his title suggests, to set us thinking not about the surface of rivers, whether smooth and shiny or turbid and rough, but rather about their philosophical significance. "What do rivers mean?" he insists on asking us at the outset, and he will not let us off easy. We cannot reply that rivers are about the endless flow of experience, or that they mirror the fluid uncertainty of our souls—such clichés will not do. For one thing, he conceives of rivers in their intransigent *thereness*, their actuality. If rivers are to mean something, it will not be because we can forget actual flows of water, with the debris they carry and the work they do. It is because we remember their material reality that we will earn the right to ask the deeper questions he wants us to consider. McMillin therefore situates us at the outset on a bluff above that quintessential American river, the Mississippi.

It is too easy for humanists, who do not often have to deal with material reality, to speak in vague generalities. This is the point at which McMillin's simplicity disarms a reader. Having asked the big questions, he builds answers to them by patiently boxing the compass of fluvial writing. It is striking to think that the perspectival array he proposes, with its prepositional modesty, might just unlock a set of precious secrets. But that is what it does. The vector of a particular imaginative approach to so common a feature of earth—so common and so essential—tells us a good deal about how we regard rivers. But it also tells us a good deal about how we view life in general. We fight the power of the river (and the world), or we give ourselves to it; we contemplate the prospect of the water's beauty and energy without quite committing ourselves to the fray; we abide by the side of a river, fixing ourselves even as it refuses to be fixed.

The Meaning of Rivers might be deemed a primer, a fundamental guide to the nature of flowing water. It is more than that, too. It instructs readers in the art of placing themselves in and upon the world. The simple directional scheme this book employs, like that thunderstorm I came across so many years ago as a kind of prelude to the great Colorado itself, has the power of a revelation. In prose that combines the same traits—profundity and accessibility—Scott McMillin instructs us how to regard, and indeed how to launch ourselves upon, the world.

Introduction | *What Do Rivers Mean?*

Standing by the upper Mississippi and casting his eye out over the river, Larry, one of my brothers-in-law, wondered aloud about the human fascination with water. What attracts us to seashore, lakeside, or riverbank? So many things bear on such a question—elements of biology, psychology, chemistry, theology, geology, history, cosmology—that it is both difficult to know where to begin and unlikely that we will arrive at an end. Metaphorically, at least, water is everywhere, figuring prominently in life's flow. Physically, there is nothing like it in terms of its role in the development of life on Earth—water, scientists have shown, "plays a part in all physical and biological processes." As the late geomorphologist Luna Leopold observed, the earth's location in the solar system allows it to have a hydrologic cycle: "The grand circle of movement of water from ocean to atmosphere to continent and back to ocean is the essential mechanism that allows organisms— including humans—to emerge, to develop, and to live on Earth." We need water, we *are* water. Still, because the question of our interest in something so fundamental as water has so many elements, it has a mysterious, even a mystical quality. To me, Larry's question seems like asking, What does water mean? And that is like asking, What is the meaning of life?

This book represents an attempt to consider such questions, and because their scope is only exceeded by their complexity, I have tried to make them approachable by reformulating them into a smaller question: What do *rivers* mean? This one too is admittedly large. In the United States alone there are about three and a half million miles of rivers and streams, tens of thousands of waterways varying wildly in size and marked by vastly different regions. By its nature, each one of these streams consists of a complex interaction of matter and energy, creating a unique form running through a distinct setting bearing a diverse content and put to myriad uses. All of those variables make it difficult to pin "rivers" down as a category of knowledge. And we also have to consider the notorious paradoxical qualities of rivers, their ability to be or do several things at once. Rivers *move*, flowing over land, through history, and among diverse groups of people, changing considerably from their source to their destination; yet they also *stay*, permanent blue lines on our maps, constant waypoints and lasting landmarks. Rivers *connect*—state with state, interior with exterior, one region with another, the past with the present; but they also *separate* nations, subcultures, and families. In short, rivers do not cede their meanings easily.

And this brings me to "meaning" more generally, its own broad problems and those pertaining specifically to rivers. Commentators representing a range of interests—from business leaders to language philosophers to scientists engaged in postgenomic biosemiotics—have suggested that we humans, having arrived at the end of the age of information, now find ourselves on the cusp of an age of meaning. The upshot of such suggestions, though it varies with context, is that we are becoming increasingly concerned with meaning, that many cultures are experiencing a crisis in meaning—as if we have been suffering from a surfeit of information and cannot process it meaningfully; or as if there are too many different ways for making sense of all that information; or as if "meaning" itself no longer means what it used to mean. Recently, some scholars of science have referred the problem of meaning to a historical disconnect in our fundamental ways of making sense of the world and our place in it, noting that "nature and culture have been sharply separated in modern thought." Separating what we do (culture) from the world in which we do it (nature), we have treated meaning as *matter*. Meaning, in this respect, is something special, either a solid entity that resides in the world (put there by God and/or evolution) and is thus discoverable by human technology or a substance that is invented by humans and overlaid on the things of the world.

I propose to address the problem of meaning by thinking of it as involving both matter and energy, treating it as a fluid, as something that flows, rather than as a stable solid to be extracted or fabricated. As such, thinking about meaning can be aided by referring to rivers. My theory is that since water is essential for life, for being, it might have something to do with meaning as well. The planet's surface is over 70 percent water, and human beings—the planet's meaning-makers—also consist of about 65 percent water; water, therefore, should be part of our thinking. Erasmus, the great Dutch scholar, wrote about five hundred years ago that we should keep our thoughts well watered. Using satire to criticize "our grim Philosophers," earnest and thoughtful people "perpetually beating their brains on knotty Subjects," Erasmus observed that the majority of thinkers lacked a certain intellectual liquidity, causing them to age prematurely: "And whence is it, but that their continual and restless thoughts insensibly prey upon their spirits, and dry up their Radical Moisture." When book-dusty scholars or grim philosophers fail to consider that water is the root of life on Earth, they miss out on an important element of meaning and lose their intellectual fluidity. Thoughts harden as mental drought sets in. A few hundred years later the American scholar Ralph Waldo Emerson also urged a watering of our meaning-making efforts. "Embosomed for a season in nature," he wrote in his first book, "whose floods of life stream around and through us, and invite us by the powers they supply, to action proportioned to nature, why should we grope among the dry bones of the past?"

Although this book deals with the past, with what others have written about rivers in the first half-millennium of American literature, I am trying to do something other than grope among dry bones. Bringing together different meanings of American rivers and ideas regarding the fluidity of meaning itself, I explore the connection to better understand the present. That, to me, is the purpose of scholarship, whether in the humanities or the sciences. If to neglect the life streaming around and through us is to bury scholarship in arid soil, then even literary study would seem to require some recognition of the watery world in which works are written and read—a proposition I have made on more than one occasion. Discussing the flow of water in Henry David Thoreau's writing at a public lecture in Grand Junction, Colorado, about a mile from the confluence of the Colorado and Gunnison rivers, I aroused the suspicions of a teenager in the audience who asked, with a mix of curiosity and exasperation, "What do rivers and literature have to do with one another?"

It's a good question. For one thing, it suggests that for some (and maybe for many), rivers and literature do not belong together. They occupy significantly different conceptual categories. We tend to separate rivers from literature in the same way we separate what we think of as nature from what we think of as culture. It also suggests to me a sense that literature—especially when written with a capital L—has been kept dry by numerous cultural devices. The proper storage of Literature, in libraries, canons, and anthologies, on special shelves in bookstores and in high school and college curricula, under the watchful eye of Men of Letters, and so on, has ensured its preservation but has also contributed to its desiccation, perhaps its ossification. Even among literary scholars and cultural theorists who insist upon placing literature in relation to the world and worldly affairs, such things as rivers, streams, and other elements of the biosphere have received less attention than matters pertaining to the social sphere. Academically considered, the physical world has been given to hard sciences, the social world to the softer sciences, and some sort of dream world remains for the humanities; we have come to think that such divisions represent common sense. In bringing rivers and literature together, I have found that both rivers and literary works have more meaning and more life in them than we commonly suspect.

Perhaps a reason for this is, as I hinted above, that the systems by which we make meaning are somewhat analogous to river systems. It's not a perfect correspondence, but meaning is like a river in that both involve complex systems. A river, according to fluvial geomorphologists, comprises three subsystems: flow (the water moving through the channel as well as the sediment load it bears), form (the shape, slope, and constitutional makeup of the channel), and the interactions between flow and form (a "process-response" system). Meaning might be said to resemble this model insofar as it involves the mind's directed energy (flow), the world of things, ideas, images, and senses (form), and especially the interactions between flow and form. Out of these three subsystems comes meaning. Literature presents a special set of conditions in which we can study meaning, and literature involving rivers offers a rich resource for understanding meaning's fluidity. In this definition, literature does not simply represent the production and preservation of works of writing that have been accorded special status; instead, it represents a way of bringing together two complicated systems, rivers and meaning, to see what each can tell us about the other. Literature, in my approach, becomes a series of events, with indefinite origins and ends, involving acts of reading and writing, yielding interpretations that contribute meaning to our efforts to understand the world in which we live.

Having thus explained why literature might be suitable for a study of the meaning of rivers, I should give some idea of how literature has been shaped for the purpose of that study. Given the range and complexity of pertinent materials to be studied, selecting and organizing the works are daunting tasks. Of those tens of thousands of U.S. waterways, hundreds if not thousands have been treated in hundreds of thousands of poems, novels, histories, autobiographies, plays, essays, travel accounts, and tales. From 1937 to 1974 a series of sixty-five books—each on a particular North American stream—appeared under the august imprint of Rivers of America. From the Kennebec River of Maine to the American River in California, these works collected the stories of some of the most prominent examples of flowing water in the continent. Even so, the series is just a raindrop in the ocean of pertinent materials. Rivers played important roles in American writings before Americans were doing the writing. To avoid a mere catalog of all applicable works or an encyclopedia of literary rivers while still considering a wide array of writings, I have limited my study to works that wrestle with rivers to make meaning and that wrestle with meaning to understand rivers. These selections don't just describe rivers or tell good stories about rivers or say something pretty; they raise questions about and in some cases deal with the confluence of meaning and flowing water.

In other words, the present work is not intended as a comprehensive literary history of American river writings. It is more of an associative field guide designed to assist two different groups of readers: (1) those who are interested in rivers but may not have given literature much attention and (2) those interested in literature who may not have given rivers much attention. To bring out the meanings of rivers and selected works that feature them, I have adopted an organizing principle based upon six different ways of experiencing a stream and its flow:

1. overlooking the river (looking down upon flowing water from some height);
2. by the river (being close to or in a particular section of a river);
3. up the river (going against the current);
4. down the river (going with the current);
5. crossing the river;
6. up and down the river.

This half-dozen can be further organized into a set of pairs that describe increasingly complex modes of river experience. Modes 1 and 2 represent the most basic experience of a river; 3 and 4 entail a more immediate and sustained experience of a river's flow, either with it or against it; 5 and 6 represent greater complexity of experience through a movement that is perpendicular to the flow (neither with nor against it) or that goes both ways (with and against the flow).

 The categories directly relate to the idea that the meaning itself involves energy. Treating meaning as having both matter and energy sets things in motion. Writers whose works concern rivers often connect to and make use of that energy to convey other meanings; the energy of rivers makes their writings particularly meaningful. Accordingly, I have selected works that use rivers to tap into that energy of meaning in its various manifestations. The chapter "Overlooking the River" explores writing that entails a removal, a distancing from the river's energy; the writer can observe the shape of the river but, in seeing it remotely, may miss out on some of its meaning. In "By the River" the river's energy flows before us, around us, or over us; the writer or character is observant of that kinetic flowing and reflects on its meaning. Struggle with the energy of the river is central to the experiences detailed in "Up the River"; in these works meaning comes from the clash of forces, the will of the writer or character pitted against the flow of the river. The movement tends to be back into the past or the forgotten wild. Conversely, the writings in "Down the River" move with the energy of the river, carried along by it, taken forward into the future, into newness and the unknown. The complex categories covered in "Crossing the River" and "Up and Down the River" involve, respectively, transversals of the flow and double exposure to the properties of its force and portent.

I have chosen literary works that represent each of these categories in a way that might be applied to the understanding of other works and other streams. Different rivers mean different things to different writers, and my interpretation of literary rivers attempts to bring out these differing connotations so that more rivers will mean more to more people. My aim, along with developing a better sense of the cultural value of significant natural phenomena, is to see how literary scholarship might better contribute to the study of nature. And this may partially explain why I have imagined two possibly disparate groups (though there are indeed many instances of an intersection between them) as a potential audience for my study. By bringing literary matters to the attention of those interested in rivers, I hope to make a case for the importance of humanistic inquiry in the understanding of nature; by bringing rivers to the attention of those interested in literature, I hope to make a case for the importance of nature in humanistic inquiry.

There are more examples of works that do the latter than do the former. For example, Prudence J. Jones has recently published a valuable study of rivers in Roman literature; Wyman H. Herendeen's *From Landscape to Literature: The River and the Myth of Geography* offers an insightful history of rivers with a focus on British literature before 1900; and two volumes by John Seelye that explore the role of rivers in U.S. literary history from the age of exploration to the early republic provide a weighty resource for historians and literary critics. These works, written for scholars in the writers' respective fields, are chock-full of information regarding the life of the past and the import of rivers in Western culture. Building off these efforts, I attempt to connect rivers and literature for a broader audience and create something full of life in the present. To do so I have spent almost as much time getting wet during fieldwork as I have staying more or less dry in libraries. In the course of my studies I have sat by, stood with fishing pole in, walked along, fallen into, canoed and rafted and pontooned on, swum in, kayaked (and at least once nearly drowned) in, waded across, ferried over, and gazed down upon a fair number of watercourses, including most of those discussed in the book. In combining the observations of the field with the findings of the library, I have sought to perform "the office of the scholar" as it was described by Emerson: to be educated by the primary "influences"—"by nature, by books, and by action"—and to fashion as true a report as I can out of those influences for the sake of inspiring and cheering on my fellow travelers to see something truly for themselves.

I do not intend my reference to Emerson here to set him up as the model scholar or to depict his Transcendentalism as the path to the truest understanding of the meaning of rivers. Transcendentalism, while in some versions escapist and abstruse, is not always such and is not inherently bad, especially when it promotes engaged attention to the world and its problems. But in bringing together a range of writings about rivers for a diverse audience, I have tried to develop a style of thinking about meaning that involves the recognition of the fluidity of nature, the questioning of prevailing ways of understanding the world, and critical and reflective imagination. It is, as I hope to show, a style of thinking that can be of use in investigations of both the meaning of rivers and the nature of meaning. These tendencies have not resulted in a comprehensive and linear literary history but rather in a selection of works that bear up well under that style of thinking, a grouping of those works meant to keep them alive, and the pursuit of a way of reading that prefers "onwardness" to stagnation.

What rivers have meant can help us think about what rivers do mean and perhaps what rivers might mean. As a culture, because of the diversity of groups that constitute that culture and because of the knottiness of the subject, we have not collectively made up our minds about what rivers mean—which implies that the possibility exists of changing the way we think about rivers. This is why I have imagined the study as fostering another grand junction, a coming together of various parties. One certainly could argue that, given the numerous problems surrounding rivers (problems of water quality and quantity as well as questions about watershed health and human well-being), what rivers *mean* is the least of our worries. In my view, however, we have a crisis in meaning to go along with serious environmental crises, and in fact these crises are related to one another. Many scientists, including Luna Leopold, believe that the people of the United States "have acquiesced to the destruction and degradation of our rivers, in part because we have insufficient knowledge of the characteristics of rivers and the effects of our actions that alter their form and process." His book attempts to correct that insufficiency from a geological perspective. That, however, is only part of the picture and does not include myriad other views and values of the rivers of America. The present work explores what we have thought about when we have thought about flowing water, to compare and disseminate those thoughts in a way to prompt further thinking.

1 | *Overlooking the River*

Our local newspaper ran a syndicated strip on the funny pages that provides a tragicomic introduction to rivers and meaning in the twenty-first-century United States. In the strip a father and his teenage son stand on a bluff looking down upon a stream as it flows through a valley, sun setting in the background, the tranquil atmosphere nearly cloudless except for a wisp of a cirrus, a flock of birds in the distance hovering above the water. The father, with his walking stick in one hand, gestures toward the river with the other and speaks to his son, who stands with hands in pockets and follows the direction of the gesture, looking out on the prospect. We cannot tell what the father is saying, for the speech-bubble of the panel is blank, just another white cloud in the sky. In the next four panels, the father becomes increasingly animated, his gestures suggesting the profound importance of the particular place in his life, but the speech-bubbles remain empty. The sequence winds up with the father's energetic embrace of his son and then (sniff) the wiping away of a tear. In the fifth and final frame the son removes an earpiece, obviously connected to an iPod or the like, and says, "I'm sorry. Were you saying something?" The father looks at his son silently, deflated and dismayed.

Perhaps because my wife and I have two sons whom we have dragged to many a fine prominence, the parental dismay strikes a chord. But the strip also interests me on an intellectual level, for in more ways than one it involves "overlooking rivers." First, the father looks out over the river and its valley, valuing the vista and wanting deeply to share the significance of the scene. He overlooks the river in the sense of enjoying an *overview* of it, a prospect of the grandeur of nature and its seemingly inherent meaning. In the son's response to the scene and in the consequent breakdown in the communication of the perceived meaning, another kind of overlooking comes to the surface, overlooking as a kind of neglect. Plugged into his personal music collection, the son misses the purport of his father's river-related effusions. Both of these types of overlooking happen frequently in North American culture, often simultaneously, and both are thus part of the meaning of rivers in this land, throughout its history at least since the presence of European immigrants. American literature is littered with examples of river-related overlook. For example, in the journals kept by Meriwether Lewis and William Clark, the explorers' seminal account of the May 1804 to September 1806 expedition into the newly acquired territory west of the Mississippi River, we often find one or both of the captains standing above a waterway, overlooking rivers for a variety of reasons: to determine where they are or the best way to proceed, as at the confluence of the Marias River and the Missouri River (June 5, 1805) or at the rapids of the Columbia River (October 24, 1805); to survey the land, its flora and fauna, and to compile an inventory (as directed by President Jefferson); but also for aesthetic pleasure, a recurrence that leads to a remarkable profusion of ways in which to spell "beautiful."

The other kind of overlooking—neglecting, ignoring, not seeing, or not recognizing the importance of a river—has an even longer history in this country. Take, for example, the Delaware River, a wide and slow-moving stream for much of its four hundred miles, stretching from the Catskills to the Delaware Bay and meeting tidewater around Trenton, New Jersey.

Overlooking the Delaware is nothing new. In his account of his 1524 voyage up the coast of North America, Giovanni da Verrazano, probably the first European to see the river, dismissed the significance of the Delaware on his way to what would become New York, as if he were late for an appointment in Manhattan. Less than a century later, Henry Hudson, in the employ of the Dutch East India Company, sailed into what became Delaware Bay and a little way up the river, but, feeling the purse strings tug all the way from Holland and finding the river a challenge to navigate, he too left the river unexplored.

Not long after Hudson poked his prow up the river in August 1609, the lives of a thousand or so Lenni Lenape were disrupted by Dutch, Swedish, and English colonizers, and the overwhelmingly "pleasant tasting water" of the river began to change. In a 1972 study engineer Robert V. Thomann observed that "from its earliest beginnings the quality of the waters of the Delaware has largely been taken for granted." Noting that all sorts of waste were discharged into the stream and its tributaries, forcing Philadelphians to seek elsewhere for unpolluted drinking water, Thomann concluded that "the country was just too busy with many more important matters than the quality of its rivers and streams."

This has changed—somewhat. In the last half of the twentieth century efforts were begun to clean up the Delaware, and some have succeeded. The Delaware, however, is not the only neglected river in the United States, and pollution is only one way (albeit the most obvious and most immediately destructive way) in which we have forgotten, disregarded, or ignored the nature of flowing water and the meaning of rivers. In the nineteenth century Henry David Thoreau quipped that his hometown of Concord, Massachusetts, was "but little conscious how much interest it has" in the Concord River and "might vote it away any day thoughtlessly." In the twentieth century, discussing the neglect exhibited by "the preeminent city on the longest river in America," William Least Heat-Moon wrote that "Kansas City, born of the Missouri, has turned away from its great genetrix." Philip Fradkin suggests that, due to the lack of care for the Colorado River, it is "a river no more." Americans, it would seem, have overlooked rivers east and west, south and north, as if overlooking were a by-product of American business, whether we take that to mean our nation's commercial and industrial activity or a general tendency to keep busy that decreases time for reflection.

The rivers of North America have not always been overlooked. In the case of the Delaware, beginning with the Transitional or Terminal Archaic peoples who lived in the region between 1800 and 800 BCE, the river's floodplains were the primary place of residence. The Lenape were drawn to the Delaware, especially near the confluence with the Schuylkill River, by the abundance of fish and game, and they called the latter river "Manayunk," Place Where We Go to Drink. Early European transplants crowded onto the banks of the river: around 1701 "practically all two thousand of [Philadelphia's] inhabitants insisted on living as close to the Delaware as they could get." Even today much of our business and some of our pleasure, for good and ill, are directly with or on rivers. But except when major floods occur, little formal attention is paid to the nature and significance of streams.

Yet another problem arises when we do pay attention due to the manner in which attention is paid. In some cases, by looking at rivers in a certain way, we miss their larger meanings. If you were to climb one of the bluffs overlooking the upper Mississippi River (say, Brady's Bluff in Trempealeau County, Wisconsin), you would obtain an outstanding view of the nation's central waterway as well as the prairie below to the north and east and the bluffs across the river on the Minnesota side, with an occasional farm silo glimmering in the distance. If you are schooled in geology, you might be able to discern an ancient history, consisting of long-ago seas covering the land and then subsiding, epochs of erosion and drainage, and side-winding river-channel migration. The scope and power of that history can overwhelm other elements of the river's meaning, including tales of human history: traces of the earliest Native American peoples found in burial and ceremonial mounds, demographic shifts due to European colonization and changing economic tides, old-time water-ski recreation and lock-and-dam construction, loved ones lost to drowning. For a family of campers at the state park or a casual hiker, thoughts might revolve around the scene's effect on the senses, a feeling of being in the presence of timeless splendor and extended horizons. Depending on the measure of interest allotted to each of us in physical sciences, social history, and scenery aesthetics, the Mississippi we see can differ mightily from another's Mississippi, and the river we see might cause us to miss another river. Even when we do look at rivers, knowledgeably and lovingly, we very well might overlook important aspects of their meaning.

Lay Low and Hold Your Breath, for I'm 'Bout to Turn Myself Loose: Craft on the Mississippi

I am not the first to observe this phenomenon of overlooking. If you had stood on Brady's Bluff in the late spring of 1882, you might have espied Mark Twain leaning out over the rail of a steamboat. Twain devoted an ample portion of *Life on the Mississippi* (1883) to a discussion of overlooking the river in the sense of missing its meaning, from historical episodes up through the contemporary period, whether due to systems of value, inexperience, poor reading skills, or incomplete thinking. Twain was born Samuel Langhorne Clemens in 1835 in the tiny town of Florida, Missouri;

he and his family moved east to Hannibal, a town on the Mississippi River, in 1839. He began training as a steamboat pilot in 1857, and his account of that momentous apprenticeship appeared in a seven-part series of articles ("Old Times on the Mississippi") in the *Atlantic Monthly* in 1875, to be reprised in *Life on the Mississippi*. That was a dozen years after Clemens had become "Mark Twain," a pen name he crafted from materials supplied by the riverboat trade, the term referring to water that was two fathoms (twelve feet) deep, just enough for navigation of larger vessels. The name, the river-related derivation of which he explained in "Old Times" and *Life*, developed into more than a pseudonym: in the transformation from Samuel Clemens, Mark Twain became a real character, that fictional self taking on its own reality. As a literary icon and one of the nation's best-known celebrity writers, Twain literally (and doubly) became a man of letters: a craftsman of literature and a man made up of letters crafted within the realm of literature.

One could argue that the difference between the man and the author, Sam Clemens and Mark Twain, is academic, of interest only to those scholars and critical theorists who have disputed such matters for thirty or forty years. *Life on the Mississippi*, however, makes evident that the issue has importance for those who delve into the meaning of rivers. Just as the invention and promotion of "Mark Twain" imply a shift in attention from a real fellow (Clemens) to a made-up figure (Twain), so too does *Life* shift readers' attention from the actual, material river to a literary, conceptual river. These shifts, in turn, suggest that meaning emerges from the intersection of the material and the conceptual; such a move does not make the river less real, but it does make literature "realer" than we usually consider it to be. And it gives authors themselves a greater material worth in two senses of the phrase: what authors do (craft things out of letters) becomes a substantial activity, something that matters; and thus their craft might be valued more highly. Clemens, shrewd man that he was, reinvented himself as Mark Twain in order to better earn a living; for similar reasons, he reinvented the Mississippi. Both of these inventions accumulated new meanings.

By looking into the river Twain crafts, we can learn something about the relations between rivers and their meaning. Although many of Twain's most famous works made use of the Mississippi (including *Tom Sawyer* [1876], which recounted Clemens's boyhood days by the river; the down-the-river escapades of *The Adventures of Huckleberry Finn* [1884]; and *Pudd'nhead Wilson* [1894], a novel examining race, social conventions, and identity in a small Missouri town on the river), *Life on the Mississippi* presented his most focused and sustained treatment of the river. To write the book Twain drew on his prior experiences in the steamboat trade but also revisited the river (accompanied by his publisher and his stenographer) long after he last stood behind the wheel. The literary-motivated return provided Twain with the opportunity to physically overlook the Mississippi again in such places as Brady's Bluff above Trempealeau and Cardiff Hill above his old hometown. It also provided the needed conceptual overlook, the chance to reconsider the river, its history, its present, and his own history with the river for the sake of crafting it all into a book. The Clemens party headed down to New Orleans from St. Louis, stopping in Cairo, Memphis, Vicksburg, and Baton Rouge, spending a week in New Orleans, and then headed upriver, visiting St. Louis and Hannibal before continuing on up to the northern reaches of the river in Illinois, Iowa, Wisconsin, and finally Minnesota. The boats he traveled in, those on which he learned piloting and those on which he voyaged years later as a passenger, serve as vessels for his authorial perspective and thus offer readers a closer view of the river from a moving standpoint as well as a firsthand lesson on overlooking rivers.

From the very first chapter of the book ("The River and Its History"), the author divulges his interest in a textual river, a river of letters. He promises that "the Mississippi is well worth reading about" and that in order to get to know the Mississippi, you must familiarize yourself with some of the various texts (historical, mythological, sociological, geographical, political, literary) surrounding the river. (Twain calls this the "historical history" of the river as opposed to its "physical history.") Crafting the Mississippi entails weaving together a multitude of facts, figures, images, and mysteries and then shaping these pieces and threads into a meaningful story. Any individual image or fact on its own does not carry much of the river's meaning; each bit must be related to the other, and the diversity of available materials requires that the resulting picture will be complex. Take, for instance, the "fact" that in 1542 Hernando de Soto became "the first white man who ever saw the Mississippi River." (Most reference sources these days make it 1541.) Twain muses that facts alone do not suffice. They must be "grouped" with others, put into relation with other potentially significant items along with an author's informed and reasonable glossing of things, and thereby formed into a text: "The date 1542, standing by itself, means little or nothing to us; but when one groups a few neighboring historical dates and facts around it, he adds perspective and color." Twain uses Soto to illustrate an important point regarding rivers and their meaning: one needs to "interpret" facts rather than merely "state" them, and meaning emerges from interpretation and the writer's ability to "paint a picture."

Twain, of course, is not saying that facts are insignificant or that the river itself is meaningless. In the same chapter he points out that the river can even change the very meanings that we give it, highlighting the Mississippi's shifting nature, its ability to restructure political boundaries and "alter its locality." The big river moves from one place to another, "always changing its habitat *bodily*," that is, changing its channel by "always moving bodily *sidewise*." This fluctuating nature can alter the relation of one town to another and even possibly affect the status of human beings. The writer relishes the river's proclivity to form "cut-offs," its "disposition to make prodigious jumps by cutting through narrow necks of land, and thus straightening and shortening itself." Discussing the nature of cutoffs, Twain connects these physical changes in the river with their geopolitical effects, delighted that the river can destabilize the world by wreaking havoc with town lines and state jurisdictions. He speculates that "such a thing, happening in the upper river in the old times, could have transferred a slave from Missouri to Illinois and made a free man of him." For Twain, the interplay between the natural history of the river (physical facts) and its social history (facts from "historical history") requires the kind of perspective that comes from conceptual overlook. This overlook enables an author to craft a text from the grouping of sundry facts into carefully designed categories, which results in a meaningful picture.

But how shall facts be grouped? According to what perspective? With the addition of which colors? Once we have accepted that the Mississippi is a river full of meaning and that facts alone do not suffice but have to be selected, combined, and ordered according to the author's judgment and preferences, we might then begin to wonder about the context in which the Mississippi's meaning is being crafted. *Life on the Mississippi* encourages such wonder by reconsidering some of the previous meanings accorded the river. There appears to be some doubt as to whether the river has any inherent "value," since the river went unwanted and unnoticed for a number of years after Soto's "discovery." Twain remarks, "Apparently nobody happened to want such a river, nobody needed it, nobody was curious about it; so, for a century and a half the Mississippi remained out of the market and undisturbed. When Soto found it, he was not hunting for a river, and had no present occasion for one; consequently he did not value it or even take any particular notice of it." Twain here suggests a connection between economics and meaning, as if the Mississippi lacked meaning because it lacked economic uses, as if overlooking (neglecting) the river were a function of the market.

Twain at once fosters and questions that connection in his account. He concludes the discussion of Soto by observing that overlooking the Mississippi's value was not remedied until "La Salle the Frenchman" came to the belief that the river would tender "a short cut from Canada to China" and facilitate trade with the East. "Why did these people want the river now when nobody had wanted it in the five preceding generations? Apparently it was because at this late day they thought they had discovered a way to make it useful." The brief chapter on La Salle and other explorers of the Mississippi concludes with France "stealing" the country from Native peoples in the name of "Louis the Putrid." The next chapter, which begins, "Apparently the river was ready for business, now," turns to a study of commercial traffic on the river. The heavy emphasis on the steady growth of both the "white population" and "commerce" serves to reduce the Mississippi's meaning to its "value" or "usefulness," though Twain's thrice-repeated "apparently" slyly (and wryly) undercuts the accuracy of these apparent facts. Readers are subtly led to wonder if each particular observation is true or if it just seems so.

Chapter 3 ("Frescoes from the Past") initially seems to answer the question on the side of economic value by providing a concise history of commerce that highlights up-and-down-the-river traffic. First it was the "great barges," the "keelboats" and "broadhorns" that floated down to New Orleans and then were arduously poled or pulled back upriver, a round-trip taking nine months, more or less, until "the steamboat intruded" and changed the nature of river trade, eventually "absorb[ing] the entire commerce." The Mississippi, now open for business, means business. But Twain shifts abruptly from these historical facts to a lengthy fictional "illustration" of boatmen's ways, declaring, "I will throw in, in this place, a chapter from a book which I have been working at, by fits and starts, during the past five or six years, and may possibly finish in the course of five or six more." The book to which the writer refers is *The Adventures of Huckleberry Finn*, and its inclusion here, along with the mention of the difficulties surrounding its production, contributes to the textual nature of *Life on the Mississippi*. The chapter ultimately ends with another abrupt shift, from Huck's fictional "adventure" to Twain's promise of a "full examination" of "the marvellous science of piloting."

What does this mean for the meaning of rivers? Twain's book on the Mississippi stakes a claim for an essential connection between the river and literature, and that claim depends upon a special definition of literature. Not merely the telling of tales, literature "brings together widely separated things that are in a manner related to each other," as Twain later wrote in his autobiography. The production of such literature requires the active intelligence of the man of letters, whose position allows him to look out over the many pieces of a river's meaning—historical facts, personal reminiscence, changing economic value, tall tales, science—and craft them into a meaningful whole. Such literature, the author hopes, will hold "pleasant surprises and contrasts" for the reader and, in the example of *Life on the Mississippi*, will help readers overcome their ignorance of the Big Muddy. The story Twain tells about the river boils down to this: you can't get the meaning of the river from history alone, or from science alone, or from adventure tales, or from an older fellow's memories. Meaning comes from the muddy mix of all these and more.

Let us further consider the mud. It would be wrong for me to suggest that Twain presents readers with a neat picture of literature or meaning; in fact, his picture is a downright mess. But, as is the case with the nutritional value of river water, the more mud, the better. A character in the *Finn* fragment—the Child of Calamity—holds that "a man that drunk Mississippi water [compared to the "clear water" of the Ohio] could grow corn in his stomach if he wanted to." Twain's river book is itself a cold glass of earth-water admixture, a mud-infused literature with nutrients aplenty. In the chapters that revolve around Twain's treatment of the science of piloting, he thickens the mud and deepens the textual nature of the Mississippi by describing his experience "learning the river"—an experience that tellingly depends upon a metaphor of literacy. Learning the river, for Twain, means learning the river like a book, as if the thick texture of the Mississippi water required a textual approach to the river. Literature provides a vantage point from which readers can survey the myriad elements of a river's meaning, delighting in the surprise connections and working through the puzzling contrasts.

Though nutritious, Mississippi mud also presents some problems. The writer commences the story of his river education by remembering some of the obstructions to truly knowing "the great Mississippi, the majestic, the magnificent Mississippi, rolling its mile-wide tide along, shining in the sun." So glorious a body of water of course commanded the attention of all who peopled it and engendered in many a longing to be a part of it, especially to participate in steamboat commerce. "Boy after boy managed to get on the river," Twain writes, and he describes how he himself "by and by" ran away, saying he "never would come home again till I was a pilot and could come in glory." The "desire to be a steamboatman" belonged to the bundle of romanticized notions that Hannibal boys toted with them; it weighed more heavily upon them than the drive to join the circus, to perform in a minstrel show, or even to become a pirate. In Twain's hands these "comforting day-dreams of the future" number among the obstructions to his truly knowing the river, along with his tendency to adopt a pose, a pronounced lack of clarity in his thinking ("I never was great in matters of detail"), and his susceptibility to be carried away by the marvelous stories of others.

The latter trait is exemplified by the tales of the first mate on the *Paul Jones*, tales that serve as a warning about the dangers of fiction. Twain, describing the effect of hearing the storyteller's "incredible adventures," recalls that he "drank in his words hungrily, and with a faith that might have moved mountains if it had been applied judiciously," but without looking carefully at the source of the stories (a man "soiled and seedy and fragrant with gin") or the style of their conveyance ("his grammar was bad, his construction worse, and his profanity . . . void of art"). Completely caught up in the tales, "speechless, enjoying, shuddering, wondering, worshipping," young Twain fails to recognize them as "low, vulgar, ignorant, sentimental, half-witted humbug" until much later. As a first lesson for one bent on learning the river, Twain's tale of the mate's storytelling serves as a warning for readers and writers of the Mississippi. Ensuing chapters make clear that Twain himself, prior to his training as a pilot, was terribly uneducated in regard to the nature and meaning of the Mississippi, despite—or perhaps because of—having grown up by the river. His sentimentalized notions of life on the Mississippi and related fantasies cause him to overlook the nature of the river.

If overly romantic ideas about either the river or himself prevent Twain from knowing the Mississippi, then a decidedly unromantic, objective, analytic approach would seem to be a reasonable remedy. Twain proposes that the "science of piloting" epitomizes such an approach and casts it as the right and proper education for those interested in "learning the river." Having finally arrived in New Orleans on the *Paul Jones* and experiencing the deflation of various dreams (and the loss of a good portion of his little supply of cash to a conniving youth), Twain contracted with pilot Horace Bixby to become his apprentice, or "cub." Bixby agreed to instruct his cub in river navigation from New Orleans to St. Louis, and Twain "entered upon the small enterprise of 'learning' twelve or thirteen hundred miles of the great Mississippi River with the easy confidence of my time of life. If I had really known what I was about to require of my faculties, I should not have had the courage to begin." As they head up the Mississippi, Bixby first tries to teach Twain that a pilot must know how to interpret the water's signs; but, lacking the context for making sense of those signs (names of particular features of the river, their effects on the water, etc.), Twain cannot process the information: when Bixby identifies a "point" (the extension of land on the inside of a river bend), Twain remarks, "It was pleasant enough information, but I could not see the bearing of it. I was not conscious that it was a matter of any interest to me." In other words, he misses the point of the point; the information has no meaning for him. This particular "point" and all the others that his teacher identifies "were monotonously unpicturesque. I hoped Mr. Bixby would change the subject." At this point Twain cannot learn the river because he cannot read it. And he cannot read it because the information he is provided does not meet the criteria that he has come to value, for he values only the picturesque, the romantic, the fantastic, and the self-aggrandizing.

Among the troubles that muddy his ability to know the river, Twain finds first that his own preconceptions need to be discarded or undone or at least marked in order to make room for new information. The lesson he receives from the pilot and passes along to his readers entails discovering that his head is full of lies, myths, and fantasies about the river; a head full of such things, he finds, is unfortunately rather empty. Admitting that his imagined Mississippi differs from the real river he has set out to learn, Twain begins "to fear that piloting was not quite so romantic as I had imagined it was; there was something very real and work-like about this new phase of it." The cub becomes painfully aware that he doesn't know anything about the river; in fact, if Bixby teaches Twain anything in those early stages of the education, it's that Twain knows next to nothing. Pleased with the fantasy river but ignorant of the actual one, he overlooks details and fails to retain those that permeate the fog of preconception surrounding his consciousness. Not long after the initial lessons, Bixby questions his cub on the identity of the first point upriver from New Orleans. Twain reports, "I was gratified to be able to answer promptly, and I did. I said I didn't know." After failing to answer a single question correctly, Twain suffers the increasing ire of his teacher. Yet another "'I—I—don't know'" from the pupil causes Bixby to storm, "'What *do* you know?'" Twain shamefacedly replies, "'I—I—nothing, for certain.'"

The young fellow's confession serves as something of a breakthrough. The realization that he has truly overlooked the river by which he has lived gives him the chance to finally learn something; all that misinformation previously inhabiting the cubbyholes of his mind has been driven out by the wrath of Bixby, who exclaims, "'You're the stupidest dunderhead I ever saw or ever heard of, so help me Moses! The idea of *you* being a pilot—*you*! Why, you don't know enough to pilot a cow down a lane.'" When Twain explains that he thought his teacher was merely trying "to be entertaining" by passing along river information, Bixby's rage reaches its limit, and he pilots the steamboat into a trading scow, causing him to unleash a mad torrent of curse words: "When he closed the window he was empty. You could have drawn a seine through his system and not caught curses enough to disturb your mother with." The writer follows the humorous image of the cuss-disburdened pilot with a key moment in the lesson: the discovery and subsequent emphasis on the fundamental connection between rivers and literacy. To demonstrate not only why "the Mississippi is well worth reading about" but also how one ought to read about it, Twain suggests ties between water and words, pilots (especially Bixby, the consummate reader of the river) and writers (especially Twain, the consummate man of letters). Those parallels make the Bixby-Twain lessons even more intriguing and the resulting text even muddier.

Just Like A B C: Lessons in River Literacy

When Bixby recovers himself, he tells his protégé, in "the gentlest way," two strikingly alphabetic pieces of advice for students of the river: "'My boy, you must get a little memorandum-book, and every time I tell you a thing, put it down right away. There's only one way to be a pilot, and that is to get this entire river by heart. You have to know it just like A B C.'" Up to this point Twain has been telling his readers about the many threads that are woven into the text of the Mississippi. He has used his craft to convey numerous aspects of the river's meaning, and now, having inserted a series of previously published writings relating to his early training on the river, he explains to readers that as a cub pilot he embarked on an enterprise that required not only that he maintain a notebook, in which he was to write every scrap of information passed along by his teacher, but also that he become an abecedarian and approach the river as if it consisted of the written letters of a language to be learned. The first of these, the memorandum book, suggests the role that writing can play in coming to an understanding of the river; the would-be pilot must translate the various physical qualities into writing, note those traits, and reread his notes in order to memorize the river's physical nature. It is not enough to hear about different elements of the Mississippi or even to experience them firsthand; if one really wants to know the river, one must listen, experience, *and write things down.*

The idea that a pilot might keep a memorandum book may not surprise us all that much, accustomed as we are to the use of writing for the sake of recording and remembering information. Yet we tend to take a language act like writing for granted. We live in language, after all: we think in language and thus usually do not think about language. Twain nevertheless appears to be pushing that particular envelope a bit further than usual, insisting that things so seemingly unrelated to language—the nature of the river, the science of piloting—require us to use our unique language ability for their proper understanding. The second part of Bixby's lesson, treating the river like an alphabet, is another thing entirely, an evocative simile that combines two rather disparate terms. The trope of "reading the river" may be familiar to boaters and fishermen, but again Twain extends the concept beyond common usage. By plumbing the depths of Bixby's figure of speech, Twain compels readers to consider just how rivers and the alphabet are alike and what we should do with that information. The ABCs are the fundamental building blocks of literacy, the roots of our literal way of processing experience within prevailing conceptual categories and thus a primary means of making sense of the world. We have to know our ABCs in order to read anything, must know the alphabet by heart so that we don't have to stop and think about particular letters every time we read something. If we did stop, reading even the most basic text would take forever. A pilot needs to know the physical features of the river in the same way he knows his letters: the things that make up the river have to be part of the alphabet with which the pilot reads the changing text of the river. The pilot makes meaning out of the river's features similarly to how readers make meaning out of a book.

Twain's account of the lesson makes Bixby's simile part of a larger education in the textual nature of rivers. Whereas Bixby teaches the lesson in order to make the river have meaning for his cub (and consequently to transform his cub into a pilot), Twain uses Bixby's lesson for a different project: making the Mississippi meaningful for his readers. The ensuing chapters comprise Bixby's lessons in river literacy, and though they make up only about a fifth of the whole book, it is a mighty potent fifth. Bixby serves as an example of a particular kind of authority on the river; as "The Pilot," he has a comprehensive understanding of the Mississippi and its many features that enables him to navigate successfully. The pilot passes along this knowledge to the cub, allowing him to become something other than an "uneducated passenger." Those lessons, however, are not without their cost, and the writer's struggles with them become part of a larger lesson for readers about rivers, literacy, and meaning making more generally.

Twain heeds his venerable teacher's advice and begins to take care of the business of learning the river by keeping a memorandum book, but difficulties soon develop. For example, Twain quickly finds that getting something down on paper does not mean that he has it down: though his book "fairly bristled" with notes, "the information was to be found only in the note-book—none of it was in my head." He also discovers significant gaps in his notes due to the fact that he only records the features of the river while he is awake. Sleeping for four hours between shifts means not knowing four hours' worth of river. Twain laments that "four hours off and four hours on, day and night," produces regular intervals of emptiness, with the result that "it made my heart ache to think I had only got half of the river set down" in his book. Make that half of a half—his heart breaks again when he realizes that he has only been learning how to read the river while going upstream; reversing course and going downstream reveals a new set of data, and it becomes painfully plain that he "had got to learn this troublesome river *both ways.*" The cub has things in his book that aren't necessarily in his head, and he becomes aware that many more things are neither in his book nor in his head.

As is common with attempting to learn something complex, the subject becomes more perplexing the deeper one gets into it. Just reading the river is hard enough without throwing in the problem of writing things down. Learning how to pay attention to the details, learning what details one needs to pay attention to, learning how to store details—not only is the devil in the details for an apprentice steamboatman, but the details themselves bedevil the student-pilot as they proliferate, diversify, and ever evanesce. Twain despairs again as he confesses to his teacher: "'I have not only to get the names of all the towns and islands and bends, and so on, by heart, but I must even get up a warm personal acquaintanceship with every old snag and one-limbed cottonwood and obscure wood pile that ornaments the banks of this river for twelve hundred miles; and more than that, I must actually know where these things are in the dark.'" In his despondence he confesses, "'I wish the piloting business was in Jericho and I had never thought of it.'"

Even as the river's vicissitudes compound and his education vexes him, the apprentice perseveres with his "note-booking," though he finds that his record is "but a confusion of meaningless names," a knot of information in which his mind becomes fitfully entangled. The sundry pieces of information that do manage to travel from notebook to head do so only to clatter about disconnectedly. Proper river literacy requires another step in the process: connecting the parts to one another and to a larger whole. In the chapter "Perplexing Lessons" Twain testifies that "at the end of what seemed a tedious while" he finally had accumulated a wealth of information, "and a curiously inanimate mass of lumber it was, too." Bixby shortly teaches him that it is not enough to pack his head full of details. The next class on river literacy revolves around the notion of shape, the larger form of the Mississippi consisting of the arrangement of those myriad details.

Knowing the shape of the river, the pilot-teacher explains, involves forming a mental picture of the sequential arrangement of physical details; it requires an imaginative rendering of the whole based on memory. The well-made picture enables the pilot to navigate safely regardless of visibility. Bixby likens it to the sense one develops of the layout of one's own home, the sense of space that lets one walk down an unlighted hallway well after bedtime without damage to limb or property: "'My boy, you've got to know the *shape* of the river perfectly. It is all there is left to steer by on a very dark night.'" Twain's emphasis on the word "shape" is noteworthy, a stress that is corroborated when Bixby uses the word five times in a subsequent paragraph that glosses what he means. The emphasis belongs to the special definition of the word in the context of river literacy, the text, as it were, created by the river's ABC. Shape in this context refers to a developed sense of how things go together, how they are arranged in relation to one another. Knowing the shape makes it possible for one to move by virtue of relation. And the shape itself results from combining various features into a meaningful whole based on sensory experience and transformed into a concept.

As the lesson continues the emphasis changes. When Twain complains that carrying around all the different shapes of the river in his head would make him "stoop-shouldered," Bixby corrects him: "*No!* you only learn *the* shape of the river; and you learn it with such absolute certainty that you can always steer by the shape that's *in your head*, and never mind the one that's before your eyes." What's the difference between "the *shape* of the river" and "*the* shape of the river"? In the context of the lesson, the shift in emphasis functions as clarification and placation; it clarifies the nature of the muddy Mississippi, explaining that there is an unwavering wholeness connecting the seemingly ungraspable "million trifling variations" and "five hundred thousand different ways" of knowing them. And this clarification is intended to placate the despondent cub. All he needs to know are the river's alphabet and the text of that alphabet's arrangement, not every minute mutation of any given letter. Details are significant, but no more so than the whole. Twain, though, is not easily or lastingly placated—he soon learns that "*the* shape of the river" actually does change, the banks being perpetually unbuilt and rebuilt by fluvial processes. To become proficient in the science of piloting, he finds, "a man had got to learn more than any one man ought to be allowed to know; and . . . he must learn it all over again in a different way every twenty-four hours."

The shape of the river, the picture formed by a holistic arrangement of phenomena, is the product of processes of perception, retention, and especially grouping. Knowing the shape is much like crafting a text out of multifarious materials: the physical traits of the moving water, the undulating and oscillating riverbed, alternations of light and shadow, the crumbling and reappearing banks, events of the recent and remote past, personal experiences and public communications. It necessitates interpretation of a host of dimensions from a plethora of angles "in all the different ways that could be thought of,—upside down, wrong end first, inside out, fore-and-aft, and 'thort-ships.'" Poor Mark Twain, only two fathoms deep, finds himself insufficient to the task of apprehending or comprehending this text: "I went to work now to learn the shape of the river; and of all the eluding and ungraspable objects that ever I tried to get mind or hands on, that was the chief." Severely challenged, he confesses to Bixby, "'I have n't got brains enough to be a pilot'"; but his teacher barks back, "'When I say I'll learn a man the river, I mean it. And you can depend on it, I'll learn him or kill him.'" And so he does—"learn him," that is. Bixby teaches Twain to do what pilots do: to read the text of the river, "to read it as if it were a book."

These lessons in water reading sink in, by and by. Twain the cub is able to overcome his tendency to overlook the river, and he does so by learning how to turn the river into a text. Twain the writer then develops Bixby's lessons into a parable of river literacy, with the following paragraph serving as the heart of the parable:

> It turned out to be true. The face of the water, in time, became a wonderful book—a book that was a dead language to the uneducated passenger, but which told its mind to me without reserve, delivering its most cherished secrets as clearly as if it uttered them with a voice. And it was not a book to be read once and thrown aside, for it had a new story to tell every day. Throughout the long twelve hundred miles there was never a page that

was void of interest, never one that you could leave unread without loss, never one that you would want to skip, thinking you could find higher enjoyment in some other thing. There never was so wonderful a book written by man; never one whose interest was so absorbing, so unflagging, so sparklingly renewed with every re-perusal. The passenger who could not read it was charmed with a peculiar sort of faint dimple on its surface (on the rare occasions when he did not overlook it altogether); but to the pilot that was an *italicized* passage; indeed, it was more than that, it was a legend of the largest capitals, with a string of shouting exclamation points at the end of it; for it meant that a wreck or a rock was buried there that could tear the life out of the strongest vessel that ever floated. It is the faintest and simplest expression the water ever makes, and the most hideous to a pilot's eye. In truth, the passenger who could not read this book saw nothing but all manner of pretty pictures in it, painted by the sun and shaded by the clouds, whereas to the trained eye these were not pictures at all, but the grimmest and most dead-earnest of reading-matter.

Occurring near the end of the chapter "Continued Perplexities," the passage completes Twain's allegorical connecting of river and book, which serves as an important component of his textual approach to the Mississippi. In the allegory the river is something to be read, a written text with punctuation and capitalization, and thus requires interpretation. Its pages are full of interest, tell a new story each day, and bear numerous readings that reveal a different set of meanings with each "re-perusal." Twain's extended metaphor promotes the river to the apex of all texts, better than any "book written by man," and lays out the almost worshipful method by which such works should be read: over and over, page by page, absorbingly, unflaggingly, with ever-renewed interest. Perhaps in holding forth on reading the "wonderful book" of the river Twain also utters some wishful thinking regarding the proper care and handling of his own wonderful books.

More to the point, Twain's allegory of river literacy describes two very different types of overlooking, two types that entail missing the Mississippi's phenomena and their effects. He expressly uses the word "overlook" in regard to "uneducated" passengers, the majority of travelers who find little or no meaning in the river. "The passenger [on the river] who could not read," a phrase Twain repeats for emphasis, merely enjoys a vague pleasure from the "pretty pictures" in this book, able to make neither head nor tail of the letters of the text. Such overlookers are antipilots, illiterate and readily distracted by colors. To the uneducated, even the most detailed and most serious "reading-matter" yields nothing more than a satisfied ooh or aah. Bixby's lessons in river literacy would seem to teach that there is plenty of meaning in every feature of the river, and with the right education even the "stupidest dunderhead" can be trained to take in those meanings. But Bixby's lessons are only a part of Twain's lessons. The second type of over-look, although another form of missing the meaning of the river, ironically results from successfully overcoming the first sort. As soon as Twain proudly reports that he has "mastered the language of this water," he finds that he may have lost more than he gained. Having learned to read the Mississippi, having "come to know every trifling feature that bordered the great river as familiarly as I knew the letters of the alphabet, I had made a valuable acquisition. But I had lost something, too. I had lost something which could never be restored to me while I lived. All the grace, the beauty, the poetry had gone out of the majestic river!"

The traded off for not overlooking.

Continued Perplexities: Losing the River, Finding the Mississippi

In Twain's ledger, gain must be offset by loss: to become a pilot by ac-quiring the analytic method of reading rivers, one must sacrifice poetic perception. "The glories and the charms" of the river no longer have value because the science of piloting reduces the available meanings of the river to those concerning navigation. Trained in river literacy by Bixby, Twain can analyze data and accurately predict outcomes. Meaning, within this system, is a function of cause and effect: "This sun *means* that we are going to have wind to-morrow; that floating log *means* that the river is rising . . . ; that slanting mark on the water *refers* to a bluff reef which is going to kill somebody's steamboat one of these nights, if it keeps stretching out like that." Various features of the river are only "noted" if they affect navigation; they "mean" something only if the reader of the river finds them valuable to that task; and they "refer" only to the particular functions of "this great science" of piloting. But in "Continued Perplexities" Twain makes clear that so wonderful a wealth of meanings brings with it poetic poverty: "No, the romance and the beauty were all gone from the river. All the value any feature of it had for me now was the amount of usefulness it could furnish toward compassing the safe piloting of a steamboat."

Viewed wholly within the context of Bixby's lessons in river literacy (i.e., from the perspective of the steamboat's pilothouse), the knowledge of the river acquired by the cub is a positive asset, free and clear. But in the context of Twain's lessons on river literacy (i.e., from the textual perspective of the writer), the positive comes with a negative, a cost that troubles the clarity of the bookkeeping. Twain likens the science of the pilot to the science of the medical doctor and asks if the doctor doesn't "sometimes wonder whether he has gained more or lost most by learning his trade." The lessons of *Life* describe a crisis in meaning that will not be resolved by the book's end, the crux of the matter involving two vastly different ways of approaching the Mississippi River. "Poetry," overly romantic, misses the point; "science," overly analytical, dulls the point. One can either be an "uneducated passenger" on the river and value it for its aesthetic qualities, or one can be a pilot and understand how the river works, but in Twain's zero-sum accounting, one cannot do both. As the writer of *Life on the Mississippi,* now neither a pilot nor an uneducated passenger, Twain "returns to his muttons," as he says, decked out as a celebrity man of letters. He reports that he lost a way of seeing when he learned to read the river like a book. He seems to regain it once or twice, as when he gazes down on the river by his old home, but this too is a moment of loss in a series of losses—of the mischievous innocence of his Hannibal youth, of the glory days of piloting, of a way of life.

Oddly enough, it is the very loss that leads to the possibility of gain. Twain's crisis in meaning creates meaning by surpassing either the romantic or the scientific and weaving them into a bigger, richer picture of the Mississippi. Youth may be too neglectful of the river, uneducated passengers too romantic, and pilots too scientific, and they all seem to be better off than the mere "scribbler of books." But writers—albeit of a certain stripe—have the opportunity for producing a truly meaningful encounter with the river. They do so, in Twain's perspective, in three ways: first, by becoming aware of the problems inherent in discrete, either/or approaches to the river; second, by not avoiding either/or approaches but instead bringing together as many as possible; and third, by reveling in but taking care to shape the mud that results from such a complex method. Even with these measures, writers will not have fully realized a river's meaning; they will have made a necessary start toward rendering the richness of a river accessible. The complexity of this approach stems from Twain's experiences with the Mississippi and also from his lifelong wrestling match with the nature of meaning, whether it was the meaning of the river or the meaning of life or the meaning that writers can convey to readers. In his autobiography he mourns the lack of significance in life, a loss of meaning evident in more than one context. The America of his day, for example, no longer means what it once meant: "Our Christianity which we have always been so proud of—not to say so vain of—is now a shell, a sham, a hypocrisy; . . . we have lost our ancient sympathy with oppressed peoples struggling for life and liberty; . . . when we are not coldly indifferent to such things we sneer at them, and . . . the sneer is about the only expression the newspapers and the nation deal in with regard to such things." The best of American principles, the truths long held to be self-evident and inviolable, have been sold down the river.

And meaninglessness troubled Twain on an even deeper level; that is, perplexities continued throughout his life and were apparently part of the Clemens genetic material. He reports in the autobiography how his daughter Susy, even as a seven-year-old, "was oppressed and perplexed by the maddening repetition of the stock incidents of our race's fleeting sojourn here, just as the same thing has oppressed and perplexed maturer minds from the beginning of time." Twain, in a lengthy lamentation, bemoans the "myriad of men" who suffer "infirmities," "shames and humiliations" as they "labor and sweat and struggle for bread," "squabble and scold and fight" and scramble. Finally,

> they vanish from a world where they were of no consequence; where they achieved nothing; where they were a mistake and a failure and a foolishness; where they have left no sign that they existed—a world which will lament them a day and forget them forever. Then another myriad takes their place, and copies all they did, and goes along the same profitless road, and vanishes as they vanished—to make room for another and another and a million other myriads to follow the same arid path through the same desert and accomplish what the first myriad, and all myriads that came after it, accomplished—nothing!

The meaning of rivers shifts depending on what one values, the values of America have lost their meaning, and human existence means nothing inherently—a bleak picture indeed, if the story ended there.

But the story doesn't end there, or at least doesn't have to end there, for a couple of reasons. One of those reasons is the river itself: the Mississippi, full of mud, keeps on flowing. The fact that it keeps on flowing and the fact that it is full of mud both contribute to the continuing perplexity, the eternal complexity of the situation. As the river keeps moving, so does its meaning; any writing about the river that dams the flow will not successfully convey the life of the Mississippi. The paradoxical constancy of the ever-changing river obliges the writer to be aware of change constantly, to allow for meaning to shift. Similarly, a style of writing that attempts to clarify the meaning of the river by purifying its waters may wind up with something in its glass, but it won't be the Mississippi, with its thick texture and many layers consisting of all manner of things. To tell the Mississippi's story, one cannot expect to let things settle, and *Life on the Mississippi*, with its "continued perplexities," maintains the possibility of meaning by keeping things muddy. If we weren't perplexed by the Mississippi, if everything was clear or if the story was done, then we might have a pretty big problem: we would more than likely be overlooking a good part of the river's meaning. If, however, we acknowledge the perpetual complexity informing its meaning, we remain capable of engaging with its changing nature. Twain's river writing fosters that capability. He seldom tries to settle things, to tell one particular story with a definitive meaning, to describe a world with any kind of clarity or purity. His is a muddy world, his America is among the muddier nations, and his river is the muddiest phenomenon of all. It's in that mud—the nutritious Mississippi mud of Twain's textual approach to writing the river—that something good can grow.

Another reason that the story doesn't end there has to do with the nature of literature. Something good can grow from river writing only if readers are willing and able to make it happen. The river's "continued perplexities" warrant continued thought, the ongoing need to exercise one's mind on the phenomena of the world one encounters daily, hourly. Because of Twain's way of writing, readers seeking the meaning of the Mississippi must read with a mind that is alive to the textuality of the river, a mind flexible and flowing instead of rigid and petrified. Recalling in his autobiography a letter he had written to a certain editor who had clearly overlooked the meaning of another text, Twain provided a helpful reminder to would-be readers. "'It is discouraging to try to penetrate a mind like yours,'" Twain remonstrated. "'You ought to get it out and dance on it. That would take some of the rigidity out of it. And you ought to use it sometimes; that would help. If you had done this every now and then along through life, it would not have petrified.'" Readers: be encouraged. Meaning is possible, if you will but stomp some suppleness into your minds and keep them from hardening by occasional use. Twain's multilayered, highly textured approach to crafting the river challenges readers to overcome the tendency to yaw one way or the other, to the overly analytic or the overly romantic; his book challenges us to think again about the Mississippi and look into its many meanings.

Those challenges can be seen in the very assemblage of the book. Twain's style of writing nearly always involves the combination of many threads and layers into a complex weave, the resulting texts consisting of multiple dialects and discourses, poses and perspectives. His personal stories and those told by others, history and news, facts and fictions—these are all crafted into a whole that defies easy categorization. *Life on the Mississippi* presents readers with the opportunity of putting things together differently. We are given pieces of Twain's own travel writing, memoirs, folk legends, fragments from novels, other travelers' accounts, bogus prison letters, social commentary, facts, folly finding, steamboat time tables, old-time steamboating, accounts of Bavarian intrigue and voting mosquitoes, Civil War ruin in Vicksburg, and scenic sunsets of Muscatine, Iowa. But the question remains as to how we will connect these sundry bits and pieces. In *Life on the Mississippi* two main forces assist the reader in tying together all the bits and pieces: the narrator and the river.

On the one hand, Mark Twain helps hold it all together—the crafter himself, his self as he crafted it in writing, the writer who had to learn the river in order to become a pilot and perhaps had to become a pilot before he became a writer. Twain does not skulk about the pages, hiding behind an impersonal and imperious Authority; he uses his well-known figure to good advantage, as part of the story of how meaning is made on the river and elsewhere. The multifarious pieces of *Life on the Mississippi* are held together by a bushy moustache and a wryly insightful eye. As the cover boy of *Time* magazine's "Making of America" issue (July 14, 2008), Twain still glares out at his reading public, the "seriously funny man" confronting us with our shortcomings and celebrating our possibilities (if not our prospects)—still America's most famous man of letters. On the other hand, the mighty Mississippi, the nation's most famous river, connects the dots. Also the subject of the cover story of a national magazine, "America's River"—or simply "*The* River," as it featured in Pare Lorentz's New Deal documentary—runs through the nation's middle from Minnesota to Louisiana, its watershed stretching east and west. The river's centrality, its bluffs and islands, its length and long history serve to make it meaningful in Twain's story and serve to make the story meaningful by linking so many different things. The Mississippi is at the heart of Twain's philosophy of grouping: everything or everyone comes back to the river. It is indeed "well worth reading about"—and worth reading well about it.

In writing *Life on the Mississippi* Twain, now the well-known writer, went back to the river for another look. His "return to his muttons" enables him again to go up and down the river, back and forth in time, to climb Cardiff Hill in Hannibal once more and overlook the Mississippi. After twenty-one years he comes back to the river in the company of "a poet" and "a stenographer." These two characters, by their titles, represent the two views of the river he calls into question. Twain positions himself as a different kind of writer, neither poet (prone to the romantic view) nor stenographer (noting everything that occurs, like a pilot), one who can bring different elements of the river together meaningfully. Though much has occurred in his long absence from the Mississippi, he rejoices to find "a thing which had not changed": the river water is as muddy as ever, and "every tumblerful of it holds nearly an acre of land in solution." He scoffs at prim strangers who must let the dirt settle on the bottom of the glass in order to drink. "But the natives do not take them separately, but together, as nature mixed them." Twain's book is like that glass. Instead of letting things settle and clarify, he gives the glass an occasional swirl, and in so doing he gives a provisional definition of literature: muddy writing, consisting of sedimentary gist, surface denotations, connotations circulating in the stream, materials transported from one time or place to another, meaning held fleetingly in suspended solution.

Such a literature would result not only from the efforts of the author, however celebrated he or she may be. Readers too make literature. In trying to tell readers something meaningful about the river, Twain occupies a position similar to the father in the comic strip with which this chapter began. We will have to unplug ourselves from the devices into which we are tuned in order to pick up what the writer is laying down. Nor do I mean to suggest that readers of literature must pick up precisely what the writer lays down, that they receive it and cherish it and never think about it again. The lessons in river literacy appear to recommend that readers get muddy when they read. To read fastidiously, as poetic or scientific purists, will get them something, but it won't be literature. Thus, the bottom line of Twain's crisis in meaning seems to be that Twain can't resolve the crisis; Clemens can't resolve the crisis; possibility for resolution now resides with readers. While the lessons of history and science teach us that we overlook rivers and their meaning at our peril, Twain's lessons suggest how and why we should look again and again at our literal streams and the life swirling in and around them.

Imagine if the comic-strip characters came to Hannibal today. They park downtown on North Street, facing the river and across from the statue of Tom and Huck. They start up the concrete stairway, up Cardiff Hill, under winter sunshine, say. Fifty-five steps to Becky's Butterfly Garden, an adornment to a narrow plaza with a view of the river; seventy-nine steps up to Rock Street; thirty-seven steps to a plateau where they stand on a large flat rock, looking southeast at the head of an island midstream across from the bottom of town; seventy-three steps more to a lighthouse built in the centennial year of Clemens's birth. They see ice floes slowly drifting downstream, the Illinois shore heavily wooded, a billboard in the middle of Hannibal: "Welcome to Hannibal—America's Hometown," with a picture of a mustachioed Twain. The river flows inexorably, it seems, steady and strong, no sign of influence from the upstream locks and dams, the water reflecting the winter sky or the wooded banks, always taking on the colors of what surrounds it, bluish or brownish or blackish, and placid in the main. In the background, even so high above the bustle, the walkers hear the intermittent sounds of saws and traffic from the nearby bridge, also dedicated the year of the author's centennial. The father does not say anything; the son is not listening to music. They look out on nestled Hannibal and the always passing, always abiding, always changing river.

After descending the steps back to North Street, where a barking beagle briefly brings Pudd'nhead Wilson to the father's mind, they pay their respects at Sam Clemens's boyhood home, pausing in the small sideyard (with a sign designating "Tom Sawyer's Fence") to look down the street to the river. Then, heading north, they drive up Harrison Hill to Riverview Park. Eating sandwiches by a statue of Mark Twain overlooking the Mississippi, they follow his bronze gaze and improve the view: upstream, islands and trees, a barge on its winding way down, father or son mentally stern-wheeling up to Minneapolis and looking even farther to the clear water at the stream's head; downstream, white circles of ice floating past the park prospect, past the town, melting on the way to St. Louis and beyond, to New Orleans, still digging out of the mud.

2 | *By the River*

How much life happens "by the river"! Throughout human history in North America, visitors to and inhabitants of these parts have fished and farmed, worked and rested, drunk and bathed, prayed and sung the blues as the river rolled on beside them. People have flirted, honeymooned, and fooled around by the river. Often they just sat there and thought, "watching the river flow," as Bob Dylan sang. Being by rivers—whether that means residing alongside them, standing or swimming in them, walking in or near them—belongs to a special category of river experience. This category does not entail enjoying an overview of the whole length or even a large section of a stream. While overlooking a river can offer perspective, it also implies distance from the river, a kind of detachment or remove, even if temporary; by-the-river works operate from closeness to the flow of water, and that closeness brings about different ways of thinking about and experiencing rivers. This unique proximity does not involve going with the flow (down the river), going against the flow (up the river), or crossing the river to the other side. In fact, it means not going anywhere, necessarily, and is perhaps the simplest, most basic, and most common way of making contact with a river. It is also a common way of making contact with our thoughts, as if when sitting by a river or standing in a shallow stream, time slows (or at least seems to slow and even stop). Picking rocks out of the clear waters of the Hurricane River or casting a line into the dark Vermilion, lying on the green bank of the Huron or sitting on a rock by the tumbling Animas, we can experience a closeness to the river, its motion and sound, that can create a sense of stillness; and at the center of that stillness thoughts form.

Of course, sometimes we sit by the river in order *not* to think, relishing release from things that demand our attention, just sitting there letting it all flow by, encouraged to dream or meditate. A fair number of American writers, however, have made use of the situation to explore the link between water and words, between streams and consciousness. In their works going nowhere and being by a river provide time for thinking, and one of the things they tend to think about is time. Being still as time and the river go by allows writers to consider the past (where the water comes from), the future (where the water is heading), or the present (the water as it flows through their point of view), as well as the continuity or discontinuity between one of those periods and the others. By-the-river writings often feature a special attention to time and timelessness; the thinking that emerges from such situations is premised on proximity to and experience of rivers and applied by writers toward the understanding of a variety of matters. The relations between flowing water and time often in turn merge with thoughts on other relations—between members of a family, between self and place, between self and society, or between human and higher truths.

In this chapter I consider some of the works that highlight by-the-river relations and the different ways in which writers have applied those relations to other problems and questions. Because this category comprises the most basic and common experience of the river, there are countless texts from which to choose. Those I have chosen represent different genres of writing and diverse periods of American literary history; they also apply the situation of being by the river to a diversity of uses. But in each work water and words are brought together to explore how relative proximity to rivers might inform our understanding of other relations that shape human experience. Each text operates on the assumption that reading about being by the river can lead to knowing something about ourselves and the world we inhabit, whether that involves spiritual elements, societal forces, or the ties among family members. The writers selected, working the connection between rivers and literature, present ways of extending the lessons of one into the problems of the other. In all of these examples time figures significantly.

Even those who have had little experience with rivers themselves have heard (and probably on one occasion or another uttered) the words, "You can't step in the same river twice." The phrase, which dates back about twenty-five hundred years to the early Greek philosopher Heraclitus, is a good example of by-the-river thinking in which the stream is used to consider a related issue. When cited nowadays it usually has two functions: either to indicate that time goes on and we can't stop the flow or, less commonly, to suggest a paradoxical situation in which "the river," as an entity, at once persists through time (stays ever the same) and constantly changes (is always different). Because little is known about Heraclitus and little of his work has survived, the exact phrase and its original context are uncertain. A recent translation of his fragments cites two possible sources, both of which change the phrase and its meaning somewhat. The first connects the perceived paradoxical nature of rivers to human identity: "We step and do not step into the same rivers; we are and are not." The second concerns time, flow, and experience: "As they step into the same rivers, different and [still] different waters flow upon them." The current phrase appears to result from historical usage having worn down the edges of the two fragments and reshaped them into a single nugget of conventional, if indefinite, wisdom.

The durability and popularity of the phrase suggest that Heraclitus might have been on to something, that rivers serve humans who puzzle over the nature of time and other cosmological concerns. During the Renaissance Leonardo da Vinci also dipped his hands into a river and drew forth a lesson in time: "In rivers the water you touch is the last of what has passed and the first of that which comes. So with time present." Leonardo's analogy posits the flow of the river as a model for temporal flow. We touch and are pressed by time: the past pushes on us from one side, the future pulls from another, and we bathe in the watery present. Western literature has long used rivers as a means of thinking about the flow of time and what we can or cannot do about it, from Greek historians' interest in Nilotic periodicity up through Henry David Thoreau's boast that time is but a stream he goes a-fishing in. Writers have set up camp by the river and curiously watched as time and meaning, struggle and recovery, gods and devils, transcendence and trouble floated by.

Close Sat I by a Goodly River's Side: Spiritual Relations

In this section I will look at three poets' use of being by the river to think about time, history, and God. Poetry, especially when it expresses an acute awareness of a concentrated experience, operates within a set of conventions that seems well suited to the theme of sitting by a river, and American poetry has often found its subject matter alongside moving water. One of the earliest examples comes from the writing of Anne Bradstreet (1612–72), who reflected on water and temporal matters in the poem "Contemplations," written around 1664 or 1665 and probably inspired by her experiences along the Merrimack River in New England. The poet, remembering a walk through the autumn woods, praises Creation and reflects on human history and the passage of time, faulting us for shortening our days by suspect practices and "living so little while we are alive." Seasonal cycles perpetually rejuvenate nature, she observes, "but man grows old, lies down, remains where once he's laid." She then remembers that the things of nature will ultimately fade, while "man was made for endless immortality." To sort out this problem (nature lives to the fullest, is ever renewed, and outlasts individual humans; the soul, however, enjoys the possibility of eternity), the poet sits down by the riverside in stanza 21:

> Under the cooling shadow of a stately elm
> Close sat I by a goodly river's side,
> Where gliding streams the rocks did overwhelm,
> A lonely place, with pleasures dignified.
> I once that loved the shady woods so well,
> Now thought the rivers did the trees excel,
> And if the sun would ever shine, there would I dwell.

The poet settles into the soul-soothing situation by the river and meditates on rivers' general excellence. In the next stanza she fixes her eye on the stream, "which to the longed-for ocean held its course," and observes that nothing can hinder the purposeful flow: "'O happy flood,' quoth I, 'that holds thy race / Till thou arrive at thy beloved place, / Nor is it rocks or shoals that can obstruct thy pace.'" The river constantly moves forward toward its goal, union with the infinite ocean, undeterred by obstacles and carrying smaller brooks and rivulets toward the desired end. Because of this the river serves the poet as an "emblem true of what I count best."

Still, just like the birds that tantalize with their song and flight, the river is but a thing of this world. Bradstreet concludes by having the poet directly address Time, "the fatal wrack of mortal things, / That draws oblivion's curtains over kings," promising that the soul "shall last and shine" when nature and other worldly phenomena are gone. The crux of her riparian "contemplations" on "the nature of the human condition in time and eternity" is that humans are caught between two choices, summarized neatly in the title of a poem from the same period, "The Flesh and the Spirit," the action of which also occurs "close by the banks" of flowing water (in this case, "Lacrim flood," a river of tears). As a good Puritan, Bradstreet believes in the superiority of the supernatural over the natural, even though she is sore tempted by the glory of the river and its environs. Sitting by the river has its merits, but those merits all belong to the world of Time, to life's unfolding or unraveling, and thus are finite. Bradstreet's "goodly river" is at its best when it functions as an emblem that represents higher meaning. The "happy flood" ultimately means little as an end in itself; it is instead to be understood as an indicator, as a finger of Creation that points to the Creator. To know the river is to know its limits and to transcend time, transferring one's thoughts to eternity and the soul's relation to the divine.

For Bradstreet, the river can teach us a thing or two about change, time, finitude, and infinity. In "Contemplations," as in much of her poetry, she represents "the struggle between the visible and the invisible worlds," and ultimately the poem redefines that struggle through its use of the river. Nature is not opposed to or a distraction from the truth but rather functions as a medium through which the truth may be obtained. Bradstreet's "masterpiece," as some scholars deem it, uses closeness to the river to exemplify a "process of meditation for the benefits of the reader," a process in which one observes, contemplates what one sees, and draws conclusions based on contemplation. In Bradstreet's example, the contemplator's focus moves from nature's cyclical time to the linear time of humans' corporeal life, finally alighting on the eternal timelessness of the soul.

Consequently, the river means two different things and demonstrates two different ways of knowing rivers. First, the river means just what we see: a clear, gliding stream, a beautiful thing in itself. Second, the river, something separate from God but a product of God's work, also has meaning as an emblem of God's glory. In other words, the river means what it is but also means what it isn't, hence the need for two different ways of relating to—being by—the river. The first method, worldly and based on vision, involves the invocation of an aesthetic sense that values nature as something pleasing to the eye. To know the river in this way requires being close enough to the physical stream to have a good view and then opening our eyes to what is before us. The second requires taking the river as a prompt for transcendent vision; this is a way of thinking by the river, alongside of it, but also using it as a tool for thinking. That thinking requires knowing the river's limits but also understanding that it offers us a chance to "glimpse redemption." Thinking by the river in these different modes is an art that entails perception, memory, imagination, reason, affection, and the will to expand the scope of our vision. Such knowledge is elusive, of course, a problem recognized by the poet amidst her meditations: "But Ah, and Ah, again, my imbecility!" Bradstreet encourages readers to persist in their meditations, presenting the river as an emblem for the soul's union with the divine. To be by the river leads to being by God.

A short distance from Bradstreet's neighborhood, the Merrimack is met by the slow-moving Concord River, along the banks of which Ralph Waldo Emerson, a century and a half after Bradstreet, added his own by-the-river meditations on topics similar to those pondered by his literary predecessor. The headwaters, in a sense, of American history, the Concord and its banks echoed with the "shot heard 'round the world," as made famous by Emerson's "Concord Hymn," and a replica of the Old North Bridge now considered "a causeway of American history," still spans the river, connecting two parking lots and guarded by Daniel Chester French's Minute Man statue. Before Concord town was founded, Nipmuck, Pawtucket, and Massachusett peoples inhabited the basin of the river they called Musketaquid. Before them, humans began hunting mammoths and the like as soon as the Wisconsin Glacier retreated about ten thousand years ago. The site to which Emerson's ancestor Peter Bulkeley came with Samuel Willard and others in the early autumn of 1635 was (as Emerson recalled in his "Historical Discourse at Concord" two hundred years later) "an old village of the Massachusetts Indians. Tahattawan, the Sachem, with Waban his son-in-law, lived near Nashawtuck, now Lee's Hill. Their tribe, once numerous, the epidemic had reduced." Emerson continues with a description of the First Peoples' wise use of the many resources "with which our river abounded."

Emerson's version of Concord's history mentions in passing the devastation that Native populations suffered in the seventeenth century, as does Lemuel Shattuck's *A History of the Town of Concord* (1835), from which

Emerson draws freely in his own writing. Both Shattuck's and Emerson's histories propose that as of 1635, one river ceased to exist and another took its place: the Musketaquid of the Indian past was converted into the Concord of the English present. The Act of Incorporation (September 2, 1635) "ordered that there shall be a plantation att Musketaquid, and that there shall be 6 myles of land square to belonge to it." The document officially decreed what the colonists' physical efforts had already accomplished— making the land speak English rather than Algonquin: "and the name of the place is changed and here after to be called Concord." "Musketaquid," a word descriptive of the grassy lowlands through which the stream coursed, is replaced with a reference to the peaceful aspirations (and supposedly well-mannered behavior) of the English people.

The history of the Musketaquid-Concord, the story of an aboriginal river replaced by a modern stream, gave Emerson material for poetic means to a transcendent end. In several poems staged alongside the Concord, he situated humans and their culture in opposition to time and nature, an opposition that is mediated by "Spirit." His well-known "Concord Hymn, Sung at the Completion of the Battle Monument, April 19, 1836," treats the river as a "dark stream which seaward creeps," working with Time to sweep away vestiges of human activity. He concludes that poem by appealing to "Spirit," depicted as something apart from and evidently above the scene, to intervene on humans' behalf and convince "Time and Nature" that they should spare Art (embodied in a monument to History). Emerson's "Spirit" is disconnected from place and time: the force to which he appeals is the same force that "made those heroes dare" in 1775. Thus, the hymn sings in praise of the actions of the men of Concord and not the land or river their ancestors had renamed.

Other poems find Emerson meditating by the Concord on men, land, river, and spirit, including one that takes the name of the old "Indian rivulet." In "Musketaquid" he depicts himself as a dreamy poet drawn to "loiter willing by yon loitering stream." In doing so, he associates himself with English farmers, "Supplanters of the tribe," whose ploughs occasionally turn up traces of the "sannup" and "squaw" who used to occupy the land. Even though the poet celebrates the wild and woody "haunts which others scorned," his work bears the same emblems of progress as that of the supplanting farmers. Their cultivated fields are kin to the rows of his writing: "What these strong masters wrote at large in miles," he now writes on the page. Both kinds of writing display "The order regnant in the yeoman's brain," which is part of the "miracle of generative force," the civilizing influence that enabled the colonists to reap Progress from the land. As in "Concord Hymn," time moves on, forever forward—the poet remembers the Musketaquid only so that it might be left behind; that ancient waterway is itself only a relic, a thing of the past to be surpassed and eventually transcended.

This brand of transcendence is ultimately attained in another work featuring his local stream. In "Two Rivers" the poet values the "Musketaquit" [*sic*] but prizes even more an unnamed river of unspeakable scope and everlasting nourishment. The opening stanza sets a tone at once innocent and knowing:

> Thy summer voice, Musketaquit,
> Repeats the music of the rain;
> But sweeter rivers pulsing flit
> Through thee, as thou through Concord Plain.

Subsequent stanzas make plain that "sweeter rivers" pour forth from a supreme, mystical source. This mysterious Super Flow courses through years, men, nature, love, thought, power, dream . . . everything. No matter how gladsome the Musketaquit, this other river is better:

> So forth and brighter fares my stream,—
> Who drink it shall not thirst again;
> No darkness stains its equal gleam,
> And ages drop in it like rain.

Just as Emerson's ancestors historically created what they deemed an improved river to replace the Musketaquid, so his brighter stream poetically eclipses the Musketaquit in "Two Rivers." Emerson moves between the present and eternity, the Concord and a greater River, the upshot being that the conceptual flow of Spirit is superior, freed as it is from time and place: "Thou," says the poet to Musketaquit, "in thy narrow banks art pent: The stream I love unbounded goes." Although "Two Rivers" implies a more complicated movement among place and perspective, nature and culture, the spiritual and the terrestrial than does either "Concord Hymn" or "Musketaquid," the tendency of all three poems is *elsewhere*—his words lead away from the local, material, familiar waters and toward a higher, more ethereal, spiritual flow. Loitering by the river, Emerson's poetry transforms the elemental nature of the Concord, turning the material, historical river into an idealized "stream . . . unbounded."

A different kind of transcendence circulates in Langston Hughes's "The Negro Speaks of Rivers," a poem dedicated to W. E. B. Du Bois, who first published it in the *Crisis* (1921). Though critical of Puritan or Emersonian versions of spiritual progress, Hughes is no less concerned with the relations of rivers, souls, and time. Where both Bradstreet and Emerson use streams as a vehicle to surpass the historical moment and physical space, Hughes employed rivers as a means of connecting to history and place, thereby establishing personal and racial identity. The poem was written not long after Hughes graduated from high school in Cleveland, Ohio. In his autobiography Hughes recalled that the one hundred or so words of the poem came to him near St. Louis as he rode a train to visit his father in Mexico and grew from his experience as the child of parents recently divorced. "It came about in this way. All day on the train I had been thinking about my father and his strange dislike of his own people. I didn't understand it, because I was a Negro, and I liked Negroes very much." Having already noted that it was "the old story of divorced parents who don't like each other, and take their grievances out on the offspring," Hughes's reflection on his father's "dislike" adds to the negative, sorrowful atmosphere of the travel recollection, and it is directly from such gloom that the critically acclaimed and frequently anthologized poem emerges.

Crossing the Mississippi at sunset, Hughes "looked out the window of the Pullman at the great muddy river flowing down toward the heart of the South, and I began to think what that river, the old Mississippi, had meant to Negroes in the past—how to be sold down the river was the worst fate that could overtake a slave in times of bondage." This put him in mind of "other rivers in our past," which led him to the words that became the poem's opening line: "I've known rivers." Jotting these down on an envelope, he wrote the rest of the poem in about fifteen minutes, "as the train gathered speed in the dusk" and rolled away from the Mississippi. Out of familial discord and racial disdain, Hughes created an incantatory, affirming expression. By repeating the opening line as well as the concluding simile that links the speaker's soul to historically prominent streams ("My soul has grown deep like the rivers"), the poem enacts a growing self-knowledge stemming from direct experience with moving water. Rivers connect "The Negro" to the land, to history, to others, and thus to otherwise disconnected parts of himself.

By announcing the speaker in the poem's title as "The Negro" (as opposed to "a Negro" or "some black folk" or "men and women of African descent"), Hughes personalizes the origin of the words yet creates a setting that spans ages, "suggesting the whole of the people and their history." The poem begins in first-person present tense, shifts to the deep past ("when dawns were young"), moves forward to the nineteenth century (Lincoln on the Mississippi), and ends back in the unspecified present. The speaker thus speaks with an authority based on the aggregation of many particular perspectives and experiences, from many places and epochs. Those to whom the Negro speaks are not asked to take the word of a single individual, in a peculiar place, from a limited moment of time; we are invited to hear a voice emanating from "a mystic union of Negroes in every country and every age," as scholar Jean Wagner observed. The creation of that union traces the people's history back to the beginning of civilization. Even though time passes, flowing from the past to the present, by having "The Negro" speak from various points in history and from different geographical locations, the speech transcends parochial boundaries and discrete periods of time.

Some of the affirmative quality of the poem comes from the uniting of a people across time and space, but the positive aspects are enhanced by the very activity of the first-person protagonist. The very first words of the title mark the breaking of a silence. Those being addressed are not in the company of a passive, quiet person. The speaker not only speaks but accomplishes a variety of tasks, chief among which is *witnessing*. "The Negro" speaks of the soul, of living by rivers, and of positive actions performed in close proximity to waterways that provide knowledge: "I bathed," "I built," "I looked upon . . . and raised," "I heard," and "I've seen." These latter two verbs, occurring by the Mississippi, are both forms of witnessing. Coming at the end of the list of rivers and ways of knowing them that begins in the deepest past and arrives in the nearest present, witnessing emerges as the primary function of the poem. To "witness" here means more than seeing something happen. In addition to being present at and observing events, witnessing involves personally experiencing events, authenticating their occurrence, and especially sharing those experiences through testimony in such a way as to lead to further action. Hughes's speaker, the spokesperson of a people, knows rivers and what happens by them. As Adrian Oktenberg has pointed out, "The Negro" speaks "with the accumulated wisdom of a sage." Here, the sage rises above time to pass along history to the audience "so that they might make the lessons of the past active in the future." Having known rivers, the speaker testifies as to what they mean.

The "ancient, dusky rivers" of which the witness speaks contribute to the timeless attributes of the poem but also represent the flow of time. The first two rivers mentioned evoke solace and parental care. The speaker uses the words "bathed," "dawns," and "young" in elucidating the Euphrates, one of the two streams making up Mesopotamia, "the cradle of all the world's civilizations and possibly the location of the Garden of Eden." The Euphrates is the archetypal river of the Old Testament, where it is often "referred to simply as 'the River' and figured abstractly as the 'waters' in Genesis." In the lands adjacent to the Congo, the largest river of Africa (in terms of drainage basin), the speaker makes his own modest home while soothed by the nearness of the river. Less comforting images surround the second two rivers, as the specter of slavery appears in the raising of the pyramids on the Nile (biblically associated with the "land of captivity") and again in the reference to Lincoln and singing along the Mississippi in the deepening South, the feared destination of slaves who had been "sold down the river." But just as the reference to Lincoln brings with it emancipation, the concluding image of the muddy river turning golden also suggests the potential improvement of conditions, perhaps even redemption.

In spite of that potential and the poem's initial affirmations, the speaker is less positive about the future or the present. A sadness surrounds the soul's increased depth, and the chronology that moves from the Euphrates dawn to the Mississippi sunset relates the events and conditions to diminishing light, waning time, and death. Nevertheless, the last image of the central stanza evokes promise and even improvement, and by closing with the simile that associates the speaker's soul with rivers, the poem creates something possibly restorative out of the apparently declining trajectory of history. And it is this act of creation, even without direct reference to divinity in the poem, that makes "The Negro Speaks of Rivers" an act of witnessing similar to that found in spirituals, to which it is often linked. Onwuchekwa Jemie believes that, by the conclusion of the poem, the union between the speaker and the rivers bears the promise of endurance and perhaps even triumph: "As the rivers deepen with time, so does the black man's soul; as their waters ceaselessly flow, so will the black soul endure. The black man has seen the rise and fall of civilizations from the earliest times, seen the beauty and death-changes of the world over the thousands of years, and will survive even this America." Out of the suffering of the race with which he identifies, Hughes testifies to an elemental meaning of rivers: in them courses the possibility of redemption to be realized through the soul's affiliation with flowing water.

Despite their obvious differences, each of the above poems exemplifies by-the-river writing in which proximity to a stream's flow leads to poetic meditation on time and history. Both Bradstreet and Emerson get close to particular rivers that carry their meditations elsewhere. For them, the meaning of rivers lies in their ability to assist humans in transcending time, in surmounting the natural world to attain a view of an all-encompassing supernatural reality. Hughes establishes a deeper intimacy with the race with which his speaker identifies but also with greater humanity, using rivers to connect all members of civilization, past and present. For all of these poets, rivers are reminders of the Spirit's own flow. Being close to rivers gives me access to elemental fluidity, informing my thought processes and the thoughts themselves. If I pause by a river, I can become aware of its motion and flow, all the more so the more still I remain, and the flow can then become a vehicle for thinking. By-the-river poetry, observant of kinetic flowing, makes use of a writer's (or character's) relative stillness in proximity to fluid motion to meditate on relations among time, spirit, nature, self, and these meditations often yield fluid meanings.

And Fear Flowed under Everything: Worldly Relations

Writers have also used by-the-river situations to discuss more worldly matters, as can be seen in two powerful works of short fiction from the same period in which Hughes's poem appeared. Neither of these short stories demonstrates interest in spiritual concerns; in fact, both are critical of religious transcendence or at least skeptical of otherworldly tendencies. Just a few years after the publication of "The Negro Speaks of Rivers," Ernest Hemingway brought out "Big Two-Hearted River" as part of the collection *In Our Time* (1925). The two-part story begins as Nick Adams, home from the war, is dropped off by train in a Michigan ghost town. Seney, once a thriving timber community with thirteen saloons, is gone, "burned off the ground." Part 1 sparingly describes Nick's arrival, his shouldering of a mighty pack through the hills, selecting a site near the river where he painstakingly makes camp with axe and canvas, fixing a canned supper (pork and beans mixed with spaghetti), and finally hitting the sack: "Nick lay down again under the blanket. He turned on his side and shut his eyes. He was sleepy. He felt sleep coming. He curled up under the blanket and went to sleep." Part 2 continues with slow, careful description of the scene: "The sun was just up over the hill. There was the meadow, the river and the swamp. There were birch trees in the green of the swamp on the other side of the river." The static predicates of such sentences contribute to a stillness by the river, a backdrop that allows readers to concentrate on even the smallest of Nick's actions, as in the three paragraphs devoted to spartan breakfast making or the paragraph in which Nick prepares his lunch, culminating with the ridiculous (well, at least far from sublime) simplicity of this declarative: "It was a good camp."

The remainder of part 2 follows Nick as he heads down to, stands in, splashes through, walks along, fishes in, and sits in the river. The story concludes with Nick, having cleaned and bundled his catch, returning to camp and looking ahead to more days of the same simplicity. Though the pared-down language resembles that of "The Negro Speaks of Rivers," Hemingway's by-the-river story is quite unlike the Hughes poem: the moment is historically specific rather than spanning ages; the main character speaks very little and has disconnected himself from others; the third-person narration has no air of mysticism; and the featured river itself not only lacks the historical prominence of the Euphrates or the Mississippi but was likely unknown to most readers. In fact, though there is a Big Two-Hearted River in Michigan's Upper Peninsula, it does not run near Seney, which lies close to the Fox River. The title, however, sets up and underscores numerous odd couples in and around the story, including the very structure of the work.

The two parts of "Big Two-Hearted River" combine to form a single story consisting of very little action in a very short span of time. The first part of the story, centered on Nick's arrival, frequently refers to the past and experiences that precede his arriving. Within this section the past itself is divided into the more distant past, with mostly pleasant memories related to camping or the river, and the more recent past, associated with trauma. Regarding the distant and arguably more shallow past, the narrator remarks on "the long time since Nick had looked into a stream and seen trout" and the return of "all the old feeling" as the fisherman watches the river life. His prior experiences in this particular place appear readily available to him, enabling him to know "where he was from the position of the river" and thus to navigate without a map. The section concludes as Nick recollects an argument with a friend ("a very serious coffee drinker") about the best method for making camp coffee, a recollection that draws forth a laugh until it threatens to take him into darker corridors of the past. Traces of more recent history have a blasted aspect, though they often remain just below the surface of the narrative, as if still smoldering. Physical reminders of the devastating fire of the year before abound, including the burned-over land and charred grasshoppers, and the fire in turn alludes to the wasteland of World War I. The weight of this deeper past is figured in Nick's need to "choke" his mind when it "start[s] to work" and in the burden Nick bears as he hikes through the woods, a pack reminiscent of that carried by soldiers: "It was too heavy. It was much too heavy."

The narration in part 1 tends to recognize or at least refer to what has come before and then to refocus on the present as it moves away from the past. Though the narrator declares that Nick "felt he had left everything behind, the need for thinking, the need to write, other needs. It was all back of him," that declaration only draws attention to that which has supposedly been left behind. As Nick plods from exiting the train to pitching camp to bedding down, history seeps into the deliberate unfolding of the action, leading readers to wonder how long the burden of the past must be borne—a concern Nick shares, as when he wonders how long the fire-blackened grasshoppers will remain tainted. Part 2, on the other hand, has left even the recent past of Nick's arrival behind, centered as it is on his remaining by the river into the indefinite future. He has no interest in heading upstream (into the current's past), and the story concludes as he considers the area downstream into which time and the river flow: "He looked back. The river just showed through the trees. There were plenty of days coming when he could fish the swamp." The two parts are framed and separated by vignettes, as are the other stories of *In Our Time,* including chapter 6, a brief scene from the theater of war in which Nick sits helpless against a church wall, wounded in the spine by machine-gun fire. The present moment is thus at once connected to and distinguished from history in "Big Two-Hearted River."

And the present is embodied in the river. Though two-hearted in name, the river is singularly pure and whole. Its water flows with clarity, taking on color only from the pebbly bottom and surrounding meadow. Clear, making no sound, running fast and smooth, the river draws together all things around it, putting the scene in motion. It is full of life and communicates "the live feeling" to Nick. Without the river's influence, informed by past experiences from which he is slowly emerging, Nick sees the world in pieces. If the river is two-hearted, that is only because of the division within Nick himself. His self divided, things around him seem to exist individually, discrete nouns lacking agency. Things do not mean; they just are. Some are kept in different pockets of his shirt or compartments of his pack, others stand in separate segments of time or in distinct places as if blasted apart by a storm or an explosive device. Like the trout he sees reconnect with its shadow, the big two-hearted fisherman returns to his senses by the river. He's mighty messed up by the recent past (heart #1), but underneath all of that burnout lies the possibility for renewal (heart #2). The river—silent, clean, alive, and ever moving forward—revitalizes Nick through its own life and that of the fish who live in it.

He is there to fish, after all. Nick is no fisher of men but a fisher of fish, angling for trout and not for symbols. As the narrator describes the scene and events, there is nothing religious, nothing spiritual about Nick's actions by the river. Nick is free from philosophical mediations, conceptual re-creations of the past, or imaginative renderings of a future beyond his present circumstances. Although at one point he wishes he had something to read, the desire stems from his aversion to the swamp; it passes quickly. Instead, the narrator's observations in part 2, including those regarding Nick's thought processes, emphasize physical interactions with the place and his sensual experiences of the day, especially Nick's contact with water. Renewal, so the story goes, comes from immersion in the water, in the woods, in the reconnection to land, home, basic acts of forging a life out of a particular spot on the earth. Wading in the water, Nick catches one fish and lets it go, watching as the released fish first hangs "unsteadily," then strengthens and holds "steady in the moving stream," and eventually revives, darting away: "He's all right, Nick thought. He was only tired." The fish serves as Nick's double, figuring his past peril and present restoration. The river is but a stream in which Nick goes fishing for time—and hooks it.

At this point in part 2, before he loses a big fish and finally lands (and keeps) two more, Nick is becoming more a part of things, connected by the river to the life of the place, its water carrying away the broken parts. Along with connecting him to the place, the river helps Nick to restore his relations with time; fishing in the river returns him at least momentarily to a deep experience of the present, affording him a sense of balance between the traumatic past and indefinite future. Critics sometimes underscore the dread with which Nick considers the swamp, a dread understood to have resurfaced in the fight with the big trout that has escaped him. But as he returns to camp at the end of the story, still wet from splash after wading to shore and sporting two "fine trout," it is the river and not the swamp he sees, flowing from the past to the future. Though he is not completely restored, Nick's process of renewal has begun; fishing for time, his line has reconnected him to the world. The earlier recognition, perhaps little more than a hope, was that the devastation he has witnessed cannot be total: "It could not all be burned. He knew that." The river proves that, at an elemental level, life goes on, that it hasn't all been burned.

Nick, of course, is a different sort of witness from "The Negro" in Hughes's poem. The two works regard entirely different rivers, treat different relations, and different meanings of the river emerge from those relations. Hemingway's story represents a kind of antiwitnessing: his narrator tells the story with an economy of language only surpassed by the protagonist's own frugality with words. The river too is silent. Hemingway strips language of all ornament and those things that lead to flights of fancy or big ideas. Where Hughes's rivers connect a people over the course of time and lead to a deepening of the human soul, Hemingway's river flows away from history and culture, away from social relations and with no reference to spiritual relations, toward a renewal of something elemental and physical. "Big Two-Hearted River" returns Nick to the world, re-creating the possibility of wholeness in a being shattered by the tensions and turmoil of human society. Hemingway offers another modern version of transcendence, not as a spiritual escape from time but as a physical and psychical process of healing. The river restores his protagonist to the present, removing him from the mire of the past and bestowing healthier relations with time.

Hemingway's fictional river renews his protagonist's emotional and physical strength, thus providing him a sounder footing in the world—a result that differs from the spiritual tendencies of the poems discussed above but that shares with them a sense of rivers' beneficial qualities. But not all by-the-river literature results from moments of quiet epiphany or exalts the salutary effects of streams, and some writers challenge the very possibility of transcendence. Rivers in such writings offer neither escape nor restoration but instead represent inexorable forces that oppress particular human groups. In Richard Wright's "Down by the Riverside" natural disaster and social injustice combine to make life impossible for an African American man and his family in the South during the first half of the twentieth century. If, in Hughes's "The Negro Speaks of Rivers," issues of activity and passivity, water and spirituals, race and history come together redemptively, "Down by the Riverside" concerns a tragic confluence of those same issues. Wright, who considered Hughes a "cultural ambassador" for African American people, followed his "forerunner" and used river-related literature as a form of witnessing. But where Hughes's speaker experiences unity and catches a glimpse of golden light on the muddy water, Wright's central character—Mann—finds himself alone and lost in the darkness except for a sporadic, dim yellow beam flickering on the surrounding, rising, "swirling black water." His "testifying" may be summed in Mann's awful plea near the story's bleak ending: "'Stop em from killin black folks!'"

The story, part of the collection *Uncle Tom's Children*, was written in 1934 and first published in 1938. (A review in the *New York Times* likened Wright to Hemingway.) Later editions of the book begin with an autobiographical sketch, followed by five stories, each of which revolves around a black protagonist reacting against brutalization by whites. "Down by the Riverside," one of the longest of the stories, depicts the struggles of "Brother Mann" as he faces catastrophic conditions: massive flooding, life-threatening complications affecting his wife's late-term pregnancy, and an alternating series of escapes and rescues that terminate with his murder by white soldiers. Throughout the chaotic events Mann repeatedly finds himself on the verge of surrendering to situations totally beyond his control, but he somehow manages to push on determinedly until dying by the river. His perseverance, despite overwhelming odds and the utter absence of justice, varies radically from the course of action outlined in the spiritual from which the story's title is taken and which is sung by the family of Mann in the first part of the story:

Ahm gonna lay down mah sword n shiel
Down by the riverside
Down by the riverside
Down by the riverside
Ahm gonna lay down mah sword n shiel
Down by the riverside
Ah ain gonna study war no mo.

The verse included in Wright's third-person narration is followed by the chorus: six repetitions of "*Ah ain gonna study war no mo.*" Yet again and again in the story Mann finds himself having to "study war" and practice it in a futile attempt at self-preservation. The riverside of the song suggests baptism in the holy waters of the New Testament and also evokes the Old Testament crossing of the river Jordan into the Promised Land, "the fulfillment of the covenant" and the promise of rebirth. To go down by the riverside is to take the first step from this world toward the next in order to be with God. In Wright's story, however, the river is far from any sign of God. The enormous, shapeless, unnamed waters, ugly and lacking in either natural or supernatural qualities, have been fed by days and days of rain; the river seems to be "everywhere," a destructive, impersonal force "producing a situation in which everything is 'down by the riverside.'" Mann's world is a "waste of desolate and tumbling waters," and what little land remains unflooded freakishly rocks and tilts as the water continually rises.

Hard times and bad luck fuel Mann's desperation in the story as he tries to preserve his family and then himself against poverty, racial oppression, and the flood "'flowin strong n tricky.'" Wright divides the story into six parts: in the first section Mann reluctantly receives a stolen boat from another family member. After an elder leads the family in prayer and in singing the title spiritual, Mann sets out with his wife, Lulu, and two others, pulling the boat against the current "over the darkening flood." The second section begins with water rustling and rising relentlessly, droning and "glistening blackly." As "fear flowed under everything," Mann becomes increasingly confused, "losing all sense of direction" and finding that "the past would tell him nothing" about where they are. He encounters the white postmaster, Heartfield, coincidentally the owner of the boat Mann rows. Fired upon by Heartfield, Mann shoots him in self-defense and finally gets Lulu to a hospital, where she is pronounced dead. Forced into service by the military, Mann performs heroically in sections 3 through 5, though he is distraught over Lulu's death and doomed for having killed a white man. When he realizes he's been sent to rescue the remaining members of the Heartfield family, he momentarily considers murdering them to save himself—they alone can implicate him in the postmaster's death—but is prevented by a sudden violent shifting of the house, "as though by gravity of the earth itself." Mann then returns to the role of savior, only to be sent to his death by the Heartfields in the concluding section.

The story of Mann tells of a struggle against overwhelming force. Probably informed by Wright's own experiences on the banks of the Mississippi in Memphis during "the terrible devastation of the great flood of 1927," "Down by the Riverside" is a soggy, nightmarish world of vicious hatred and racial inequality where geographical features are erased and an imbalance of power stands out starkly. Its protagonist is not just any man or Everyman but a certain kind of man: an impoverished southern black man who "undergoes his ordeal with courage, intelligence, and resourcefulness" but at last succumbs to circumstances beyond his control. If scholars such as Kenneth Kinnamon are correct—that the story as a whole demonstrates the ineffectiveness of either faith or individualism in "coping with white oppression," thus suggesting the need for collective action, then what about the river that runs throughout the story? How does it figure in the brutal events of the brief life of Mann?

Though the date of the story and the setting of its events cause readers to assume that it is the Mississippi River in flood, as in Bradstreet's poem the river is not named, which suggests that what matters most is the river's function rather than its precise identity. Neither the shape of the river nor its course is clearly defined; its banks are long gone by the time the story begins, and we know only that its current moves generally toward the "South End" of the unnamed town. In fact, the river is less of a particular stream than a vast tide of "wild waters" covering everything, sweeping away humans not fortunate enough to have a boat, and ripping human structures off their very foundations. We only know the river by what it is not (e.g., the Jordan, to which it is compared by the story's title and song) and by what it does. For some readers, the flood of the story symbolizes fate, while for others it represents a world of "unrelieved bleakness" and "epitomiz[es] Southern racial relations." In either case, the flooding river is the emblem of an unstoppable force; its primary role is that of elemental antagonist. We learn of its force through Mann's battle, his struggle against its current—the one struggle he wins, much to the surprise of white soldiers, who cheer his achievement even as they dehumanize him with racist epithets.

The few qualities of the water that do appear—depth, sound, and color— mostly refer to the river's adversarial role. In section 1 it rises from four feet deep to six feet to twelve feet; in the fourth section it is still rising "'at the rate of five feet an hour.'" The narrator frequently remarks on the ominous "droning" of the water, except when the levee breaks, causing "a wild commotion" all around Mann: "Behind him were shouts, and over the shouts was the siren's scream, and under the siren's scream was the loud roar of loosened waters." And from the very opening of the story the narrator's attention turns most often to the color of the water, which changes throughout the day, in the morning beginning as a "deep brown" and then in the afternoon becoming "a clayey yellow. And at night it was black, like a restless tide of liquid tar." Yellow only in the first section, the water remains black through most of the action (sections 2–5), turning brown in the conclusion as the narrator focuses on Mann's corpse and ends with ellipsis points: "one black palm sprawled limply outward and upward, trailing in the brown current . . ."

Color, as other commentators have pointed out, is terribly important in the story: white people, white boats, white rage and dehumanizing discourse; black people, black fear, black acquiescence and resistance. But what of the "black waters"? The flooding river is yellow before Mann sets out on his tasks, black during his prolonged and agonizing fight, brown when he's dead. By insistently pointing out the water's blackness during Mann's struggle, the narrator associates Mann's battle against nature with an interior battle against certain aspects of his own blackness, even as the protagonist draws strength from other cultural traits of the oppressed community to which he belongs. Mann must strive against the current, of flooding water but also of tendencies toward submission and/or deep desperation that fragment his community. The color-time scheme extends the one poetically painted by the forerunner Hughes, in which the Mississippi changes from "muddy" earlier in the day to "golden" at sunset. Wright's story takes readers into the world of the river after the sun has gone down, into the dark night of black Brother Mann's soul. In that darkness Mann cannot realize the spiritual unity experienced by Hughes's "Negro." Social, political, and economic forces intervene, leaving individuals to scrape and scrap for themselves.

The narrator's description of Mann's death down by the river presents a sort of witnessing different from that of the by-the-river poetry. Where the poets found the possibility of a redemptive understanding down by the river in a vision of the world that transcends time, for Wright time is one of the impersonal forces that can overwhelm struggling humans. In the morning following the apocalyptic events of the flood, as the rains cease, the waters begin to subside, and "the darkness was thinning to a light haze," Mann looks out on verdant slopes and prays to the Lord for salvation. But in Wright's story the "blurred dawn" in which Mann prays is but a false dawn; time offers no relief from his woes. Redemption will not come from the river or from supplication to God, not from nature or from the prevailing structure of society. Redemption, if available at all, will result only from collective human effort to surmount natural and social conditions. Elder Murray's "Down by the Riverside" asks singers to surrender; Wright's story rewrites the spiritual by remaking the river into an impersonal force of godless nature, emblematic of other forces that push members of a community to the verge of oblivion. Readers are asked to pick up sword and shield, to carry on Mann's struggle. The final ellipsis points pose a question: How will you act in the postdiluvian world?

We Sat on the Bank and the River Went By: Familial Relations

There are countless ways in which literature and rivers merge in the investigation of the relationship between self and other. By-the-river writings, while often concerned with spiritual meditations and societal issues, also take up matters of lesser magnitude, and in some cases writers return to the river to consider personal and domestic problems. Instead of starting by the river and moving beyond to grand questions, these writers come back to the riverside to think about the nature of family and home. Once again by the river they gather their thoughts to sort through their relationships with people and places. In two examples the writers turn away from their academic professions to explore the meaning of rivers and produce literary works of beauty and power. Both works—a collection of essays by a professor of philosophy and a novella by an English professor—lead readers to flowing water, and both feature questions about life, meaning, and family. In each case a scholar turns to literature in order to devote significant energy to thinking by the river in two different senses: thinking alongside a river and thinking by means of rivers. Their writings, premised on autobiographical experiences with streams, pursue questions of interpersonal relations; they connect water and words to discuss other connections, those that persist and those that do not—connections between members of a family, between humans and the world, and between life and language.

The epigraph of Kathleen Dean Moore's *Riverwalking* comes from the eminent British philosopher R. G. Collingwood and likens the "life of the mind" to "the flow of a torrent through its mountain-bed." Moore, who teaches and writes about such topics as environmental ethics and critical thinking at Oregon State University, moves beyond disciplinary boundaries in *Riverwalking*. In one of the twenty brief essays that comprise the book, each titled with the name of a river, she recalls being drawn to the study of philosophy because its "essential value was clarity," whereas such fields as the study of literature seemed awash in ambiguity. But she goes on to find that the insistence upon clarity and the pursuit of objectivity offered by the discipline of Western philosophy have their limits, as she explains in the preface, tracing the book's origins to relations with her husband, a biologist at the same institution, and their experiences off-campus. Having found that their "professional lives . . . fragment our studies into discrete objects and focus our attention on answerable questions only," Moore writes that streams reconnect their lives and experiences: "We come together on rivers where biology and philosophy, body and mind, experience and idea, flow side by side until they cannot be distinguished in a landscape that is whole and beautiful and ambiguous. This book is about what I have seen and heard in that land." For Moore, academic departmentalization, visible in the brick pathways separating buildings and disciplines, results in opposition, fragmentation, "discrete objects," and distinct foci. Her literary efforts, though informed by her training, belong to life outside of the institution. While rivers are a vehicle for taking her off-campus, these literary essays serve as a vehicle for taking her beyond her professional training: in the discipline of philosophy, she has found, important matters are kept apart from one another for the sake of clarity. Literature allows her to celebrate ambiguity.

All of the essays of *Riverwalking* pertain to thinking by the river. Each takes up an experiential or conceptual topic as a problem, connects the topic to a river (even if a few of the connections are rather loose), and moves toward some sort of resolution, whether that entails simply identifying more precisely the nature of the problem or a more advanced response, say, solace, understanding, hope ... The connection of topic with place plays an important role in Moore's approach to "thinking." Following up on the suggestion of the limits of academic disciplines outlined in the preface, Moore recalls her experience as a beginning graduate student, being shamed when discussing the first paper assignment with her philosophy professor. Wanting to write about Descartes and the events of his life that may have informed his approach to philosophy, the student was chided by her teacher: "'Philosophy is not about life. Philosophy is about ideas. Life and ideas are not the same.'" After twenty years of working in the field that her professor helped demarcate, Moore uses *Riverwalking* to offer a different approach to ideas, philosophy, and thinking. Life and ideas may not be the same thing, but they are, in Moore's book, related to one another. The essays turn to rivers in order to think about life and frequently use the notion and experiences of "family" to consider relation. And while they can't quite be called philosophy, at least not by Moore's professor, these essays are nevertheless philosophical (loving or aspiring to or seeking out wisdom), a kind of writing that promotes reflective inquiry and creative propositions.

One reason for Moore's turn away from philosophy and toward literature and rivers becomes explicit in the essay "Winter Creek," which features the "art of poking around" in the neighborhood of moving water. Whereas for Moore formal systems of philosophy employ precision and abstraction for the purpose of clarity and certainty, too much is left out of consideration (e.g., questions of "home," land, "work"). A literary approach to life and its vicissitudes, informed by rivers and their environs, permits a more truthful

though less consistent way of thinking about place, people, and the relations between them. Philosophical approaches to problems can improve
our understanding by sharpening methods of inquiry, but they can also
obstruct understanding by interrupting the flow between life and ideas.
Moore's solution is a literary experiment in which she takes the critical
reflection out of the philosophy department, out of the building entirely,
and sets up camp with it down by the river.

She is by no means the first such experimenter. Henry David Thoreau,
whom Moore conjures in "Winter Creek," complained in *Walden* that in
his day there were only professors of philosophy instead of philosophers.
"Poking around" at the edge of Winter Creek, Moore uses Thoreau and his
essay "Walking" to call for a kind of thinking that involves examining one's
world in a less disciplined but still engaged manner. With her reference to
Thoreau and an emphasis on "wonder and hoping," Moore reminds readers that hers is a literary endeavor. Because literature is governed by rules
different from those that govern philosophy, *Riverwalking* enables Moore
to take thinking on a different course. Writing "by the river" allows for poking around; it nearly always involves questions of relation and encourages
a critical and creative response to those questions. As we will see in later
chapters, discipline, direction, and purpose are necessary characteristics of
downriver or upriver narratives. Going up or down, there is seldom time
for poking around, and there are too many dangers if one does. By-the-river
literature, however, often results from a writer coming to a momentarily
stable point of reference from which she or he sifts and sorts through such
matters as the purpose of life, the nature of suffering, questions of time or
language or family.

"So I poke around at the frozen edges of Winter Creek," Moore explains,
"in the late afternoon when the sun comes in low over the oak knoll and
throws a long, rippling shadow from each dried cattail across the creek and
up the farther bank." In her casual investigation of the margins of Winter
Creek, Moore celebrates the place as well as a lively "method" of engaging
with it; the method, if it can be called such, requires that one temporarily
abandon destinations and step out of directed endeavor. Moore defends
what would otherwise appear to be an idle and trifling pastime, "an avocation for the dissolute," proposing that it is the proper enterprise for the
philosophically inclined: "Everything interesting is complicated. Since truth

is in the details, seekers of truth should look for it there." Being by the river rather than going with the flow or fighting against the current, we are well situated to examine life and its properties; just far enough away from but yet close enough to the flux and forces of life's rush, we can observe and ponder the meaning of events.

Moore exemplifies by-the-river thinking in an essay following the death of her father. "Salish River" connects experience with the recent funeral to thoughts on time. She recalls the difficulty of choosing passages suitable for memorializing her father, a scientist, who acknowledged the spiritual possibilities of "life everlasting" while devoting himself with greater passion to the earthly processes of life. Her contemplations in the essay resemble Anne Bradstreet's but ultimately turn in the opposite direction, back to observations of time and the river, away from questions of eternity and the soul. Moore finishes "Salish River" sitting by the stream, not knowing what else to do, thinking through her father's lack of interest in the afterlife, thinking of the salmon who provide the measure of the "times of a river," and finally rises to walk along the river, associating herself with the spawning salmon.

The type of thinking developed in *Riverwalking*, like that in many of Thoreau's works, depends largely on the meaning of foundational words, terms on which we build our conception of the world. Throughout the book Moore connects words and ideas to rivers and watersheds in an effort to improve our understanding of meaning, of what matters to humans and why. While thinking by the Salish River uses closeness to the stream to consider notions of "time" and the seasons of human life, "The Willamette"—the very first essay in the book—is based on ideas of "family" and "home." The essay begins with an italicized section (one of three) that recounts a family camping excursion. This part of the essay takes place by the river and describes Moore's intellectual and emotional preparations for the departure of her young daughter on a trip abroad. They have set up camp by the river as part of a secular ritual to mark her daughter's coming to adulthood and to ensure her return to the family after her travels.

The italicized segments are woven into a discussion of the nature and meaning of home. Moore uses autobiographical experiences with rivers to thread the past and present together, tracing the mother-daughter's lineage back to England, where Moore's own mother "was born in a river town" in

Yorkshire. These thoughts on the motherland establish the maternal origins of "a long line of people with strong homing instincts": faced with postwar unemployment, her mother agreed to emigrate from Yorkshire to Cleveland, Ohio, only after insisting that, poor as the family was, she would be allowed to "go back home" every four years. Moore follows this emigration with her own removal from Cleveland, not long after the infamous burning of the Cuyahoga River, to Oregon, "because it had clean, cold rivers." Her memories of her own holiday homecomings to Cleveland are associated with "the homing instinct in garter snakes," who return to "ancestral homes" they have never seen, to "a place they have never been," and what scientists know about such instincts in other animals (bees, salamanders, pigeons, songbirds). These thoughts bring her to the essay's "essential issue: What will draw our own children back home?" What instincts, principles, or traditions will keep families whole? Are there essential qualities of modern humans' "home" that will draw us back or help us return, even as our culture becomes global and our families disperse? Is there really any such thing as home to which we might go?

That last question brings up the problem of meaning and stems from Moore's philosophical concern that meaning is not an essential property of things, even things so seemingly natural or instinctual as "home." Citing the French existentialists, she proposes that, though we daily "walk out into a world we think makes sense," the sense that the world makes, the meanings that we accord to the things of the world, are "baseless, arbitrary, floating." "We think we understand what things are and how they are related. We feel at home in the world." Those feelings, however, may not always persist over time and can shift in a moment with the slightest prompting from events or our surroundings. "Suddenly, without warning, the meaning breaks off the surface, and the truth about the world is revealed: Nothing is essentially anything." Despite personal losses and the general lack of an essential "home," Moore proposes that we can repair a sense of "at-home-ness" in the world through the thoughtful creation of meaning in relation to a particular place: "When the feeling comes over you, you have to go home, knowing that home doesn't exist—not really, except as you have given meaning to a place by your own decisions and memories."

"Home," in other words, will only have meaning if we make it meaningful, and that involves working with our instincts and abilities. Moore's solution to the crisis of meaning has something to do with the Willamette, where the essay returns us at its conclusion. After watching her daughter make tea at the edge of the river, Moore cites research in biology on homing instincts. "Scientists say" that a wasp can return to its hole in the ground after a day's work, "zigging and zagging" for miles and miles and hours and hours and then "flying straight home." In one experiment a biologist observed an individual wasp return each day to three rocks framing its home hole; when the scientist removed the rocks and arranged them in a different place, the wasp "wandered around, stupefied" upon its return. The rocks were there, but the hole was not. Comparing the wasp's difficulties to her own returns to her Oregon home after occasional Cleveland visits, Moore writes, "My three rocks are the Willamette River." The Willamette serves as a homing device for her thoughts, allowing her to draw a sense of "home" from that place but also to imbue that place with the meaning that makes "home." The river is a symbol, a sign of where home might be; but it is also the thing itself by virtue of the writer's meditations at its edge.

Family relations and the rivers of home are at the center of one of the best-known by-the-river writings of the late twentieth century, Norman Maclean's novella *A River Runs Through It* (1976). The variety of uses to which the very words of the title have been put testify to the work's familiarity: followers of Maclean have proposed that a river runs through everything from brain mechanics to the formation of the universe. Although the popularity of the phrase may have as much to do with the success of Robert Redford's film version as to the book on which it is based, in each case something is flowing *through* something else, connecting sundry parts and creating a watershed of relationships. Relation, embodied in that preposition, is what matters most. And "relation" is the central question of Maclean's story, whether it regards the strained ties between siblings or the intricate play between words and water.

A River Runs Through It belongs to a line of literature dating back at least to Izaak Walton's *The Compleat Angler* (1653), a work mentioned early in Maclean's tale—even if Walton, "'an Episcopalian and a bait fisherman,'" is one of those disparaged as a "bastard" by one or both of the main characters in the novella. Like Walton's, Maclean's "little book," as he calls it, concerns fishing. On one level, the story concerns how fishermen know rivers, how fishermen fish, and how fishermen relate to one another; it is about the dif-

ference between big-fish fishermen and little-fish fishermen and the extent
to which fishing can help men as they deal with life's problems. Centered
on the events in the lives of two brothers—the narrator and his brother,
Paul—in the summer of 1937, the story begins and ends in the vicinity of
the "great trout rivers in western Montana." Because of the absence of distinct sections or breaks in the narration, events flow from one to the next,
even when the narrator's view shifts back to the past and then returns to
the present. Four fishing trips structure the events and function like pools
in a river, places where movement slows and a fisherman stops, expecting
to catch something.

On another level, the river on which they fish organizes the narrator's
meditations on humanity, the human condition, and the role of storytelling
in treating that condition. Fishing, family, and religion are the terms by which
Maclean structures his autobiographically based account of the attempt to
derive meaning from the river that runs through all, and the significance
of those terms is signaled in the very first sentence of the book: "In our
family, there was no clear line between religion and fly fishing." Each of the
four outings examines the fluid relationship between fishing and religion,
with "family" functioning as the basic unit, the fundamental relationship
mediating others. The closeness of the Maclean family reaches into both
the spiritual realm (exemplified by the Presbyterian church in which the
father preaches) and the natural realm (the river). The Big Blackfoot River,
where most of the fishing occurs, "is the river we knew best," the river that
the brothers have fished for almost thirty years and that their father had
fished before them, and the river regarded by all of the Maclean men "as a
family river, as a part of us."

But even before the river is introduced in Maclean's story the narrator
signals the importance of love and family and their place in the world. He
remembers, for instance, that "painted on one side of our Sunday school
wall were the words, God Is Love. We always assumed that these three words
were spoken directly to the four of us in our family and had no reference
to the world outside, which my brother and I soon discovered was full of
bastards, the number increasing rapidly the farther one gets from Missoula,
Montana." Later in the story the narrator highlights the import of this sign of
a sacred love with a profane sighting: he and his brother stumble upon the
narrator's brother-in-law (another "bastard") sprawled naked by the river

with his illicit lover, on whose backside is tattooed "LO|VE" (LO on one cheek and VE on the other, "with a hash-mark between"). The appearance of the word in other contexts serves to reinforce the significance of love among the Macleans; in subtle ways, the narrator pursues an understanding of love throughout the story, the river playing an important role in that pursuit.

Love in *A River Runs Through It* is indicative of Maclean's interest in the nature of relations. Relations—within the family, between religion and fishing, between the family and others, between the world and the Word—are central to the book, the narrator using the four trips to catch more than fish. Like many by-the-river works, there is a great deal of life but little dramatic action. The brothers fish the Big Blackfoot; they reluctantly escort people from outside the family fishing; and, finally, they cheerfully return their father to a favorite spot on the family river. The most dramatic event occurs "off-camera," as it were: in the final pages the narrator remembers driving with a police sergeant "down the length of the Big Blackfoot River" to inform his parents of his brother's death by pistol whipping. What matters most is what does *not* happen or, rather, how the characters in the story struggle to make sense out of what happens. Being by the river, watching events float past, the narrator contemplates the river and all that moves along with it. Perhaps even more so, the narrator contemplates contemplation; he thinks about thinking, about what he does and does not know. Although his brother, Paul, is a most winning character, a fetching, masterful young man "at the height of his power" (when he is not confined to a drunk-tank or losing dangerously at the gambling tables), the story is more concerned with the narrator's inability to understand Paul than it is with Paul himself.

The differences between the two brothers can be seen in their approach to fishing. While each one is a "big-fish fisherman, looking with contempt" on those who settle for the "little ones," the brothers' approaches to the art diverge. From the very first, Paul splashed onto the scene as a fisherman of daring, prone to action rather than contemplation. "If he studied the situation he didn't take any separate time to do it." He never seemed to stand around, never reclined on the bank; he jumped off rocks into the current of the mighty Big Blackfoot, swam and wrestled fish athletically, was always the first to cast and the last to quit. The river spray "emanating from him" wreathed him like a "halo"; awestruck onlookers muttered "My, my!" and

"Jesus!" in admiration of his prowess. As a result of his mastery "the whole world turned to water." Before the narrator fished, on the other hand, he "studied the situation" and always "had to do a lot of thinking before casting to compensate for some of my other shortcomings" as a fisherman. Fishing, for the narrator, entails thinking, circumspection, second-guessing, and still more thinking.

The different approaches lead to similar ends, however, as both fishermen enter into an intimacy with the river, an extension of their relationship to each other. On that first fishing trip Paul's seemingly unstudied actions enable him to merge with the Big Blackfoot. Throwing himself into the stream, he partakes of water, and everything becomes vapor and spray by virtue of Paul's physical unleashing of the river's potential energy. The process takes longer to unfold for the narrator: on the third trip, sitting in contemplation by the river after catching a few "nice-sized" fish and a smaller one, he watches the Big Blackfoot until "eventually the watcher joined the river, and there was only one of us. I believe it was the river." Further thoughts—on the glacial nature of the Big Blackfoot, on its straight and fast run through rapids, on the places where it slows and deposits rock and sand—deepen his intimacy, and he finally "becomes" the river by arriving at an understanding of the principles that underlie its formation. Thus, both brothers merge with the waters of the Big Blackfoot, Paul physically and the narrator intellectually.

The narrator, that is to say, follows in the tradition of by-the-river writing, sitting on the bank and contemplating as life courses past. Much of *A River Runs Through It* consists of the narrator's description of his thought processes as he tries to understand what is happening. His thoughts, especially his thoughts on thinking, dominate the scene; but in spite of this propensity he spends a great deal of time in uncertainty. On the first fishing trip he stumbles along, "studying the situation," mentally wandering from wondering to association, from conviction to doubt. On the second trip he thinks until "all that existed of me were thoughts." Fly fishing, he muses, is essentially "looking for answers to questions." As a result, his story consists largely of one long Bradstreet-like "Contemplation," with less rhyme and more ribaldry. More often than not, however, the contemplator fails to understand what is happening around him, why it is happening, or what he can do about it. There are some things he just doesn't want to know (details of Paul's dissolution, for example) and some things he simply cannot understand. Between the first two fishing trips, driving alone at sunrise, he tries "to find something I already knew about life that might help me reach out" and assist Paul, but he cannot come to any understanding. However strong may be the instinct to help, it remains "futile" and "haunting" due to his inability to know how to help. The day dawns, but the narrator is left in the dark. He continues to fret and intellectually fumble on the second fishing trip, near the end of which he succinctly states, "I still do not understand my brother."

Just before the final trip, discussing the problem of helping Paul with their father, the narrator summarizes the insufficiency of his thinking: "'I don't know, that's my trouble.'" Thinking by the river, for the narrator-writer of the story, is like fishing: the thinker tries to catch understanding but often fails to hook it. Time and the river rush on, and it is not until long after events have occurred that knowledge takes shape. When it does, it does so through creative, imaginative reengagement with facts and perceptions, through a literary activity that reexamines and reorganizes things into something meaningful. Recounting the final fishing trip, the narrator recalls Paul's theory of thinking: "'All there is to thinking,' he said, 'is seeing something noticeable which makes you see something you weren't noticing which makes you see something that isn't even visible.'" Unfortunately, this theory of knowing does not enable Paul to save himself; it does seep into the story, however, and ultimately enables the narrator to understand something. Throughout most of the novella the narrator lacks understanding because his thinking lacks creativity. He worries about comprehending, about getting his head completely around a problem; he struggles for precision and angles for the truth, trying "with each step to leave the world behind" and replace it intellectually with "a world perfect and apart," disconnected from life but distinct, clear, and knowable. It is only later, when he begins to connect events, perspective, and experiences by turning them into literature, that the truth takes shape.

In other words, the narrator eventually realizes Paul's theory of knowing through writing a fictional story of autobiographical events. Understanding, he learns, involves paying attention to something he has noticed, using this sight to see things he had not already noticed, then developing his critical vision further through creative insight. The latter stage allows the narrator to begin to understand that which cannot be seen—meaning, principles, conceptual truths that transcend the material facts of reporting (what, where, who). I said earlier that the story is more concerned with the narrator's knowing than with that which he would know (his brother and how to help him); the story is ultimately about stories and about this story in particular: how it started, the reason for telling it, and what it might yield. *A River Runs Through It* is the narrator's attempt to understand the events and people of his life by moving beyond autobiographically reporting a true story to telling a fictional story that helps him see more truly.

During the third fishing trip the narrator traces the story's origins to the Big Blackfoot itself and a quiet moment during which thinking *by* the river led to identification *with* the river:

> As the heat mirages on the river in front of me danced with and through each other, I could feel patterns from my own life joining with them. It was here, while waiting for my brother, that I started this story, although, of course, at the time I did not know that stories of life are often more like rivers than books. But I knew a story had begun, perhaps long ago near the sound of water. And I sensed that ahead I would meet something that would never erode so there would be a sharp turn, deep circles, a deposit, and quietness.

Reflecting back on the birth of the story, the narrator understands it to have come from a joining of patterns and images, of imaginative perception and riparian reflections. The attention that the narrator gives to the story's origins belongs to a theme developing throughout the narrative and explicitly articulated in its concluding pages: the intimate relationship between words and water.

The final fishing trip features a set of significant confluences, religion and family running together again, fishing and thinking, water and words, all forming streams that merge in the end. Near the start of the trip the narrator comes upon his father, who has finished fishing and sits "reading the New Testament in Greek." Pondering the part that "'says the Word was in the beginning,'" the preacher tells his son, "'I used to think water was first, but if you listen carefully you will hear that the words are underneath the water.'" "The Word" of God is connected to "the words" of humans; both Logos and language precede the waters of the river, a story that the river itself now tells "'if you listen carefully.'" The narrator disputes his father's interpretation and suggests that Paul would do so as well, believing that "the words are formed out of water." "'No,' my father said, 'you are not listening carefully. The water runs over the words. Paul will tell you the same thing.'"

The minister does not further explicate his aquatic theology, but a subsequent moment of the trip also involves water and words; here it is the language that water itself speaks. After Paul makes "one big cast for one last fish" as the other two Maclean men watch, a magical and even electrical moment results in "the last fish we were ever to see Paul catch," a moment full of Paul's beauty. All three men then sit by the river, listening to it and understanding its words: "We sat on the bank and the river went by. As always, it was making sounds to itself, and now it made sounds to us. It would be hard to find three men sitting side by side who knew better what a river was saying." While the earlier episode puts water and words in relation to one another, wondering over which came first, the second episode shifts to the words that water speaks, to the river's own words and what they might mean. For all the river's eloquence, however, meaning is yet elusive, and uncertainties remain: the narrator remarks, "A river, though, has so many things to say that it is hard to know what it says to each of us." These uncertainties spill over into the following spring, when the narrator remembers the absence of understanding surrounding the circumstances of Paul's death.

At the end of the final outing the father pushes the narrator for a clarifying tale to be made of the fishing, the family, and the words over which the Big Blackfoot runs. The minister asks his son, "'You like to tell true stories, don't you?'" The narrator modifies the question somewhat by responding that he likes "'to tell stories that are true,'" prompting his father to suggest that he try "'mak[ing] up a story and the people to go with it.'" "'Only then,'" he explains, "'will you understand what happened and why.'" Reverend Maclean's cryptic suggestion intimates that an act of literature is necessary to ascertain truths otherwise unavailable to our usual means of making sense of things. It is an addendum to Paul's theory of knowledge, apparently spurring the narrator to develop the requisite creative insight that leads to better ways of knowing. Coming from the minister-father, the advice has biblical as well as familial implications; but in the larger context of the story it belongs to the theme of water-and-word relations. The drift seems to be that, thinking by the river, one can best understand the difficult past by exercising imagination and piecing things together creatively for a general audience—that is, through literary activity. The minister's minihomily effectively brings to a close the remembrance of the past. Back in the present, the narrator, now "too old to be much of a fisherman," concludes his story with those words about water that have become part of our cultural lexicon: "Eventually, all things merge into one, and a river runs through it." This image of unity and the connectivity of the river, followed by references to "the world's great flood," the rocks of "the basement of time," and "the words" underlying everything, makes up a puzzle or parable for the reader to consider, punctuated by the book's last sentence: "I am haunted by waters."

A River Runs Through It thus exemplifies by-the-river literature, which is characterized by a fundamental connection between flowing waters and formative words. Premised on that connection, by-the-river writing is nourished by and further nourishes thinking about some of the most basic questions regarding our condition: questions of time, truth, identity, God, self, other, suffering, evil. In pursuing these questions, by-the-river writers don't need to go anywhere; they stand or sit, thinking, as the river goes by. The final two paragraphs of the story underscore the idea of relation, with particularities merging into an indefinite whole and the river standing out as the vital reality at the center of things. The narrator's thoughts bring the events of the deepest past into the present, all things blending into the grand unity through which the Big Blackfoot River runs. The waters running in the river today, he tells us, are related to the waters receding from the Flood; the words of his family members, all those he "loved and did not understand" when he was young, are related to the Word. But the conclusion of his story-about-a-story also represents a special property of literature—a quality that can lead us to see relations in seemingly distinct entities and disjointed events. A river runs through everything for Maclean, a life-giving force that fuses all things to one another and thus serves as an emblem of relation, a concept figured as God's love in the minister's preaching and placarded on the Sunday school wall. Literature, in this story, is a mode of thinking that facilitates our understanding of the meaning of the river.

3 | *Up the River*

Who goes up the river? As our idioms indicate, we might find ourselves up a certain creek without a paddle or sent up the river to prison, but we seldom go upriver of our own volition: it can take an awful lot of volition to paddle, swim, or even wade against the stream. The force of the water, the pull of gravity, the course of time, the call of destiny—nature itself seems to lead us down the river. Because opposing these forces requires considerable effort and energy, we seldom (if ever) go up the river accidentally or casually; we go upriver because, for some reason or another, we must. Going against the stream is a purposeful endeavor, often dependent upon an external power source (a good tailwind in the sails, at least, or steam, once upon a time, and, for the present, an ample gas tank) and almost always driven by a profound desire to obtain something reputed to reside somewhere up the river. The contemplative atmosphere to be found by the river is left behind in striving against the current, there being little time to pause and think about relations or anything else when the earth itself seems to be pushing against the upriver traveler. While anyone can hang out alongside a river and leisurely ponder the flow passing by, only the man of action goes against the flow and fights his way upstream.

I certainly do not believe that only men can go up the river, but it is nevertheless the case that men have figured predominantly in upriver texts. This may have something to do with the relatively small number of such texts. While both being by a river and coming into contact with a particular section of stream are among the most common means of experiencing streams and their flow, going against that flow is surely among the least common, a fact reflected in American literature. But it is also true that those few narratives based on upriver movement often operate within a martial and/or colonial context. Going upstream provides a means of exploring and commanding territory, of gaining supplies or power, of surmounting nature and staking a claim on behalf of a culture. Especially in early American literature, upriver travel often entails colonial captains penetrating the "virgin wilderness," and the sexual politics of this arrangement lies at the center of one of the nation's most durable myths—the story of Pocahontas and John Smith. Such narratives tell the story of the brave soldier, a cultural standard-bearer, battling against nature and forging his way into the savage, sylvan "darkness," ever away from the light, the known, the certainty of civilization and customary ways of understanding the world.

Another reason for the relative paucity of upriver narratives is that travelers almost never go upriver and stay there. When I have ventured upstream, walking up the Hurricane River near Lake Superior, say, or paddling up the Sudbury in Massachusetts, I have always had to walk or float back down. In Lorain, Ohio, a friend and I paddled up the Black River under a hot September sun, starting from a concrete launch, passing piles of coal and gravel, loud clangs and horns and other industrial alarms, large machines lumbering on the banks. Occasional pieces of trash drifted on the greenish brown water of the Black, a wide and deep river at its mouth with little current. As we proceeded up the river, we saw more and more great blue herons on the shores, a couple of cormorants on a rock midstream, gulls and geese, kingfishers and turkey vultures, turtles, an osprey, a red-tailed hawk, silver sparks of tiny fish leaping ahead of us. But we had no commission, and we had other things to do, so we circumnavigated an island and headed home.

In keeping with the categories I have constructed for this study, such a journey is not, strictly speaking, upriver but rather up and down the river. There is a subtle but significant difference between the two categories. In upriver texts the writer emphasizes upriver movement and events that occur upstream, giving little or no attention to the return; though the *voyage* may go both ways, the *story* is primarily unidirectional. Up-and-down-the-river stories, on the other hand, give more or less equal attention to the going forth and the coming back, making a special point of the two-sided trip. For Lewis and Clark, ascending the Missouri River was an important achievement, as was descending the Columbia to the sea; but their successful return back up the Columbia and down the Missouri made the mission complete and the story compelling. The tales I consider in this chapter feature a commissioned voyage and have three main sections: a prelude, providing the reasons for going upriver (the terms of the commission); a description of the movement against the stream; and an account of what occurs at the end of the upriver journey, dwelling mostly on the action at the top of the river and sometimes adding brief mention of the return trip.

Because streams provided the primary way into the continent, some of the earliest writings about North America tell the story of upriver adventures. Jacques Cartier left a vivid record of his exploration of the St. Lawrence River, including the first upriver voyage to Hochelaga (now Montreal) in 1535. The St. Lawrence, which took its name from a misreading of the manuscript of Cartier's account, flows from Lake Ontario to the Atlantic Ocean; the French explorer described it as "without comparison the largest river that is known to have ever been seen." In a series of voyages to that area, Cartier and his men reconnoitered what he believed was "the land God gave to Cain," seeing unfamiliar life-forms (walruses, for example—"fish in appearance like horses") and sampling strange plants, such as tobacco, which the Native peoples puffed to stay "warm and in good health." "We made a trial of this smoke," Cartier reports. "When it is in one's mouth, one would think one had taken powdered pepper, it is so hot." Cartier spends most of the account describing their considerable effort "to make our way up the river as far as we possibly could"; on the return they find themselves beset by a strange disease (a form of scurvy) and "frozen up in the ice," stuck from mid-November to mid-April in ice two fathoms thick with snow four feet deep. Twenty-five men died before Cartier and company eventually breezed down the river and back to France in a couple of pages.

In all of the upriver narratives of early America, the voyagers are just about always looking for something in particular (the Northwest Passage, gold, pearls, food), and they just about always find Native peoples whom they fear, whom they are charged to convert, with whom they trade, and whom they cannot understand. Cartier, for example, writes of Donnacona, "the lord of Canada" and his tendency to "harangue" the French, "moving his body and limbs in a marvellous manner." Cartier never captures the precise meaning of Native harangues, nor do they deter him from pushing upstream "as far as possible." The marveling works both ways, of course; Cartier reports that, after his company complied with a request for a show of artillery, his "much astonished" hosts "began to howl and to shriek in such a very loud manner that one would have thought hell had emptied itself there."

Wonder and fear comprise the atmosphere of most early American upriver narratives, and these stories are full of hazardous conditions, unthinkable practices, hard work, ravaging illness, and the violence of clashing world-views. That clash results in profound misunderstandings: gestures, motives, and meanings are often lost in the translation from one culture's worldview to the other's. Accordingly, up-the-river tales emphasize struggle, usually between self and other, though often the self's struggle with itself, and always involve the struggle to understand a world utterly different from the explorer's own.

This Riuer of Moratico Promiseth Great Things: Lured into Ambiguity

A half-century after Cartier and over twenty years before Henry Hudson sailed up the stream that now bears his name, the Englishman Ralph Lane penned an upriver narrative based on his experiences as the leader of the first Roanoke colony (August 1585–June 1586). As is the case with Cartier's reports, to read Lane's "Discourse on the First Colony" is to make a kind of interpretive upriver journey, against the flow of history into an unfamiliar time of great uncertainty. The worldview reflected in the "Discourse" and Lane's style (and spelling) as a writer combine to make it an almost foreign literature requiring an act of translation. Strange occurrences, often brutal actions stemming from firmly held beliefs, and wholesale uncertainty in frequently life-threatening conditions—early American literature is not for the dainty reader, those faint of heart or weak of stomach. The body of writings often connect us to an interpretive heart of darkness, a world of rapid change inhabited by a people fearful of change, a people culturally biased toward a particular idea of order and the immutability of God's Creation but confronted by phenomena that severely challenged the categories with which Elizabethans made sense of the world. One of Cartier's commentators has observed that the French explorer "attempted to understand the new world through similarities rather than differences," and the same may be said of Lane and other early upriver narratives. In these works the New World, assumed to be an unfinished version of the Old, can best be understood by what it is not. Things of the New are likened to things in the Old and found wanting, in need of improvement, and the land is as full of promise as it is of terror. God often lends a hand to the writers of these accounts in their day-to-day affairs, the Devil lurks behind the next tree, and the Native peoples alternatively are gentle children of the forest or double-dealing diabolical agents.

Lane's "Discourse" (written for Sir Walter Raleigh, the sponsor of this colonial enterprise) describes "the particularities of the imployments of the English men" from August 17, 1585, to June 18, 1586, and attempts to explain the failure of Lane's mission, attributing it to "our weake number, and supply of things necessary." Rivers figure prominently in Lane's reconnoitering and provide much of the drama of his account. Exploring the Chowan River in March 1586, his party encountered Menatonon, "the King" (or "Weroance") of Choanoke, "a man impotent in his lims, but otherwise for a Sauage, a very graue and wise man." Menatonon, whom Lane had taken prisoner (apparently his customary mode in dealing with "savages"), provided useful information about the land, the people, and "the commodities that eche Contrey yeeldeth," including an exceedingly enticing view of riches to be found "three dayes iourney in a canoa vp his Riuer of Choanoke" (today called the Chowan). Lane designed to voyage up the Chowan and fortify outposts in the vicinity of the headwaters; his half-baked plan never materializes, however, dependent as it is upon additional men and supplies that never arrive. Instead, his attentions were given to another waterway, "a most notable Riuer, and in all those partes most famous, called the Riuer of Morotico."

The Morotico—now the Roanoke—River runs from near the city of Roanoke, Virginia, in the Blue Ridge Mountains some four hundred miles to Albemarle Sound in North Carolina. The Roanoke is presently dammed several times, and at these sites the river becomes lake, but in Lane's time it flowed unimpeded: "This Riuer of Morotico hath so violent a currant from the West and Southwest, that it made me almost of the opinion that with oares it would scarse be nauigable." Comparing its lower reaches to "the Thames betwixt Greenwich, and the Ile of dogges," Lane determined to do battle with this "most violent streame" and travel against the flow and up its length, even though Menatonon and "the Sauages of Morotico themselues doe report strange things of the head of that Riuer." As with most upriver accounts, the world becomes stranger and stranger the farther Lane ascends. His informants told him it would be a long and arduous voyage, thirty to forty days, but Lane expected it to be well worth the toil: "There is a Prouince to the which the sayd Mangoaks haue recourse and traffike vp that Riuer of Morotico, which hath a marueilous and most strange Minerall." Gazing far up the river into the darkness of this New World and his colony's future, Lane saw Chaunis Temoatan, a proverbial land of riches. Here, he has been told, he would find "Wassador," a copperlike substance that he suspects might even be gold.

Spurred by the prospect of wealth, Lane "tooke a resolution with my selfe . . . to enter presently so farre into that Riuer," having established relatively amicable relations with some of the Native peoples living beside the river and thus counting on them for trade and support along the way. The company set out in late March, on a "voyage vp the Riuer"; for three days they rowed against the strong current, struggling one hundred miles into the interior, according to Lane (though scholars point out that he often exaggerated distances in his writing). Their supplies diminished as the party advanced, but Lane "could not meete a man, nor finde a graine of corne in any their Townes." He suspected that Pemisapan, a leader of the Native inhabitants of Roanoke Island who had changed his name from Wingina as tensions escalated between the Roanokes and the English, had betrayed Lane and had spread a rumor among river peoples that the English came to kill them. As a result, all of those living by the Morotico "abandoned their Townes along the Riuer, and retyred themselues with their Crenepoes [women], and their corne." According to his account, Lane explained their plight to his men—that they were several days from their base with only "two dayes victuall left"—and asked them "whether we should aduenture the spending of our whole victuall in some further viewe of that most goodly Riuer in hope to meete with some better hap, or otherwise to retyre our selues back againe." Sleep on it, he told the men, and give me an answer in the morning.

There are many curious aspects of Lane's story. For one, he writes that on the following day his men expressed the firm resolution to push on up the river; oddly, Lane himself, though their "resolution did not a little please mee," states that he "pretended to haue bene rather of the contrary opinion." In part, this demonstrates to his patron the convictions of the colonists and their earnest efforts to accomplish Raleigh's goals; it also shelters Lane somewhat from their lack of success. They continue up the Roanoke River but never encounter any trading partners, nor are they ever able to procure their own victuals from the land. Instead, they are fired upon by unseen attackers, abandon the upriver exploration, and resort to eating a stew made of two bullmastiffs that had made the journey with them. The account of the trip concludes abruptly at "the riuers mouth . . . , hauing rowed in one day downe the currant, as much as in 4. dayes we had done against the same." The voyage, an experience "not without both payne, and perill," results in something short of success, though as Lane summarized the events, "God was pleased not utterly to suffer vs to be lost." Ambiguity abounds up the river. Within months of their failed upriver venture, the colonists had hastily climbed aboard Sir Francis Drake's ship and headed back to England, having completed enough investigation to compile a significant survey of the territory they were calling "Virginia," having peacefully treated with many Native peoples and wiped out a large number of others (sometimes through fear-driven slaughter and sometimes through accidental infection), until "some people could not tel whether to thinke vs gods or men." Or devils maybe?

Success and failure, incursion and retreat, Lane's upriver mission is replete with the warring of light and darkness. In his report to Raleigh he explains why he has "set downe this voyage somewhat particularly": to show that "there wanted no great good will from the most to the least amongst vs" in furthering the colonial cause. All they lacked was better luck and better provisions from their superiors. And if presently the situation were perilous and painful, the future was no less bright. Though they had not completed the mission, though much remained to be done in discovering and securing the riches of the land, they had verified that "this riuer of Moratico promiseth great things," including what they believed was possible access to the Pacific Ocean. Through upriver exploration a luckier and better-supplied company would someday discover either "a good mine" or passage to the Pacific, and with the discovery of either one, Virginia would no doubt become a garden spot, with "the most sweete, and healthfullest climate, and therewithall the most fertile soyle, being manured in the world." A most fascinating aspect of Lane's up-the-river narrative, just like Cartier's account before it, is the extent to which the trip into the unknown obfuscates almost as much as it illuminates. As Karen Ordahl Kuppermann has observed, both stories "diverted attention from the problems of settlement to the dream of riches and access to the South Sea and further confused sixteenth-century European attempts to come to terms with North America." Uncertainty and conflict, the struggle to understand, and the struggle with others—as the river narrows the farther up one goes and trees close in, darkness overtakes light. The upriver traveler who leaves the boat steps out into a world of ambiguity, land tight on the water, water swamping the land.

Infinite Impediments, Yet No Discouragement: Up the River and into the Swamp

The Chickahominy River begins north of Richmond, Virginia, and meanders southeast through the state, heading due south its last six or seven miles before emptying into the James River. At the mouth, river blends with river, and both register the effects of the sea (not forty miles distant), indefinite boundaries more distinct for an observer of a map than for an observer situated near the confluence. At this point the Chickahominy, now wide and tidal, invites the eye as it does the sailboat, its channel narrowing only well beyond view. The ebbing or flooding waters flux, sometimes slowly lapping the swampy shores where the knobby knees of bald cypress roots project up through the water. Straight-trunked trees standing in slow-flow shallows surrounded by bony fingers pointing to the sky—such a scene symbolizes the upriver story to me: forest-choked waters, water-overrun trees, mingling of matter and forces, facts swamped and the truth elusive, clarity caught in glimpses through shadows and sticks, the ecotones and contact zones into which history sluices and out from which it seeps.

really?

As one moves up the river, slow footed along the mucky and tangled banks, the course tightens. The low and level margins of the river, full of conifer and holly, stump and vine, rotting trunks and bird twitter, do not yield vistas lightly. Only occasionally does one find a bump of a bluff for an overlook or espy a turkey vulture high above the snarl of growth and morass of decay for vicarious perspective. And farther upriver the going slows in the funky stillness, the way more choked, darkening in either direction, especially under early-winter clouds. In this portion of the river—about twenty-five miles from the mouth as the crow flies and almost twice that as the bass swims—Virginia Historical Highway Marker E-12 marks the spot where "in Dec. 1607, while exploring the headwaters of the nearby Chickahominy River, Capt. John Smith and his party were captured by a hunting party consisting of members of the Paspaheghs, Chickahominies, Youghtanunds, Pamunkeys, Mattaponis, and Chiskiacks." Traffic on U.S. Route 60/State Route 33 (also called the Pocahontas Trail) rumbles by every now and then (nothing like the racket of nearby Interstate 64), but the peace was broken long ago. And to look at the black-and-white sign now, with its all-caps headline ("CAPT. JOHN SMITH CAPTURED"), is to render history present in a strange way, more so even than at the reenactment villages and information centers at Jamestown and Williamsburg. Although the historical marker is black and white, history is not. To venture up this river does not solve matters but rather leads to a material reminder of the boggy beginnings of significant events and portentous processes.

Sometime during the shortening days of early winter in 1607 John Smith set out from Jamestown, the first lasting English settlement in the New World, with a small group of men. Conditions at the fort, which was little more than six months old, were terrible. The English were dangerously short of supplies after the long voyage, having not only "spent our victuall" on the five months at sea but also "lost the opportunitie" to plant crops for harvest in the fall, all of which Smith attributed to "the unskilfull presumption of our ignorant transporters, that understood not at all, what they undertooke." Beginning in July 1607, rampant disease afflicted the colonists, along with occasional attacks by Algonquin peoples, malnutrition, mismanagement, and a lousy water supply. In August alone nineteen men died, and Smith reported that from May to September "fiftie in this time we buried." After a brief reprieve from extreme difficulties in their first autumn, the colonists' want and political infighting intensified that December. Having been thrust into a leadership role (or having finagled one), Smith readied a trading party for a voyage up the Chickahominy River, where he had already met with commercial success on three similar trips in November, though without having made it all the way up the river. Whereas Ralph Lane ventured forth in search of mines or passageways to the Pacific, Smith went upriver for relief, for salvation, for corn, basically, but also to get away from those

Lane goes upriver to escape mutiny

who "muttered against Captaine Smith, for not discovering the head of the Chickahamania river" already.

Into the interior he went, accompanied by nine men on a barge and making it forty miles "up the river, which for the most part is a quarter of a mile broad, and 3. fatham and a half deep, exceeding osey [oozy], many great low marshes, and many high lands." When the barge could go no farther upstream he left it in the care of seven men, anchored in a small bay, while Smith himself proceeded up the river with two others and two hired Native guides in a canoe the next day. At this point Smith and company "put our selves uppon the adventure: the country onely a vast and wilde wildernes." After another dozen or so miles on the water, the trees greatly encumbering the way, the party paused "to refresh" themselves. "Never get out of the boat," an upriver traveler would observe three and a half centuries later, but Smith did, to explore the "boughts" (bends or curves) of the river and shoot some game for dinner. Picking his way through the "quagmire," he was "beset with 200. Salvages." Throughout his several accounts of the attack, Smith defended himself valiantly (if using his Native guide as a "barricado," or shield, may be considered valiant): he fired upon his attackers, slaying two, before misfortunately stepping into the "bogmire" and having to surrender (on good terms, at least, thanks to his guide's quick-witted testimony that Smith was "the Captaine" and thus deserving of special treatment).

Behold the bemired Captain Smith: waist deep in Chickahominy muck, he is about to provide an important lesson on the nature of upriver narrative. It is a lesson in foundering, in foundering as founding. When he was finally pulled from the bogmire by his captors, Smith stepped from one fen into another—the swamp of history, a series of mist-draped events to which Smith himself added shades of mystery. The captain's accounts of what happened demonstrate an essential element of American upriver writing: the crux of the story comes from events that occur somewhere upstream, usually at the uppermost point of the journey. Writers seldom devote much attention to the process of going against the current or the nature of the waters themselves; what matters most about these rivers is what happens *up* them, at points far from the civilized place from which the voyager has set out. The river's meaning derives from what it connects, and it is usually some form of "culture" being connected to "nature": a voyager representing "civilization" uses the river to complete a mission (e.g., obtaining riches or information) and encounters some version of the "wild." The Chickahominy, whatever else it might do, connects John Smith to Powhatan and also to Pocahontas, and both of these "Salvages" (a word that customarily signified "wildmen") figure as foundations of peculiarly American stories.

In the earliest version of his adventure, Smith is removed from the muck and marched about the countryside, well fed and entertained by his captors, even though he expects every minute to be "executed." After several days of travel and sundry stops, he is delivered to Powhatan, the "Emperour" of the region. Smith reports that he astonished Powhatan in the same manner that he had dazzled Opechancanough, his initial captor: with a "discourse" on the roundness of the planet and the courses of various bodies in the heavens. His "much delighted" host responded warmly. According to Smith, Powhatan asked him to "forsake" his own people and live with the emperor "upon his River." The host promised to give his guest "Corne, Venison," and other food supplies in exchange for "Hatchets and Copper wee should make him, and none should disturbe us. This request I promised to performe: and thus having with all the kindnes hee could devise, sought to content me: hee sent me home with 4. men, one that usually carried my Gowne and Knapsacke after me, two other loded with bread, and one to accompanie me."

This upriver narrative, first appearing in Smith's *A True Relation* (1608), full of tension between the English and the Native inhabitants of the land, nevertheless ends happily, with mutual respect between the captain and the emperor and the promise of amicable relations between the peoples they represent. Such an outcome, however, occupies only a corner of the swamp of history, for Smith wrote a later version of the story that has then been retold countless times in every form imaginable. In the revised tale, penned in the third person, the Chickahominy connects the captain not only to Powhatan but to Pocahontas as well. Smith again describes the upriver travel (though with less detail), adds color to the incident of his capture, and observes again that, subsequent to the "many strange triumphes and conjurations they made of him, yet hee so demeaned himselfe amongst them, as he not onely diverted them from surprising the Fort, but procured his owne libertie" and gained their "estimation" and admiration. He greatly elaborates on the demonstration with which he amazed his captor, "the King of Pamaunkee": in addition to the geological and cosmological lesson, he informs the Algonquians of "the diversitie of Nations, varietie of complexions, and how we were to them Antipodes." In remarking on the antipodal relationship between the English and Powhatan peoples, Smith puts the whole world between them. In the view expressed by the captain, there are two kinds of people in the world: the wild savages, nature's children, who live upriver in the interior of the New World, and the captain's civilized Old World colonialists, bearers of culture.

The second version of his captivity stresses the difference between the parties. Before being taken to Powhatan, Smith witnesses behavior he cannot understand, as when "strangely painted" people "cast themselves in a ring, dauncing in such severall Postures, and singing and yelling out such hellish notes and screeches." Playing heaven to their hell, Smith confounds his preliterate captors by writing a note that is carried to Jamestown and produces the results he has predicted to the Algonquians, as if "he could either divine, or the paper could speake." The "most strange and fearefull Conjurations" persist, and Smith quotes a translation of Seneca to describe the experience: "*As if neare led to hell / Amongst the Devils to dwell.*" His antipodal opposites are "hellish," "most strange," "devils," "fiends," "ugly," painted in red and black and white, adorned with snakes and weasels, skins and feathers. They want to plant his gunpowder and grow their own, he reports. He is taken to Powhatan at Werowocomoco, and "Here more then two hundred of those grim Courtiers stood wondering at him, as he had beene a monster." Even after Smith's "rescue," when he is treated with "esteeme," "Powhatan disguised himselfe in the most fearefullest manner," looking "more like a devill then a man," and Smith was "still expecting (as he had done all this long time of his imprisonment) every houre to be put to one death or other."

Instead of relieving the tension between the hellish and heavenly parties with demonstrations of mutual respect between emperor and captain, as he did in the first version, Smith augments the distance between the two parties in the second version. A third party is needed to mediate between the two opposites and mitigate the heightened tension, and that's where Pocahontas comes in. She is, like her father and his other "grim attendants," in a "natural" (i.e., "unsaved") state, but she proves to be nonetheless kindly and compassionate, an inexplicably salvational savage who comes to the rescue because—well, we don't really know why "she hazarded the beating out of her own brains to save" Smith, as he mentioned briefly in a letter to Queen Anne eight years after the publication of *A True Relation*. In fact, we don't really know *if* she did (let alone *why* she did) what Smith says she did in some of his accounts, the most elaborate being *The Generall Historie of Virginia, New-England, and the Summer Isles* (1624), the one I have been calling the second version. It is this account that sets in motion a foundational American myth, the quintessential upriver story.

In *The Generall Historie* Smith's "Famous Chickahominy Voyage" ends with a climactic image wrought from the stuff of legends:

> The conclusion was, two great stones were brought before Powhatan: then as many as could layd hands on him, dragged him to them, and thereon laid his head, and being ready with their clubs, to beate out his braines, Pocahontas the Kings dearest daughter, when no intreaty could prevaile, got his head in her armes, and laid her owne upon his to save him from death: whereat the Emperour was contented he should live to make him hatchets, and her bells, beads, and copper; for they thought him as well of all occupations as themselves.

It is a stirring story of selflessness on the part of the Indian maiden, whom Smith thought to be "a child of twelve or thirteen years of age" at the time (though she may have been even younger, as Smith intimated in other versions). But since Smith was the only person on the scene who could make "paper speake," and since he made paper say two quite different things about this peculiar upriver occurrence, we are left with murky evidence on which to base an understanding of the events.

Philip Barbour, Smith's most respected biographer and editor of his *Complete Works*, writes: "What really happened when Pocahontas 'saved Smith's life' we can never know; but Indian customs provide an explanation, and the exercise of tact for the benefit of the Virginia Company in London could explain the seemingly contradictory accounts." Barbour and other scholars suggest that Pocahontas played some sort of role in a well-established ritual that served to initiate Smith into the community. Prior to that interpretation, through much of the seventeenth, eighteenth, and nineteenth centuries, Smith's second version held sway, with commentators

giving value to Smith's own heroics and Pocahontas's miraculous interven-
tion; in the early 1900s the event became increasingly romanticized, with
writers underscoring (and readers thrilling to) a love-motivated, Romeo-
and-Juliet escapade involving the Indian princess and the dashing captain
(to the dismay, perhaps, of the progeny of Pocahontas's actual marriage
to John Rolfe). Around the time of the Civil War, Northern historians
(e.g., Charles Deane before the Civil War and Henry Adams after) opened
a frontal attack on Smith's second version. Citing the discrepancy in his
own accounts and the lack of corroborating evidence for the Pocahontas
rescue, they labeled Smith a liar, a belief that reigns today in some scholarly
circles.

While some scholars have defended Smith's veracity and movies continue
to make much of the Pocahontas-Smith romance, I am most interested
in three related aspects of this upriver story: what we do not know, what
we do know, and the meaning of the Chickahominy as conduit between
the two. First, I am intrigued by what we do not know about Smith's adventures: what really happened, exactly why he varied his accounts, what
type of man he was, and so on. The uncertainty surrounding that "unsolvable contradiction" enables us to make our own sort of upriver journey
against the current of events and accounts and into the swamp of history.
Smith's upriver writings take readers into a morass of contested grounds
and conflicting accounts. On such terrain it is difficult to lay factual foundations. Instead, we are reminded that foundational tales often emanate
from complex circumstances and that making sense of them requires that
creative interpretation be mixed with such historical accuracy as we can
muster to understand events and characters.

Terrence Malick's recent film treatment of Smith's American adventure,
The New World (2005), "based on actual historical events and public records,"
portrays the captain (Colin Farrell) proceeding up the mucky Chickahominy
to be overwhelmed by fleet-footed "Naturals" while fighting most ineffica-
ciously under armor in the marshy marge of the river. This Smith, however,
proves to be an ambivalent seeker, both a man of action and a man prone
to mystic musings. Increasingly smitten with the peaceful, loving ways of
Powhatan's people (and particularly with Pocahontas herself), Smith learns
(alas, too late!) that the forest life of these people, which appeared to be
some sort of dream, is actually "the only truth." His brief upriver existence—

truer, more "natural," and thus in a sense more real—had been rendered a dream by Smith's cultural circumstances and consequent worldview. The apparently false reality of English civilization has conquered him, as it will conquer land and inhabitants in the New World.

Second, I am drawn to consider what we know about Pocahontas from Smith's dubious accounts. Pocahontas stands for the possibility of something other than antipodes, antipathy, and armed conflict. When she does appear in Smith's versions—and the appearances are generally brief—she is a child of the wild who nonetheless possesses traits thought to belong only to the unsavage: compassion, pity, selfless generosity. Though she does eventually convert to Christianity, take an English name, marry an Englishman, and give birth to a son who leaves a physical legacy of antiantipodal relations, she doesn't need to do that to signify portentously in Smith's Chickahominy story. There, as yet undeveloped, she is simply (and for whatever reason) *good*. Some subsequent renderings would make her into a "historical point of origin" and a common heroine. Disney would make her over into an hourglass-figured postpubescent model in scant buckskin who uses rivers for extreme sports and cavorts with other tame creatures of the wilderness. Malick's Pocahontas functions as a true go-between who connects English civilization to an unencumbered land of innocence and promise. In Smith's own writings she is an unexpected minister of the wild who saves the hapless representatives of culture, an emblem of inexplicable compassion. If Lane's narrative, as John Seelye has written, showed that "Art and Nature would seldom work in tandem in America," Smith's stories of Pocahontas hold open the possibility that nature's art could alter culture.

And finally, through all of this drama and murk, the Chickahominy slips quietly by. Against it the traveler struggles; through it the traveler is introduced to other worlds; along it the traveler runs the risk of having himself or herself undone. The meaning of the Chickahominy River, like that of its counterparts in other upriver stories, is largely derived from its function as a channel for human movement and a course of action. Going upriver means access to potential boon: trade, *wassador* (mineral riches), the Northwest Passage. But while upriver writers tend to treat the water as a means to an end, a route for a necessary journey or mission, other possible meanings arise from these stories for those who read them. Up the Chickahominy literature and nature come together suggestively. The intersection makes evident that the story of the English foundations of America is an upriver story, that upriver stories tend to be antipodal accounts, and that culture and nature serve as fundamental antipodes for those stories. In the case of the Smith-Pocahontas tale, "the ur-myth of American literature," the captain and company bring culture to nature and attempt to establish it in the New World; the agents of culture suffer, and their suffering is relieved by the agents of nature, who play the role of "the accommodating savage" in the myth; relations between these parties quickly fray, a war of opposites looms, then an intermarriage brings the two parties (tenuously) together. And from that mythical beginning flows history. In that foundational story the river represents an element of nature, a way into the heart of the pure wild, enabling the mission of remaking the New World into a resource for the Old. Rivers both are nature and open up nature to culture's tinkering, representing both a problem to be fixed and an instrument for fixing the problem.

Writers of upriver stories, premised on an antipodal idea, must explain their experiences within the oppositional paradigm, and Smith's two different versions demonstrate some of the difficulties that arise in the process, as if rivers resisted the effort to sequester them. Pushing toward sea level and relative equilibrium, rivers require that agents of culture struggle against that force to accomplish their mission. In addition, as ex–Virginia colony president Edward Maria Wingfield noted at the time in regard to Smith's voyage, "The river the higher grew worse and worse." Banks narrowed, canopies descended, headwaters spread into swamp. The upriver operative "muddles rather than marches along, slog-slog-slogging through the muck of the wild, wet woods." Upriver literature sheds some light on the darkness into which culture has marched, the stories that emanate from the swamp of history, and our methods of construing the meaning of those stories.

Looking out on the Chickahominy near Chickahominy Shores, the day after Thanksgiving four hundred years later, my family and I stood somewhere downriver from where Thomas Rolfe, the son of Pocahontas and John Rolfe, built a fort. An elderly man at a marina told us that when he came to the area in 1981, he heard that just up the road, on an island in the river, was the spot where Pocahontas rescued Smith. The island—called Smith Island by some—is actually closer to the spot where the captain was captured; but we followed directions and drove up the river on a gravel road along railroad tracks to Colonial Harbor. A fisherman floated nearby, though most of the bigger boats bobbed in dock. The sky clouded over the wide water, and the slow current made the water especially reflective, wind rippling the surface just enough to blur the island bald cypress and blacken the evergreen understory of the other shore. Here the stillness was more moving and the overcast sky more illuminating than the downriver recon-structions at "Historic Jamestowne." At that national park we had crossed the Pitch and Tar Swamp and walked beneath the pointy Tercentennial Monument amid other centennially commemorative markers from this and that association, passed a huge statue of a commanding Smith (whom a schoolgirl described as "ugly") towering over the tourists on a high pedestal, passed another statue of Pocahontas, supplicant, much closer to the earth on a low, flat rock, her arms open and palms shiny, though the rest of her is stained by history. At the site of Jamestown and in the visitors' center we found much information; but up the Chickahominy we felt closer to what we cannot seem to know.

Never Get Out of the Boat—Absolutely Goddamn Right: Ending Up at the Beginning

Even considering recent remakes, Smith's writings have not exactly touched off a cottage industry of upriver narratives. There are some but not many, testifying perhaps to the struggle such movement (and thinking about it) entails. With the prevailing cultural bias in the twenty-first-century United States being toward ease and speed, and with powerboats able to head upriver as easily as down, interest in bucking the current would seem to be a thing of the past. Lack of interest also could be attributed to the lack of need: we can make our way nearly anywhere without waterways; we can probably order *wassador* on-line. Faced with the "infinite impediments" of upriver journeying, we're likely to shrug our shoulders and turn on the Travel Channel. Or perhaps the paucity of upriver narratives might have to do with the nature of authorship in the United States. Early in the nine-teenth century writer Henry Marie Brackenridge observed that authors, whom he deemed "abstract men," have no particular place or purpose in this country; they are not "men of action" who undertake such things as going against nature. In his estimation captains—of industry or of the

army—are too busy to write, and writers are too "abstract" to act. This may
no longer be the case, as bookstore shelves teem with firsthand accounts
on getting ahead, blogs boom, and assisted autobiographies of achievers
abound. But Brackenridge uses himself as an example: hoping to hang
out his shingle in the newly acquired territory of Louisiana, the budding
lawyer discovered that "prospects of success in that part of the world, were
not such" as he wished, that he was "in no small danger of becoming an
author" (and "a professed author in our country, alas! is pitiable indeed"),
and that he would be just as well served in heading up a river as he would
in "tak[ing] up his abode next door to starvation."

The result was that rarest of the rare: a narrative of an upriver journey
undertaken without having been commissioned and more or less for the
heck of it, for "mere gratification" and "an idle curiosity," in the writer's
words. Brackenridge's *Views of Louisiana; Together with a Journal of a Voyage
Up the Missouri River, in 1811* was relatively well known at the time and was
read with interest by future river travelers, including Henry David Thoreau.
The party was led by fur trader Manuel Lisa and consisted of some twenty
men and Sacagawea, the heroine of the Lewis and Clark expedition. Though
he lacked both the impetus of a mission and the dramatic conclusion of
Smith's adventures, Brackenridge ventured up the river with a conceptual
map every bit as antipodal as the captain's. His removal from civilization
and the familiar into a savage land overwhelmed him at times, as when they
passed "the last settlement of whites," roughly three weeks into the trip.
Brackenridge admits that he "almost repented of having undertaken this
voyage, without an object in view, of suitable importance." He only managed to cheer himself by presaging that "there is no spot however distant,
where I may be buried, but will in time, be surrounded by the habitations
of Americans," by which he meant white folk such as himself.

Brackenridge vividly records both the marvels of the vast plains surrounding the Missouri and the obstacles to the party's upriver progress: "The
current of that vast volume of water rolling with great impetuosity," high
water from spring floods, banks eroding into the stream, snags and floating
log piles (*embarras*) slowing them down, misanthropic mosquito swarms
and menacing bison, widespread rumors of heightening Indian threat, and
the ever-increasing distance from home. A month after the initial moment
of despair he extols the "beauty of the scenery" yet laments that "there

appears to be a painful void—something wanting—it can be nothing else than a population of animated beings." As with all true upriver narratives, very little attention and space are given to the return voyage. After reaching as far up as the Mandan villages, "1640 miles from the mouth of the Missouri," and subsequently celebrating the Fourth of July, Brackenridge and a small party "set off, to return once more to civilized life," succeeding a page and a half later. Contrasted with the painstaking description of the upriver portion of the journey and detailed observations of a week-long sojourn in the Arikara village (which leads him to declaim that "the savage state, like the rude uncultivated wastes, is contemplated at most advantage at a distance"), the return trip is but a punctuation mark. They came, they saw, they conquered. They also went back home, but that's not the point—the point is that they bested the river and braved the savages, beating nature the whole way. Early in the party's progress Brackenridge illustrates the method by which the crew overcame a Missouri "ripple," all hands exerting themselves with cordelle (towline) and pole. Driven back several times, they kept at it, "and thus by perseverance became conquerors."

The fur traders gather furs; the naturalists (including a "Fellow of the Linnean Society") collect specimens; the hunters kill fowl by the flock and sundry mammals by the herd; and the author abstracts a narrative from that voyage up the Missouri River. Brackenridge characterizes his task as a travel writer as describing "the face of nature in its primitive state." Finding fault with European models (the French are too fanciful, the English "loaded with sluggish prejudice"), he holds that Americans are best situated to write impartially and authentically about their travels, and therefore his unbedizened journal should be read as truthfully depicting the sylvan land and savage peoples upriver. Brackenridge observes differences between tribes, finds some (though few) good qualities in their ways of life, and suspects that he may repulse them as much as they repulse him. The moments of self-reflection in upriver stories are rare, however, since the work is hard and the task clear: the "painful void" must be platted someday with the streets of civilized Americans, and the "ignorant and savage man, can only be ruled through the means of fear." Aside from passing along that important "lesson," as he calls it, the author only desires to write "in such a manner as to enable the reader to participate in the agreeable parts of my peregrinations."

Like that of most of the upriver writers before him, Brackenridge's progress up the river is also a regress, back into time. He makes quite clear in his
journal that he and his party carry civilization with them, that he is proud
to be the bearer of these tidings and certain of his culture's future spread
(while leaving open the question of its inherent or universal "beauty"). As
another one of those magicians able to make paper speak, Brackenridge
conjures a tale of bringing the present/future to the primitive past and
preparing to remake it into something new, something modern. It is the
work of supernatural beings, gods or devils, who can convert the primitive, the "natural," the "savage" into the civilized and thoroughly modern,
into the America of destiny. Those processes will continue long after the
fur traders have come and gone, well into the nineteenth century, having
been set in motion by colonialist crossings of the Atlantic and subsequent
upriver probing. At the end of that century Joseph Conrad wrote an upriver
narrative that questioned the spatial and temporal aspects of European
progress and its strange movement: *Heart of Darkness* illuminates some
of the unsound methods bedeviling the colonial enterprise and raises the
specter of the imminent danger that the wild and primitive will overcome
the very nature of the would-be civilizer and modernizer.

Though *Heart of Darkness* is undoubtedly the best-known upriver writing in English of the last one hundred years or more, I mention it here only
briefly and mostly in relation to its late-twentieth-century interpretation
by an American film director. Conrad was born in Poland in 1857, worked
for a while in the French merchant navy, and eventually sailed (and wrote
fiction) under the British flag. His novella describing a mission up the Congo
River (though the river is not named in the story) originally appeared in
three installments of *Blackwood's*, a prominent British magazine, in 1899.
In *Heart of Darkness* Conrad's unnamed narrator tells the story of a man
named Marlow telling a story. The framing or outermost story begins and
ends in the "mournful gloom" downriver from London on the Thames,
where Conrad's narrator, Marlow, and three others "wait for the turn of
the tide" to take their yawl out to sea. That tale, however, consists mostly
of the narrator quoting Marlow as he spins one of his yarns, with only brief
pauses and whiffs of interruption. In the first third Marlow describes going
to Africa in search of adventure and employment, setting out on a mission
for a colonial company trading in ivory, then traveling the coast for some

thirty days before a two-hundred-mile trek inland along the "big river" to a station where he must retrieve a steamboat from the bottom of the river and refurbish it even before embarking on the mission itself.

The introductory section includes Marlow's thoughts on colonialism and its kin, conquest. Discussing the latter in establishing the context for his upriver mission, he observes: "'The conquest of the earth, which mostly means the taking it away from those who have a different complexion or slightly flatter noses than ourselves, is not a pretty thing when you look into it too much.'" For Marlow, colonialism differs from conquest in that it substitutes efficiency for brute force—that is, the means differ, though the end may be the same. His voyage up the Congo belongs to the colonialist enterprise of transferring African resources to European control, that enterprise not being confined to any one nation. (In his case, he is a British citizen employed by a Belgian concern.) As his mission unfolds, the play of darkness and light increases. Though the civilized, white-skinned man travels deeper into a land of savage, dark-skinned people, he does so as part of a project that he describes in hellish terms. The further Marlow becomes involved in his work for the Company, the more closely he acquaints himself with "a flabby, pretending, weak-eyed devil of a rapacious and pitiless folly," with greedy, "insidious" ministers for the prince of darkness, as if he were moving deeper from one "gloomy circle of some Inferno" to the next.

The culmination of Marlow's journey, Mr. Kurtz, is a proto-European, an insane product (though apparently a logical extension) of the colonial impulse. "'All Europe contributed to the making of Kurtz,'" says Marlow. Half-English and half-French, educated in England and a successful trader for the Belgian Company, Kurtz, whose bald white head shines as bright as the ivory he accumulates, operates way upriver at the heart of *Heart of Darkness*. His haul of ivory is only exceeded by the horrors he has inflicted on others while pursuing it. Marlow tells us that Kurtz's own heart has turned dark because of his time in the jungle, its effect on his methods, and his "'nerves [going] wrong.'" Marlow (in the middle of Conrad's narrator's story) and Kurtz (in the middle of Marlow's story) both contribute to shades of meaning, assisted by the recurring play of dark and light images. "'Going up that river,' says Marlow, 'was like travelling back to the earliest beginnings of the world.'" He attends to the slow progress as they "'penetrated deeper and deeper into the heart of darkness,'" closer and closer to the source of ivory, until reaching "'the farthest point of navigation and the culminating point of my experience. It seemed somehow to throw a kind of light on everything about me—and into my thoughts. It was sombre enough too—and pitiful—not extraordinary in any way—not very clear either. No, not very clear. And yet it seemed to throw a kind of light.'"

Kurtz's ivory-like head and his dark heart are what lie up the river, and they are emblematic of the depth of depravity, the height of rapacity, the light of culture (good intentions), and the gloom of greed (evil deeds). While the middle portion of Conrad's story consists almost entirely of the actual upriver travel, in the final third Marlow reports evidence of Kurtz's brutality as well as his brilliance. His tale ends with Kurtz's death, the group's return, and Marlow's visit to Kurtz's widow. The framing narrator then closes the book with the *Nellie* seaworthy, as the Thames "seemed to lead into the heart of an immense darkness."

The novella traces the upriver narrative to its fin de siècle conclusion, attempting to illuminate what usually remains in shadow. *Heart of Darkness* suggests that upriver tales—all tales of a voyage against the flow of time and nature—attempt to go back into the primitive wild of the human past or into the jungle where that savage past is presumed present; that such stories also entail an exploration of the little-known interior of the European self where art, efficiency, and liberal ideas compete with the rapacious drive to conquer, still evident in the colonial impulse, and with lingering vestiges of the wild. Because of the numerous manifestations of "darkness" and the different levels on which it appears, such tales themselves are "not very clear . . . not very clear" at all, and it's their lack of clarity that "throws a kind of light." The illumination, however, serves mainly to remind readers of the depth and persistence of darkness. That is what is nearly always found up the river: a darkness that no light can penetrate. In other words, such literary works do shed light on the interior, but only to show an interior that we do not usually regard, the result being not illumination per se but a heightened awareness of the darkness.

Conrad's contribution to upriver literature is immense, his story reaching into both the genre's past and its future. Though not *American* literature, his story about darkness and its hearts assists us in meeting our own upriver devils: those we place at headwaters, those that inhabit our notions of the wilderness, and those we carry within us. His fictional treatment of colonialism, culture, and deviltry raises its head among the sundry kingdoms of the dead in American-born poet T. S. Eliot's "The Hollow Men," which opens with an epigraph referring to Kurtz's demise. Eliot's critique of modernity, peopled by "the hollow men / the stuffed men," concludes with an image of unraveling: "This is the way the world ends / Not with a bang but a whimper." Both "The Hollow Men" and *Heart of Darkness* reached deep into the American twentieth century, adopted and adapted by John Milius, Francis Ford Coppola, Michael Herr, and others for the film *Apocalypse Now* (1979), which translates Conrad's Congo River adventure into a film about American involvement in Vietnam. In Coppola's film Marlow becomes Captain Willard (Martin Sheen), a secretive assassin of the Special Forces assigned to "terminate the . . . command" of Kurtz (Marlon Brando), himself a Special Forces officer accused of employing rogue methods to establish a small, bloody principality of darkness just inside Cambodia.

In his voice-over narration Willard explains at the outset that he was to travel "hundreds of miles up a river that snaked through the war like a main circuit cable, plugged straight into Kurtz." One of the primary functions of the fictional Nung River is as a means of connection, much like the Moratico and the Chickahominy; in Willard's case it not only connects him physically to Kurtz but also suggests a greater similarity between the insane (if effective) colonel and the capable (if confused) captain. Willard foreshadows that similarity early when he says that there is no way to tell Kurtz's story without telling his own. Both stories depict the main characters as products of a war that sacrifices reason, an absurd war in which wrong and right continually exchange uniforms. Traveling upstream, even though the engines of the navy patrol boat readily overcome the slack current, is fraught with difficulties: obtaining fuel and other supplies, maintaining sanity amid the multilateral menace of war, confronting the deepening dangers of dark nature. But the Nung provides the only means of accomplishing the mission. As in *Heart of Darkness*, even to get to where the voyage begins requires struggle: Willard's boat and crew can only set out after a cavalry of helicopters (led by one bearing the motto "Death from Above") and a vast quantity of napalm have cleared the way. The Nung's muddy waters, the twisted wreckage of war along its banks as the boat moves slowly on, the thickening jungle, and the looming madness at the end of the river reprise Marlow's spectral movement into increasingly gloomier circles of hell.

At each hallucinogenic stage of the journey, Willard and the navy crew delve deeper into a darkness alleviated only by momentary flashes from mortar fire, LSD, grenade launchers, marijuana joints, and tracer bullets as the boat churns up the Nung. Under way after the Wagnerian-scored attack on the Viet Cong at the mouth of the river, where Lieutenant Colonel Kilgore (Robert Duvall), the leader of the air cavalry, refers to the enemy as "fucking savages" and asks for assistance in blowing them "back into the Stone Age," Willard and Chef (a crewman played by Frederick Forrest) walk into the jungle looking for mangos; a tiger springs on them from the dense foliage, chasing them back to the boat in a frenzy, Chef whimpering maniacally, "Never get out of the fucking boat! Never get out of the fucking boat! Hi, tiger! Bye, tiger!" Seeking supplies at a military station, the crew stumble upon a USO-like show in which *Playboy* bunnies, scantily dressed in a cowboys-and-Indians motif, whip hundreds of GIs into a fearsome fever. Pushing farther upriver, the navy boat pauses briefly to investigate a sampan, which leads to the chaotic massacre of a Vietnamese family. On an acid-laced reconnoitering of the last army outpost on the Nung River, Willard and crew are told they're in "the asshole of the world," a carnivalesque theater of war where no one is in command and a bridge must be continuously rebuilt after being continuously blown up. Just upriver from that scene snipers kill one of the crew while a tape from his mother plays telling him the news from home. Another ambush from the jungle-covered banks, this one consisting of toy arrows, concludes with a spear thrown through the boat's pilot's heart. The river narrows even more, the banks grow higher, shutting out light, occasional torches flicker on a crop of skulls, and the darkness closes in on Willard and two surviving crew members as they seem to come to the very end of the river, a lagoon with no visible outlet where white-painted aboriginal men in loincloths (played by the Ifugao people of Banaue in the Philippines), blank-staring GIs in shredded uniforms, and war-painted half-clothed Green Berets quietly, warily watch the boat's arrival. On the wall of an ancient temple, spray painted, we can read the "motto" of Kurtz and his "children": "Apocalypse Now."

"This is the end, beautiful friend, the end"—a Doors song plays at the beginning of the film and again in the last scene as Willard slinks into the river, emerges slowly, and slays Kurtz. The song reminds us that, as the title indicates, Coppola's story is most deeply concerned with The End. When Willard first arrives at Kurtz's headquarters, he finds severed heads strewn about the steps and landings of the temple, the hacked bodies of Vietnamese, Viet Cong, and Cambodians everywhere, corpses dangling from trees. "This was the end of the river all right," he says, and signs of apocalyptic unwinding abound. Brando's Kurtz, at first just a voice in the darkness until his white bald head emerges from the shadow, slowly bathes his head while questioning Willard about the mission to "terminate" his command. Later, while Kurtz reads the opening section of "The Hollow Men," the photojournalist–psychedelic court jester (Dennis Hopper) jumps ahead to the poem's last lines on the world's whimpering out. After the ritualistic killing of Kurtz, Willard returns to the boat, having chosen to displace but not replace the evil king. The command is terminated, the screen goes dark, Kurtz's dying whisper ("the horror, the horror") is repeated, and the audience hears rain.

At the beginning of the film we hear "The End," and at the end we hear rain, the source of rivers. But Coppola's finale does not refer simply to ancient archetypal cycles, nor does it offer a fortune-cookie koan such as "The end is the beginning, the beginning is the end." *Apocalypse Now* epitomizes upriver stories in that it depends upon a beginning-end reversal to give the river meaning. The end or goal of the upriver traveler is the beginning of the river. The river has meaning only insofar as it connects the voyager, the seeker, the man on a mission, with the source, the primitive, the wild. Meaning comes not from a vista overlooking the river or proximity to a certain section but from the experience of moving from the river's end back to its beginning. On the Nung River "apocalypse" refers to final destruction and catastrophic conclusion but also to revelation. Willard's river journey reveals the horror of modern warfare, some of the absurdities and hypocrisies of "civilization," and the need to confront national and personal devils. Whether an explanation or a critique of colonialism and conquest, upriver literature involves a mission in which a representative of culture uses the river to go back into nature, back through time, back into the dark origins. The river, the only way in, is also the only way out, and that is why one must beware getting out of the boat.

"The boat" in these writings is culture's vessel, the carrier of civilization. "Getting out of the boat" is a euphemism for going native as well as for taking up the role of a supernatural caretaker of savages. When Chef and Willard barely escape the jungle tiger, the captain is spurred to reflect on his mission and upriver journeys in general: his sober voice-over comments, "Never get out of the boat—absolutely goddamn right. Unless you were going all the way." Get out of the boat and you won't complete the mission; stray from the stream and you won't make it back. But then again, upriver stories do not place much emphasis on or derive much significance from coming back down. What matters most is what is found up the river. The river introduces us to sundry devils, those we have placed in the darkness and those we carry within.

4 | *Down the River*

I think I was in junior high school when my parents took me to Washington, D.C. It was mostly a standard self-guided sightseeing tour of memorials and monuments, leaving me with a general impression of the nation's grandeur and few distinct memories. The one souvenir that remains, after thirty-some years, is a set of eight-by-twelve-inch reproductions of Thomas Cole's series of four paintings called *The Voyage of Life*. I do not recall precisely what it was about Cole's paintings that captured my adolescent attention—maybe the ornate majesty of the actual paintings, each at least six feet wide and over four feet high; maybe the allegory, with a story line I could easily follow; perhaps the allegory's reassurance—in each painting a guardian angel accompanies the voyager on a river journey from childhood to youth, on into manhood, and finally to old age, at the end of which another angel awaits to welcome the voyager to heaven. I do not remember being particularly fascinated by Cole's river of life.

The river, however, plays a portentous part in the paintings' story line. It issues from a cave and begins as a pleasant, placid stream with green, flower-bestrewn banks that contrast sharply with its mysterious mountain source. In *Youth* the stream's floodplain widens, while its course at first appears to head straight toward a domed dream castle shimmering in the sky; not far in the distance, however, the river makes a hard right and enters foothills, the rocks of which create mild whitewater. Storm clouds with furious faces loom over *Manhood* as the stream flows precipitously into a perilous rapid featuring a frothing hole of unknown depth. And finally the River of Life concludes by issuing into the black sea, with a brilliance breaking through the clouds over the offing. The physical features of the male voyager of course change throughout the voyage, as does the boat on which he rides and the relative position of his guardian angel: first ebullient child (angel at the helm, boat filled with flora and fronted with a prominent seraphic bowsprit), then beardless youth (voyager at the helm, boat prominently ornamented with wings, angel on the bank bidding farewell). Next, the poor bearded man prays as his helmless boat enters the rapids (while the angel watches from on high); finally, bald and white bearded, in a boat with neither helm nor bowsprit, the voyager is rejoined by the angel, who points heavenward.

Cole's voyager experiences the River of Life from beginning to end in what is commonly considered the "natural" way for streams, moving from top to bottom with the flow of water and the pull of gravity. Writings that overlook the river may very well be detached from the flow of things. By-the-river stories usually feature a close but stationary encounter with a limited section of the river; the stream's current in such writings may have significance, but primarily as something that enables the watcher to contemplate relations among a variety of elements or parties. Up-the-river stories run counter to natural forces, underscoring oppositions (culture versus nature, self versus other, light versus dark). Although down-the-river writings also consider such topics, they tend to do so against the meaningful backdrop of going with the flow. Downriver works draw much of their meaning from the fact that they go somewhere, and especially from the fact that they go there by dint of the river's force, which causes them to run in a certain metaphorical direction: from birth to death, from the past to the present, from order to chaos, and so on. While they may sometimes resemble upriver narratives by venturing from the known to the unknown, downriver tales tend to raise questions regarding truth, fiction, and their correlatives.

In *The Voyage of Life*, for instance, the artist suggests that human lives are shaped by fictional versions of reality, including the illusion that we are alone, that we can alter our course by our own actions, and that we can reach an imaginary Land of Grandeur shimmering in front of us. In other words, we take what we "see" as reality, but that reality is merely a product of our limited ways of seeing. What is truly real, according to Cole's extended down-the-stream metaphor, is that we are accompanied by an unseen spirit who guides and guards us, that our ultimate destination is the "Ocean of Eternity" governed by a "Superior Power," and that the River of Life is but a means of transporting us from our "earthly origin" in the "mysterious Past" to the "Haven of Immortal Life." In its guide to the paintings the National Gallery of Art recognizes the Christian allegory at work in *The Voyage of Life* but adds another possible reading in which "Cole's intrepid voyager" represents "a personification of America." The fiction, the gallery speculates, entails America's materialistic pursuit of treasures on earth and the ill-conceived dogma that the river of "unbridled westward expansion and industrialization" will lead to palaces and pleasure domes. The unfortunate reality, however, is that the dream building is merely "a cloudy pile of Architecture, an air-built Castle," as Cole himself explained; the "adolescent" nation's "feverish quest for Manifest Destiny" leads to the same destination as everything else while having "tragic consequences for both man and nature."

Downriver stories such as Cole's flow over a bedrock of truth, relying on the incontrovertible fact that water flows downhill as the substratum for other meanings. The most interesting of these stories use the facts of nature as a primary meaning from which they explore secondary meanings, moving from terra firma into other regions, some testing the validity of fables and myths, others investigating personal identity and cultural practices. Frequently, down-the-river texts connect primary and secondary meanings to form foundational theories on the creation or formation of the world itself as well as on the place of humans in that world. All such stories proceed by an interplay between truth and fiction, whether the storyteller works within an objective or a subjective frame, similar to the "scientific" and "poetic" frames treated in *Life on the Mississippi*. Since I spent considerable time on Mark Twain's Mississippi in chapter 1, I will give it a rest in this chapter. I must note, however, that Twain's *Adventures of Huckleberry Finn* is a first-rate down-the-river tale in which truths and fictions are ever running into one another. Huck begins by observing that the eminent writer "Mr. Mark Twain" "told the truth, mainly," in an earlier book about Tom Sawyer. "There was things which he stretched, but mainly he told the truth." Huck follows his critical observation with an account of his own adventures that no doubt includes "some stretchers" and that uses the slow, constant flow of the Mississippi to shape the adventures themselves, to escape slavery and its permutations, to examine the accuracy and hypocrisy of fundamental cultural truths, and to provide the lead-up to Huck's eventual "light[ing] out for the Territory." His downriver journey serves as a springboard to the Wild West so that he might avoid another bout of being "sivilized" back home at the end of the river journey.

Huck and Jim travel the Mississippi to escape *from* something; other downstream writings follow the courses of rivers to escape *to* something, to discover something, to understand a place or people, or to find the self. In all of these accounts the writer-narrator or main characters run rivers. Action, speed, danger, and commotion flood the page as writers take readers through rapids, around bends, and over waterfalls into unknown lands. Trials abound, and the river's force—the force of nature—plays a key part in the drama. Interpreting these texts, we need to resist being carried away by the force of the narrative in order to consider the layers of meaning that underlie and surround it. Cole's paintings use the river's flow, from source to sea, as the primary meaning. That flow is connected to the course of human life, which functions as a secondary meaning from which come tertiary meanings—God's grace, America as misguided youth, nature serving as benign medium, and so on. These layers of meaning, from the seemingly objective base to the subjective strata higher up, add complexity to Cole's story and significance to the unknown. In *The Voyage of Life* human experience is colored by unknown beginnings, unknown ends, and unknown twists, turns, and falls along the way. Cole does not render the unknown known; he only acquaints viewers with how little we know.

Numerous other down-the-river stories, especially those set in the American West, feature strata of meaning, movement from known to unknown, and subjective-objective interchanges. In up-the-river narratives much remains unknown; even after the story's end, a mystery still emanates from the land upriver, an impenetrable darkness still envelops events and eventualities. Down-the-river works tend to begin in the known, move into and through the unknown, and arrive at the end with the travelers having gained knowledge. In many instances, unlike Cole's voyage, the unknown is subsequently known, named, measured, and parceled for communication to others. Often, however, the apparent stability of the ground on which the traveler stands at journey's end begins to shift. Subjective layers crumble, objective layers buckle, tributaries of fiction flow into the truth, and the meaning of the river changes course. Like Cole's paintings, however, many such writings use the river to tell a particular story, even those writings classified as nonfiction. Cole's River of Life is highly idealized, an amalgam of real rivers converted into an imagined whole for the sake of allegory; real rivers, however, are put to similar uses.

Take the Colorado River, for example, the largest river in the American Southwest and the seventh longest in North America (1,450 miles) as well as the largest desert river on the continent. The principal source of water and power for an enormous portion of the United States and part of Mexico, the Colorado is put to a variety of uses (agriculture, mining, generation of electricity, municipal and residential needs) in a number of states and fuels the growth of such cities as Denver, Las Vegas, Phoenix, and Los Angeles. The closing of the Glen Canyon Dam floodgates in the early 1960s began a "complete physical and biological alteration of the river." By the end of the twentieth century, the Colorado River had "become a single, vast, complex plumbing system." Scientists report that "the Colorado River drainage is one of the most regulated rivers in the world, with over 40 large flow-regulation structures and countless diversions." According to Ivo Lucchitta, regulating the Colorado and especially curtailing maximum flow means that "the river no longer can clear its throat," resulting in worsening rapids and increased beach erosion. Even with all such human uses, the Colorado retains an allure, a reputation for wildness that draws thousands of people each year to float significant portions of it.

Especially in that part of the river that runs through the Grand Canyon, the Colorado affords both colossal thrills and meditative solitude to those who float amid the spectacular landforms surrounding it. The quiet water can soothe one's soul as the boat bobs slowly down the river; the white-water of the rapids—so furious that boaters and geologists were forced to develop a special scale by which to measure the danger of the run and the skills necessary for a boater to make it through—can blow one's mind. Calculating the force of the Colorado rapids, Larry Stevens proposes a vivid equation: at a healthy flow, "1000 tons of water are moving through the river channel every second. If an average elephant weighs about five tons, this means that the flow of the river is equal to 200 elephants skipping by every second." Such figures hint at the river's power to elicit stories, ways of making sense of it all and attempts to convey some sense of the river's effect on humans. These stories also put the river to use, and to tell them writers also require a different sort of scale, one that features a shifting balance between truth and fiction.

There are two main types of writing that occur in down-the-river works: description of the river and the land through which it flows and description of characters' experience of going with that flow. Guides and textbooks exemplify the first sort, and Ann Zwinger's *Downcanyon: A Naturalist Explores the Colorado River through the Grand Canyon* (1995) represents some of the best work in that category. With maps of the lower river (from just below the Glen Canyon Dam to the Grand Wash Fault), an appendix of mileages marking significant sites as one moves downriver, and drawings of rock formations along the way, Zwinger attempts to provide a thorough depiction of the Colorado as it flows through one of the most sublime places on the earth. Organized by seasons instead of by a single trip down the river, *Downcanyon*—"a book not about fascinating people but about a fascinating river"—is designed to present a "year-round picture" of the Colorado. That it does so from the perspective of a naturalist matters greatly to the meaning of the river that emerges; making repeated trips over the course of time and observations from a variety of points, Zwinger tries to construct as comprehensive, as true, a view of the river as possible.

Zwinger tries to give readers direct access to the world viewed with as little mediation by the writer's presence as possible. She patiently and meticulously strives to get it all down, to accumulate as much detail as possible of the Grand Canyon and the life between its walls, as she does in a chapter at the center of the book, "Badger Creek and Running Rapids." Here the reader finds careful, objective descriptions (what "one sees" instead of what "I see") of the river and its environment, including definitions of geological and hydrological terms for features of the environment (dikes, eddies, hydraulic jumps, haystack waves) and measurements of rock and water: the varying speed of the current, the drop in elevation at Badger Rapids (fifteen feet in a sixth of a mile), statistics for the total fall of the river through the Grand Canyon (nineteen hundred feet), average fall of the river through the Grand Canyon (eight feet per mile, twenty-five times that of the Mississippi River), percentage of the total fall accounted for by rapids, and so on. Zwinger also gives an explanation of processes (how rapids form) and procedures (how to run rapids in a boat), a brief history of boating (where the names of rapids come from, different trips down the river, different ways to run the rapids, types of boats used), and formulas and ratios of the river's hydraulic work.

Much of *Downcanyon* consists of artfully conceived compilations of data highlighted with vivid imagery, while the artist herself tries to reduce her own presence and hence her effect on the perceived scene. While the writing sometimes involves colorful similes (as when she likens the spray from whitewater to the undergarments removed by burlesque dancers) and gives readers glimpses of the writer herself, it frequently relies on catalogs of information conveyed through straightforward, passive construction, declarative sentences. In the same chapter, while Zwinger's party scouts Hance Rapid prior to running it, the naturalist surveys the scene and finds a Grand Canyon rattlesnake, coiled "like a cinnamon roll." Explaining that "the markings of an adult Grand Canyon rattlesnake are distinctive," she provides a minute description before explicating the process by which the rattle developed and detailing the snake's proper habitat in textbook-style language familiar to viewers of *Animal Planet* or *Mutual of Omaha's Wild Kingdom*: "Although rattlesnakes are usually thought of as inhabitants of dry, rocky places, the canyon rattler, *Crotalus viridis abyssus*, often occurs in riparian habitats within feet of water and dens in tamarisk thickets."

Zwinger journeys down the river toward knowledge, acquiring more and more information with each trip. Lessons in natural history expand into deeper geological history, shot through with veins of cultural history. Using the viewpoint of the naturalist, her writing presents rock-solid information as the setting through which she passes. Identification, definition, and explanation—the naturalist's primary tools—construct a stable, apparently unadulterated truth regarding the river and its surroundings. The writer tries to avoid constricting the meaning of the Colorado by reducing the effect of her "I" on the river, as if the goal of her downriver writing were to shift readers' focus from interior to exterior concerns, from the personal to the environmental.

If the project of the naturalist may be said to entail "naturalizing" (recording the nature of) the river and its environs, for Zwinger this process entails denaturalizing the self, or at least minimizing the self and its effects on a place in order to present as objective a picture as possible. The rapids almost accommodate the dismantling of the subjective perspective—running House Rock Rapid, Zwinger is very nearly undone: "Sitting high on the back hatch of a dory, I look down into a hole that transmogrifies into a huge obese wave and buries my present, my past, and my future being."

In a way, though, for her project the self of the naturalist is an unnecessary encumbrance. Accomplishing the naturalist's mission—explaining natural history, accustoming herself to a different environment, introducing readers to nature so that they too may flourish there—requires an objectifying of the subject. The topic of study and the student studying merge into the material world of nature and its processes. Zwinger's *Downcanyon* uses the downriver movement as a means of journeying toward the truth.

The second kind of down-the-river writing differs considerably from the objective approach of the naturalist, as one can see in Edward Abbey's "Down the River," a chapter from his *Desert Solitaire: A Season in the Wilderness* (1968). Although Abbey too writes of floating down the Colorado River, his subjective perspective takes center stage. Whereas Zwinger tries to get out of the way so that readers can have direct access to the river, Abbey features himself, showcasing his "impressions of the natural scene." He too wishes to provide a true picture of the river, explaining that he has "striven above all for accuracy," operating from the belief that "there is a kind of poetry, even a kind of truth, in simple fact." But while Zwinger as a naturalist moves toward the truth, Abbey's journey down the river is more of an escape, a movement away from the false.

"Down the River" records a leisurely journey with a friend (Ralph Newcomb) on a stretch of the Colorado upriver from the Grand Canyon, just prior to the construction of the Glen Canyon Dam. The river's impending doom is deeply important to the essay, making the story a first-person narrative of a last voyage on a section of a grand river soon to be turned into just another "enormous silt trap and evaporation tank" of use only in further lining the pockets of "real estate speculators" and agribusinessmen. Whereas downriver writing of the Zwinger type uses different methods of organization to present an objective picture of the river (e.g., seasons), subjective down-the-river writings—even nonfiction—are usually organized into a "plot" that follows the downriver progress of the traveler. The story unfolds as Abbey and Newcomb put in near the town of Hite, 150 miles upriver from "the new dam already under construction," and float down the Colorado in flimsy inflatable boats with little planning and only basic supplies, hoping to enjoy a "very intimate relation with the river" and restore their faith in (or at least "renew our affection for") humanity by being shut of it for a while. The plot, in other words, follows the travelers as they fulfill what appears to be their main purpose: getting lost. They embark with an inadequate map, which they promptly lose, indicative of the travelers' "ignorance and carelessness," which Abbey calls "deliberate," so that they might escape the "multinefarious delights of what Ralph calls syphilization."

On this particular stretch, at least for the time being, the river leads away from the "incredible *shit* we put up with most of our lives," as Abbey enumerates in an early soliloquy, including under that profane heading such things as "*domestic* routine," "degrading *jobs*," "the *insufferable* arrogance of elected officials," "*crafty*" and "*slimy*" business practices, "tedious wars," "diseased and *hideous* cities," "the constant *petty* tyranny," the "*intolerable* garbage," and the "utterly *useless crap* we bury ourselves in day by day." The narrator's anger-laden list is prompted by his "first taste of the wild," just after casting off. Though embarked on a leisurely and carefree trip, Abbey portrays it nonetheless as something of a mission, the accomplishment of which requires precisely carefree, leisurely progress, away from the false world of "the Authorities" and "all their rotten institutions" and toward the truth. Truth, for Abbey, abides in the wilderness. Well under way, "deep in the wild now, deep in the lonely, sweet, remote, primeval world, far far from anywhere familiar to men and women," he meditatively pokes the word "wilderness" with a stick to see what (if anything) it means. For a couple pages he repeats the word as if mumbling it while musing, describing it as a place, italicizing it, removing italics, adding an ellipsis, providing a definition from "government officialdom" to underscore the inadequacy of such definitions.

The meaning of "wilderness" poses problems in Abbey's story, because of the problem of "meaning." In one sense, "meaning" itself is linked with the world he and Newcomb are leaving behind—the world of authorities and institutions with its stories of God and dams. For Abbey, wilderness is the absence of meaning, the antithesis of human activity of all sorts, as he explains near the end of the essay: "Under the desert sun, in that dogmatic clarity, the fables of theology and the myths of classical philosophy dissolve like mist." After describing the landforms, atmosphere, and flora of a particular spot and their effect on the senses, he writes, "What does it mean? It means nothing. It is as it is and has no meaning. The desert lies beneath beyond any possible human qualification. Therefore, sublime." Although his approach to downriver writing differs dramatically from Zwinger's, Abbey too is something of a "naturalist" of the wilderness. They both produce nonfictional accounts that move down the river and attempt to represent the world through which they move to readers. But where Zwinger's naturalist writing relies on objective description and explanation, Abbey's subjective naturalist ventures away from familiar systems of meaning. Those systems, he suggests, are actually meaningless, a parade of false meanings led by a false notion of God and consisting of fictional stories that "screen" humans from the world. To this he opposes "the river and reality."

Abbey uses the downriver journey to take readers into the sublime wilderness; rather than describing the exterior world as accurately as he can, he tries to represent an interior experience of the exterior world while doing so outside the usual systems for making meaning. The "living river" takes him away from those systems and gives "coherence and significance" to the world by ushering him into the wilderness, where he believes a kind of primitive meaning resides—or perhaps resided. The river makes possible both an escape and a search for something lost. Written after the closing of the dam gates, as Abbey makes clear in the introduction, "Down the River" centers on a river already in ruins: "The beavers had to go and build another god-damned dam on the Colorado," the essay begins. He reminds readers periodically that his is a "last voyage" on the river before its alteration, concluding eventually with "a last lingering look at the scene which we know we will never again see as we see it now: the great Colorado, wild and free." Their trip is—or was, as he points out—a voyage "deeper into Eden," "rebirth backward in time and into primeval liberty," a temporary return to "the only home we shall ever know, the only paradise we ever need." But since the river is already gone before the essay begins, Abbey's downriver writing cannot simply recover what has been lost. Like the book to which it belongs, "Down the River" is a "memorial," a "tombstone"—a point underscored by the sign from the Bureau of Reclamation cited at the very end of the essay, threatening prosecution to those who do not "leave [the] river," a sign that "bears a message and it is meant for us." The sign is the tombstone's tombstone, double marker of the river's death.

Between the foregone conclusion of the introduction and the finality of the boxed-off proclamation by the Bureau of Reclamation at the end, the river provides the plot for the essay and serves the voyagers in a variety of ways, giving them drinking water, coffee, baths, fish, clean laundry, clean dishes, and entertainment. Unlike upriver writings, which usually describe the river as a means of transport and an opposing force to be overcome but offer little description of the river and its surroundings, downriver writings make the stream a central character among the dramatis personae as well as the vivid scene of much action. The ongoing, forth-flowing river, ceaseless in its movement to the sea, models and enforces a kind of natural emergence and unwinding. Abbey describes the experience of going with the flow as the fulfillment of a dream. *"Floating down the river"* gives the floater a sense of bliss, however temporary it might be.

And temporality is very much at issue in the Abbey type of downriver writing. The bliss he and Newcomb experience is as intense as it is brief and a thing very much of the past. Time has already run out on Glen Canyon by the time Abbey writes of their journey through it down "the splendid river," "the steady, powerful, unhurried, insouciant Colorado." While the type of downriver writing represented by Ann Zwinger's *Downcanyon* tells a story of gain (especially of knowledge but also of delight), the Abbey version of down the river tells a story of loss and longing. The human beavers have already built their dams and posted their signs, effectively ruining the river for good. Zwinger focuses on making the river *present* for readers; the flow of the river is a central feature in a description of creation and the processes that cause it. Abbey uses the river to represent something *absent*—God, paradise, the river itself. "Down the River" functions as a memorial to something we will never get back and a testimony to nature's lapse, hastened by human actions and artifices. Time goes on, things fall apart, the end is nigh, so get outside while you can.

On Our Way Down the Great Unknown: Form and Unconformity

Abbey and Zwinger represent different types of down-the-river writing and different uses of the river; both, however, claim a common ancestor, and that ancestor's downriver account conforms to neither of the categories I have described. Maj. John Wesley Powell was one of the first European Americans to explore the region of the Colorado River, and his book on descending the Colorado River is one of the best-known examples of downriver literature and nineteenth-century nature writing. Powell captured the attention of the post–Civil War nation with his exploits, and his writing continues to interest river runners and historians; but his down-the-river work—perhaps *the* down-the-river work in American literature—raises important questions about the relations between truth and fiction, the known and the unknown, and the meaning of the Colorado River. Both Abbey and Zwinger refer to Powell frequently in their works, as does any writer who travels down the Colorado, and Abbey makes much of the contrast between his "last voyage" on the river that Powell was the first to descend. Because of his work's prominence in downriver literature but even more so because as a writer Powell adopts a complex strategy to describe an unnervingly complex experience of the river, his book on the Colorado River serves as the focal point for understanding downriver texts.

Black, orangey brown, dark green, sundry purples, rust red and sand yellow, graying white—the colorful walls of the Grand Canyon comprise layer upon layer of limestone, sandstone, shale, and schist. Down through these layers the Colorado River has cut. Descending a trail from the South Rim toward the river, one likely begins atop a crust of Kaibab Limestone (about 250 million years old) and can wind up a billion years earlier standing on Vishnu Schist. Intervals of ten, twenty, fifty million years pass as one walks, traces of ancient seas underfoot, canyon jays and ravens in the scrub along the path. In certain sections near the river one can encounter a geological "unconformity"—a place in the earth's strata in which a rock layer of a more recent period meets that of a much older period without record of the periods that come between them. The term "Great Unconformity" refers to sites where rock layers have worn away, allowing the relatively new to connect with the almost unthinkably old. In the Grand Canyon, for example, Precambrian Schist (approximately 1.7 billion years old) meets Paleozoic Tapeats Sandstone (approximately 550 million years old), and the intervening eons of rock are gone.

Unconformity occurs, generally speaking, when things do not agree, when they do not belong together or conform to a perceiver's expectations; it is a lack of harmony, an incongruity. On the surface the Great Unconformity may not be all that striking, a shadowy site of contrast between brownish red and black, but considering what these colors represent and thus being confronted by this staggering lack of conformity, one can be reduced to brow-furrowed head shaking, to confounded muttering of expletives, to outright awe, especially when the confrontation happens at the bottom of the Grand Canyon. As the delightfully literary geologist Clarence Dutton put it, "Probably there is no instance to be found in the world where an unconformity is revealed upon such a magnificent scale, and certainly none amid such impressive surroundings." His story of the Grand Canyon's unconformity includes familiar elements and agents of geological change: vast ancient seas, detrital deposits, faulting and flexing of the earth, volcanic uplift, and, in a starring role, erosion, the great grinding god of wearing away whose force is demonstrated by absence.

Another way of thinking about "unconformity" highlights its contradictory nature—it is a situation in which things that we believe should not be together are nevertheless found together. Both kinds of unconformity, the geological and the paradoxical, surface in Powell's downriver writing on the Colorado River. In 1869, long before damming and even before reliable mapping, the Colorado River was an excellent embodiment of the phrase "force of nature." The scope of the river, the velocity and volume of its flow, the harshness of the land through which it flowed, and the great, difficult distance separating much of the river's course from "civilization" had helped maintain it as a wild, relatively unexplored phenomenon. Major Powell in 1869 was a largely self-taught amateur naturalist and one-armed Civil War veteran, a wiry midwesterner with little or no whitewater experience and a lack of knowledge of much of the Colorado's course and region. One would not expect to find the river and the man together, at least not then. But they did come together that year and in following years, and Powell's literary accounts of his scientific adventures helped put both the major and the river on the map.

Like the walls of the canyon he studied, Powell's writing has more than one stratum of meaning. One layer, consisting primarily of objective facts and scientific explanation, regards the nature of the river and the formation of the earth; established in a lengthy introduction that takes up a fourth of his most popular work, this layer, characterized by definitive declarations, bears the imprint of the patient professor: "Let us understand what this means. Over the entire region limestones, shales, and sandstones were deposited through long periods of time to the thickness of many thousands of feet; then the country was upheaved and tilted toward the north; but the Colorado River was flowing when the tilting commenced, and the upheaval was very slow, so that the river cleared away the obstruction to its channel as fast as it was presented, and this is the Grand Canyon." Another layer, more literary and subjective, involves a dramatic account of adventure and discovery, as when an expedition boat "breaks away and speeds with great velocity down the stream. The 'Maid of the Canyon' is lost!" Powell brings these two layers together in his exploration narratives, and most readers take them as forming some kind of seamless whole. Because these layers do not quite conform, however, a different story emerges from the depths of the Grand Canyon when the unconformities of Powell's work are considered.

Wallace Stegner deemed Powell's Colorado River Exploring Expedition "the last great exploration within the continental United States." Such grand claims for the mission are not uncommon. Upon the party's return from the river, news accounts joyfully declared that Powell, as expedition "Chief," having made "his adventurous descent of this remarkable river," had successfully "performed his task and made a complete exploration of the path pursued by that stream." Almost a century later the 1960 Disney version (the film *Ten Who Dared* and a comic book based on the film) labeled it "one of the most perilous journeys ever attempted by man." Stephen Pyne, calling Powell's account "surely one of the great adventure stories in American literature," writes that the major's return from the successful voyage was received with "the acclaim normally reserved for war heroes or, at a later age, for astronauts." The original expedition—ten men, four boats, and not nearly enough food—was led by an inquisitive thirty-five-year-old specimen collector. At the beginning of the Disney renditions, which resemble in tone the newspaper coverage by the popular press in Powell's day and capture the widespread interest in his trip, a reporter asks, "Major, my newspaper would like to know why you think *you* can lick the Colorado River when nobody else has?" The major replies, "I'm a geologist! I believe in science! I've made careful calculations!" Powell's fundamental belief in science serves as the base layer of his downriver writing, atop of which run strata of romantic adventure and mythical quest.

In one of his earliest narratives of the trip, the major described the expedition's origins with a provocative metaphor. Having studied the region of the Colorado Basin for a number of years, he recalled that "the thought grew in my mind that the cañons of this region would be a book of revelations in the rock-leaved Bible of geology. The thought fructified, and I determined to read the book." Geological science is depicted as a biblical source of truth, and the canyons of the American Southwest serve as a book of the New Testament. Powell's metaphor, viewed in the context of his life and writings, proposes that scientific understanding of the nature of Creation supplements (and perhaps even supplants) theological versions of that nature. The rock-leaved Bible of geology provides a more solid, weighty truth about the genesis of the earth than do the stories of the paper-leaved Bible.

The passage also announces Powell's determination to "read" the book of canyon country, suggesting a connection between scientific and literary endeavors. Powell's expedition was a geological attempt to study a different kind of Bible, to harvest the forbidden fruit of knowledge. The goal was revelation through geographical interpretation. Where other geographical surveys of the era sought railroad routes or mine sites or military redoubts, Powell wanted to read the earth's writing in order to know the Colorado River and its canyons, to "add a mite to the great sum of human knowledge," as he wrote humbly to the *Chicago Tribune* on the eve of departure. He was out to replace that disturbing word "unknown," written across the far-off region of the Colorado on all existing maps, with its simpler and far more reassuring antonym, an act of amending the text of the American West. The coming together of literary and scientific elements, of reason and faith, creates fertile unconformities out of which Powellian thoughts spring naturally or "fructify."

The original Colorado River Exploring Expedition departed May 24, 1869, from Green River Station in what was not yet the state of Wyoming. The major's crew numbered nine men in four boats: John C. "Jack" Sumner, William Dunn, Walter "Old Shady" Powell (the major's brother), George Bradley, Oramel and Seneca Howland, Frank Goodman, Billy "Rhodes" Hawkins, and Andy Hall. This odd lot of Civil War veterans, mountain men, and excitement seekers floated down to the junction of the Green and the Grand and from that confluence down the Colorado through the Grand Canyon to the mouth of the Rio Virgen in what is now Nevada, where the six remaining members of the party dragged their raggedy selves and two remaining boats from the river on August 30. Major Powell made other trips, down parts of the Green and the Colorado in 1871 and 1872, as well as general explorations of the region, during which he was more concerned with ethnographical than geological studies, spending a great deal of time with the Paiute, Ute, Hopi, and Navajo peoples. Throughout the period he also made side trips to Washington, D.C., for money, to various places for provisions, and home to reconnect with his wife and daughter. All of this travel would inform and be folded into the narrative of that first river excursion in an obviously literary act with particular rhetorical ends, featuring an array of devices designed to achieve those ends: the downstream movement of the party, heroically hell-bent down the river and down into the earth, an act of "penetration," as Powell repeatedly put it; the mighty river itself, dashing and ripping and roaring through the canyons; and always a region increasingly unfamiliar and mysterious, increasingly unforgiving and forbidding, majestic, perhaps, but also, at least by some measurements, totally useless. "Country worthless to anybody or anything," as boatman Sumner wrote in his journal at the end of July.

In all of his literary accounts of that first trip, Powell manipulated rivers, river running, and region to tell a story of the arid West and terra incognita, of the perilous search for knowledge, and of the triumph of science. The first such account appeared in William Bell's *New Tracks in North America* the same year as the initial trip down the river. Next, giving way to pressures of being scooped by a member of the second voyage, Powell prepared "The Cañons of the Colorado," a series of articles for *Scribner's Monthly* in the January, February, and March issues of 1875. The one-sentence penultimate paragraph of the *Scribner's* version declares simply, "The exploration of the Great Cañon of the Colorado was accomplished."

A more scientific version, written at the urging of Congress and the Smithsonian Institution, came out as *Exploration of the Colorado River of the West* in 1875, and finally Powell partially revised and expanded this version into *Canyons of the Colorado* for a popular press in 1895. Beginning with the 1875 government publication, the exploration narrative purports to follow, in diary format, only the May 24 through August 30 first descent of the Colorado, though it uses information from other trips without identifying the members of the second river party—an authorial choice that to this day disturbs a shipload of people. The problem arises from the unconformity between the scientific elements and the more notably literary elements. Readers who expect the truth and nothing but the truth in Powell's text grumble about "omissions, inaccuracies, and errors." Those who treat the narrative as a literary composition, on the other hand, seldom pursue the significant consequences of Powell's combination of fact and fiction.

In the day-by-day narrative section of the report, Powell writes as if other trips *did not* happen and as if the 1869 trip *is* happening. That narrative, however, belongs to a longer text, one that is revised over time by the writer. The larger work is assembled long after the initial voyage, but the writer imaginatively re-creates the first trip in order to report most effectively on the land and its formations, to tell the story of the West and how it was formed. Powell perpetually emphasizes the primacy of the expedition, as on the numerous occasions in which the narrator remarks on the naming of landforms. Being first highlights the strangeness of the places, the danger of the undertaking, and the greatness of the accomplishment. By stressing that the land is unknown and unnamed, Powell continually reminds readers that the very movement of the party *reveals*.

As one might expect, "The River" plays a hugely important role in Powell's drama of discovery, and the actual rivers navigated by the party were well cast. The Green River presents Powell's audience with an introduction to rivers' versatile nature. As Tim Palmer has written, it is a "landmark river of the West": with its headwaters in the Wind River range, it begins as a mountain river, becomes a high prairie-land river, changes back into a mountain river below Flaming Gorge Dam, and finally, at Lodore Canyon, turns into a desert river. Through such variable terrain (and, nowadays, despite being dammed more than once), the Green flows over seven hundred miles, joining the Colorado River in southern Utah. Powell's descriptions of the Green usually serve his story by foregrounding contextual (e.g., geological) information or navigational qualities. Chapter titles, taken from particular reaches of the river ("From Green River City to Flaming Gorge," "From the Mouth of the Uinta River to the Junction of the Grand and Green"), organize the river in terms of the party's downstream experiencing of its course, and the river so organized in turn organizes the narrative. Powell uses the river to structure his account, which presents a certain view of the river.

Description of the land through which the river and boats run is crafted to intensify the effects of the adventure tale and to convey a lesson in the formation of the earth. At the conclusion of the first chapter of the narrative, in an entry dated May 29, Powell uses river miles to chart his expedition's progress: "The distance from Green River City to Flaming Gorge is 62 miles. The river runs between bluffs, in some places standing so close to each other that no flood plain is seen. At such a point the river might properly be said to run through a canyon." Here, as he does elsewhere at the end of chapters, Powell summarizes a section of the river (including the miles covered by the expedition), provides a setting for the expedition's adventure, and offers basic terminology in earth formation. The next chapter follows up on the geological lesson: "One must not think of a mountain range as a line of peaks standing on a plain, but as a broad platform many miles wide from which mountains have been carved by the waters." The narrative's scientific layer describes the work of water in shaping the world out of rock and also forms the background of the adventure story.

The canyon-creating power of the river adds to Powell's tale in different ways. As an explanation of the origins of the setting of the tale, it contributes both setting and mood. Canyons are adumbrated by mountain majesty, a darkness made darker as the scene shifts from the glory of the mountaintop to the gloom of the chasm. The geology lesson on orogeny (mountain making) comes from a kind of third-person, omniscient narrator's perspective of the sort one would expect to find in a textbook. In fact, the textbook serves as a frame for the exploration narrative: Powell's third-person, detached view is established in the first four chapters ("The Valley of the Colorado," "Mesas and Buttes," "Mountains and Plateaus," and "Cliffs and Terraces") and brings the story to its conclusion in chapter 15, "The Grand Canyon." By recurring to this knowledgeable and descriptive perspective within the narrative of the river trip, Powell transports readers from the scene of action to a vantage point above the scene and even above time, looking down on a world as it is formed. Such a vista is juxtaposed with the events of the expedition, as in the final section of the chapter "From Green River City to Flaming Gorge" at the start of the narrative, which takes place in the depths of a canyon created by the carving waters. By moving back and forth from the third person to the first person, Powell's narrative makes the depths deeper, the canyon darker, the rock walls tighter, the setting more tense, and the action more exciting.

The movement between narrational perspectives also bolsters the world-making aspect of Powell's account. "Flaming Gorge," for example, is a name bestowed on the land by the Powell party and represents another aspect of the creation of the world. Whereas the third-person narrator objectively describes the shaping of the earth's crust by elemental forces (water, etc.), the first-person narrator highlights a subjective role in shaping our understanding of a place by naming the features of the land. Powell's first-person account constantly reminds readers of the expedition's "firstness." Being first is important to the revelatory action of Powell's expedition, which is in turn important to the version of the American West his narrative creates. These two aspects of world making, the elements that form the world and the Adamic naming of those elements, frequently operate in tandem, and their cooperation is central to Powell's story of creation. In the entry dated May 26 he writes: "The river is running to the south; the mountains have an easterly and westerly trend directly athwart its course, yet it glides on in a quiet way as if it thought a mountain range no formidable obstruction. It enters the range by a flaring, brilliant red gorge." The description of the setting provides background information for the nominative act that follows: "This is the head of the first of the canyons we are about to explore— an introductory one to a series made by the river through this range. We name it Flaming Gorge." The river made the canyon, and the Powell party named it. Along with demonstrating their "firstness," the party's naming also functions to mark the land, making it known. The new world takes shape as the explorers progress.

As Powell takes readers down the Green River, different layers of the text become increasingly visible. On top of the story of creation he has laid for foundation, he adds first-person descriptions, third-person explanations, rocking rhythms, and color tones. The trip commences with fanfare: the citizens of Green River City cheer from the banks, and the expedition members hoist their "little flag," push away from the shore, and give themselves over to "the swift current." After some early wrinkles (the party's progress is halted by a sandbar, an oar is lost in the process of avoiding a large rock, two more oars are dropped into the river amid confusion), the movement of the party settles into a pattern of undulation: downstream movement alternates with cliff climbing and side-canyon reconnoitering, the water smoothes and then turns turbulent, the scene alternates between dark and light as the boats pass in and out of shadows, speed increases and decreases, dramatic action gives way to scientific observations and meditations on grandeur, and the narrative perspectives continually vary, all creating the perfect staging of an encounter with the "Great Unknown."

The highs and lows of these undulations set the stage in several ways. For one, Powell's literary patterns reflect the travelers' sensations as they move downstream on rivers like the Green and Colorado with their regular riffle-and-pool frequencies. On the river one experiences this geological pattern of alternation as periodic fluctuations in velocity, fast water giving way to slow water, slow water quickening into a rapid. The changing pace is accompanied by a sound pattern of roar followed by quiet, providing the downstream traveler with a set of rhythms, a waltz of tranquility-activity stepped to the music of noise-silence amid the play of canyon shadows–desert light. The rhythms of moving down the river become part of the story's layering.

These strata make plain just how literary Powell's account is. While the textbook frame and the first-person memoranda suggest that the work is an "exploration," a "history," or a "report" (all of which appear in early titles), Powell's writing is very much a *story*, employing numerous narrational devices and informed by a philosophy of storytelling similar to that which Powell attributes to another member of the trip. Introducing the cast of characters at the commencement of the adventure, Powell says of young Andy Hall, "He can tell a good story, and is never encumbered by unnecessary scruples in giving his narratives those embellishments which help to make a story complete." Powell's admiration of Hall's ability informs the major's approach to writing up his own report. Some "scruples," of course, are necessary, or the work would disconnect from historical truth entirely. But Powell jovially declares that certain scruples might be "unnecessary." Although undiscriminating scrupulousness is what one would commonly expect to find in a Smithsonian "report," Powell discards "unnecessary scruples" and provides the Institution and future readers with a textual unconformity—part scientific report, part literary narrative.

Powell's own "embellishments," which contribute significantly to the layered effect of his writing, complicate the objective truth of his report and demonstrate the literariness of his project, the role that literature plays in shaping his thought, his findings, and his means of communication. Literature's role in Powell's narrative entails more than mere references—as when, for example, Powell likens boatman Oramel Howland to King Lear.

As is the case with the 250-plus illustrations included in the Smithsonian and later versions, such layers help "make a story complete." Many of these layers come into view in the Canyon of Lodore, just two weeks into the narrative. Powell ominously records their situation in camp with one of his rhythmic alternations, beginning with the description of a moment of repose after a good climb from which he sees that "the canyon opens, like a beautiful portal, to a region of glory." But even as he moves his pen across the page, day turns into night and the scene changes: "This evening, as I write, the sun is going down and the shadows are settling in the canyon." Powell then uses the shift from day to night to underscore the portentous, precarious uncertainty of the party's situation. The "portal to a region of glory" has become "a dark portal to a region of gloom—the gateway through which we are to enter on our voyage of exploration tomorrow. What shall we find?"

With the artifice of the diary-like notation "as I write" suggesting the immediacy of the account, the encroaching gloom foreshadowing events that will occur farther down the river, and his suspenseful question highlighting the precariousness of the party's situation, Powell artfully prepares the reader for "The Canyon of Lodore" (chapter 7). After explaining the manner in which they run the rapids of the canyon, the narrator describes his difficulty in falling asleep after "the excitement of the day." He picks up the story the following morning with an episode of naming: "One of the party suggests that we call this the Canyon of Lodore, and the name is adopted." Powell doesn't explain that the name was taken from Robert Southey's well-known poem "The Cataract of Lodore" (a name suggested by Andy Hall, the artful embellisher). In any event, "Lodore" resonates with "door," as emphasized by the accompanying illustration—an etching titled *Gate of Lodore* that shows the battle of shadow and light played out on the Green, from the boulders in the foreground to the winding river itself as it passes along the many-lined walls, all the way up to the ominous clouds gathering above the towering rock. Through these portals, some of glory and some of gloom, the heroes must pass.

As they proceed Powell continues to layer his account: scenes of their progress topped by objective observation of the setting, subjective impressions of the setting tucked underneath high drama, dramatic action relieved by a vein of humor. Throughout it all the author exploits the diary format to heighten the tension and deepen readers' connection to the story's action, increasing their interest in the expedition's success. Though there is scant evidence that such a journal even existed, and though most of the published versions came out long after the actual trip, Powell's "diary" purports to tell the story as it happened. As a "journal" these pages appear to be true accounts of the day-to-day affairs, an actual log rather than a carefully crafted story. The entry for "June 9," for instance, builds tension gradually, mimicking the movement of the party itself: "Very slowly we make our way." There follows a general description of the formation of calm areas at the head of rapids that relies on adverbs ("usually," "often") to extend the scene and descriptors to color the moment with tranquility ("quiet water," "ease"). The scene is set. Powell has brought readers to "the brink," using the apparent diary format to veil what is about to occur.

A desperate call comes from the men of the *No Name*. The Howland brothers and Frank Goodman have missed Powell's signal to land and now rush out of control toward "the narrow, angry channel below"; the boat's "going over is inevitable." In the ensuing commotion, depicted in what we nowadays call "real time," Powell's self-reported actions help create a scene of uncertainty and confusion. After hearing the shout and "looking around," the major breathlessly "run[s] to save the third boat," then "scramble[s] along" to get a look at the *No Name*, pauses briefly to look downstream, where "the river tumbles down again for 40 or 50 feet, in a channel filled with dangerous rocks that break the waves into whirlpools and beat them into foam," and next "pass[es] around a great crag just in time to see the boat strike a rock and, rebounding from the shock, career and fill its open compartment with water"—all of this in the space of a paragraph not yet concluded.

The pace of the action quickens, the confusion deepens, and Powell continues to run about frantically, with the prose of his account trying to keep up with him—"This seems a long time as I tell it, but it is quickly done." The combination of diary, present tense, and sudden excitement accentuates the danger and drama of the scene, with the help of action verbs descriptive of violence ("striking," "broken," "strikes again," "dashed to pieces"), until the narration catches on the image of "Frank Goodman, clinging to the rock with a grip on which life depends." To heighten the color of the dramatic adventure layer, Powell delineates various substrata:

the awesome forces of nature that cause havoc for human endeavor, acts of courage and ingenuity by which humans can surmount those forces and restore order, light comedy that offsets the dramatic darkness. After the calamity of the *No Name* in "Disaster Falls," some of the men volunteer to search the wreckage for instruments crucial to the mission. Sumner and Dunn work the rising river valiantly and to Powell's delight "set up a shout, and I join them, pleased that they should be as glad as myself to save the instruments." "The boys" bring back the implements of discovery, the loss of which would have imperiled the expedition, and also an illicit "three-gallon keg of whiskey. The last is what the men were shouting about," admits the major.

Powell uses the diary format as a thick and colorful layer in his account of triumph over the unknown. Because it functions as a day-to-day actual record, the diary obscures the fact that a tale is being told, making the action more immediate and more real, situating events in a numbered chronology that locates them at a particular moment in time, thus using time as a seemingly reliable measure of the account's truth claims. The days go by, the party progresses, obstacles occur and are surmounted. By paying attention to the layers, however, readers can make out a story different from the one Powell tells. Describing a side trip he takes with Bradley on "June 18," Powell gets himself stuck on a cliff face with nowhere to turn until his partner rescues him (by the unexpected act of taking off his trousers). Exploiting the present tense, Powell conveys a breathless struggle with the elements and the ultimate victory of human ingenuity. Written in the past tense, as it was in the *Scribner's* version, the scene loses much of its suspense. Changing to present tense enabled Powell to decrease the temporal distance between writer and reader, making the action more immediate, more dramatic, faster, and thus seemingly more real.

But beyond the use of present tense to increase dramatic tension, the episode is, in yet another way, an example of Powell's narrational tampering with temporal matters, for according to Bradley's journal (widely regarded as more reliable with respect to dates, in part because it truly is a diary, a daily record of the expedition), the episode happened much later in the trip, on July 8. (Bradley is customarily more economic in his version: "In one place Major having but one arm couldn't get up so I took off my drawers and they made an excellent substitute for rope and with that assistance he got up safe.") Powell's account situates the event three weeks earlier than Bradley's. I won't try to guess the major's intentions in doing so, but the result is that much of the more action-packed drama is grouped together, on the Green River in the earlier stages of the narrative. After the high drama of June 18, Powell's account tends to derive its dramatic tension less from particular moments of excitement than from the increasing desolation of the setting, the dwindling supplies of the party, and ultimately the depth of the party's encounter with the unknown. Thus the shift of the trouser rescue from July 8 to June 18 attaches the reader to Powell and party through more obvious peril and daring heroics, peril and heroism that become more subtle as the expedition courses on. Powell utilizes many means to make his story complete, including moving scenes around in the sequence of events and diarizing the narrative, tinkering with time and playing the cliff-hanger card for all it's worth. By the time we get to the Grand Canyon proper, Powell's story has the reader hooked, eagerly awaiting the next revelation.

Layer upon layer, a story takes shape. It is not just a story of a region or a story of an adventure; these are strata of meaning that pile up into a grand story about the world and ways of understanding it. Powell combines these strata carefully, attempting to make them conform to one another and to the greater story. The unknown can and should be made known by reason and empirical pursuit of the truth. The moral of the story is that science and technology can overcome the mysteries of nature, and various elements of the story are made to conform to that moral. Each of the different versions of his story, from the earliest to the latest, adds another layer. The major writes the report initially to guide governmental interests in the Colorado Plateau and procure support for continued exploration. By the time the story reached its final form even more layers had accreted, and they apparently added up to a seemingly straightforward picture: the region was unknown; Powell and his men made it known by exploring, describing, and explaining it.

The Grand Canyon functions as a key layer in the picture, the deepest, remotest, most sublime home of the unknown. To accomplish the expedition's mission, the Grand Canyon must be conquered and its secrets revealed. Powell's most emphatic use of the word "Unknown" occurs in an "entry" under the heading "August 13." For the expedition, the Grand Canyon/"Great Unknown" begins at the mouth of the Little Colorado, and

Powell marks the occasion with his most memorable sentence: "We are now ready to start on our way down the Great Unknown." After describing the party's condition—nervous, nearly out of supplies, but trying to make the best of a bad (and rapidly worsening) situation—he next places them, though with no great specificity, on the river. "We are three quarters of a mile in the depths of the earth, and the great river shrinks into insignificance as it dashes its angry waves against the walls and cliffs that rise to the world above; the waves are but puny ripples, and we but pigmies, running up and down the sands or lost among the boulders." Temporal exactitude (i.e., the more or less precise coordinates of the party in time, the morning of August 13) contrasts with spatial inexactitude (somewhere on the verge of the "Great Unknown"). Even "the great river" loses significance or meaning in such a setting. Powell's narrative emphasizes the chronological and historical nature of the party's progress, which works with the dangerous uncertainty of their whereabouts in a powerful play between the known (what Powell and crew accomplished and when) and the unknown (where they were and what was coming next). The diary format allows Powell to maintain the fiction that he does not know where he is or whether he will complete his mission; such a narrative strategy maintains the connection between readers and the narrative's present, suspending us in the positive-negative, known-unknown tension.

At this stage of the narrative, where the party *is* matters much less than where the party *isn't*. They know, for example, that they are at the foot of the Little Colorado River, which they also refer to as the Flax River, "a lothesome [*sic*] little stream, so filthy and muddy that it fairly stinks," according to Bradley, "as disgusting a stream as there is on the continent," in Sumner's words. At first, cloudy skies prevent them from establishing their coordinates, but eventually Powell is able to figure the latitude and determine that the course from this point on will mostly be westward. The men are also painfully aware that by now their rations have run almost as low as their spirits. Noting their paltry rations, Bradley confesses, "If Major does not do something soon I fear the consequences." The rapids are worsening, as the explorers have emerged from Marble Canyon and are about to enter "the granite" (meaning the steep, high walls of Vishnu Schist, which Powell also refers to as "gneiss") for the first time. At this point, the explorers are literally between a rock and a hard place, and they know this all too well. In the depths of the earth, no longer a part of the known, they have been deposited into a netherworld, and their subsistence there is shaky.

Powell labors to impress upon readers that progress from this point means moving ever deeper into the unknown, into a kind of negative space: "We have an unknown distance yet to run, an unknown river to explore. What falls there are, we know not; what rocks beset the channel, we know not; what walls rise over the river, we know not." The ominous, dramatic repetitions take readers ever deeper into terra incognita, to somewhere below the bottom of Powell's down-the-river tale on which the story's meaning ultimately rests: the undiscovered, the undetermined, the not-yet-known. The diary format, with its temporal specificity and chronological order, deposits a positive layer of time over the negative space of the unknown, providing readers with a temporally arranged map of the Colorado River and the Grand Canyon.

As the expedition enters the deepest, darkest part of the unknown, it becomes clear why Powell referred to the Grand Canyon as the "Sockdolager of the World." It will be over two weeks, almost two hundred rough river miles, and a drop in elevation of more than a thousand feet before the take-out, but time and space collude at the head of the Grand Canyon to pack a peculiarly powerful punch. Though originally descriptive of the whole Grand Canyon, "Sockdolager" was eventually bestowed on the first rapid to be found on the Colorado River as it enters the granite. The rapid looms into view on "August 14" in Powell's narrative, as various layers of rock and text are exposed. Viewed from above while hiking down from the South Rim, the gorge appears as a steep V cut into the Vishnu Schist, which rises vertically thousands of feet from the river, the towering black rock face deepening the gorge's gloom. On an outcropping above Sockdolager one can see the Great Unconformity, where the schist is overlain by brownish red sandstone, marking "widespread geologic upheaval" and age upon age of deposition and erosion, strata of presence and absence on a nearly unimaginable scale. In the rapid itself water seems to explode from the river's bottom, birthing a chaos of waves bouncing off walls and crashing over rocks, creating a constant roar heard clearly even from a good distance. Hance Rapid, just upriver, is a more difficult run for boats, as is Lava Rapid farther down; but the depth and closeness of the walls at Sockdolager, the river's brief rage, and the lack of options for voyagers make it dark and foreboding, "a perfect hell of waves."

In the major's narrative Sockdolager exposes more than the Great Unconformity. Describing the "awe-inspiring" setting and the boats' arduous movement through it, Powell builds slowly toward a scene of violence and disorder. The walls rise and tighten, the pace quickens, until "about eleven o'clock we hear a great roar ahead, and approach it very cautiously. The sound grows louder and louder as we run, and at last we find ourselves above a long, broken fall, with ledges and pinnacles of rock obstructing the river. There is a descent of perhaps 75 or 80 feet in a third of a mile, and the rushing waters break into great waves on the rocks, and lash themselves into a mad, white foam." In Powell's actual log kept during the trip, the "perhaps 75 or 80 feet" was recorded as 30 feet, and today boatmen and geomorphologists measure Sockdolager's fall at 19 feet. It would seem that, in order to heighten the drama, Powell deposits a thin layer of inflated numbers to cover what is nonetheless a significant drop on fast water through a narrow crack in the earth.

And that's part of what intrigues me about Powell's writing. As if the downriver trip weren't eventful and exciting enough, he plays with time and space to create another story, one that lies atop the day-to-day, real-life adventure of the expedition. Some have reckoned that he turned truth into fiction as part of a self-aggrandizing campaign or, in a more generous assessment, for the benefit of continued study of the West. But I don't see the major as replacing one story with another. Different versions of the story, told at different times in different tenses; elements of different stories combined into one; different perspectives folded into one another; layers of adventure, layers of illustrations, layers of instrumentality and measurements—Powell tries to form a kind of whole out of all these various parts, make a grand, panoramic story of the river, the canyon, and the region that can then be passed along to readers. For the most part, that story is a tale of science and reason, of humanity's use of courage and ingenuity to shine light on the wild darkness and discover truth. To "make this story complete," to make the truth more immediately accessible to readers, Powell uses "embellishments." But always, at a yet deeper bottom, lies the unknown, and though in most places it is covered by the multiple layers of storytelling, in some places unconformity is exposed.

Though Powell is generally understood as replacing the unknown with the known, the downriver movement, faster and faster, into deeper and darker regions, reveals a more complex world that continues to unfold as Powell continues to think about it and write about it. He tries to make fiction conform with truth to tell a tale of how the earth was formed, how it needs to be read, and how it needs to be treated, but upheaval and erosion continue. Faults surface, exposing other layers; the ground shifts, unsteady underneath us. New layers form, old layers wash away, and where this happens, the distinctions between known-unknown, truth-fiction, become less relevant. Maybe Powell began to suspect that if we separate one element out with a rock pick, its meaning changes, as would the meaning of the layer from which it has been taken. Each belongs to the multilayered picture of the truth that is revealed to the literary geologist and that the literary geologist tries to pass along to readers. As I mentioned earlier, in the 1875 version of the expedition serialized in *Scribner's* the story concludes with a definitive pronouncement that the exploration of river and region "was accomplished." In later versions, however, Powell shifts from the past tense to the present tense, and, along with the other literary incongruities, these unconformities undercut the successful completion of the mission.

We can see evidence of increasing unconformity as Powell rewrites his account. Beginning with the Smithsonian version and later in the popular book, Powell brings the narrative to an end with much less grandiosity and flourish than he does in the *Scribner's* series, commenting that "our arrival here is very opportune," and once again describing their dangerously diminished supplies. In the Smithsonian version the conclusion of the trip is but halfway through the whole report, two-thirds through part 1 ("History of the Exploration of the Cañons of the Colorado"), followed by a detailed study of "the physical features of the Valley of the Colorado" and finally by zoological treatises by Elliott Coues and G. Brown Goode (which are omitted in later publications). The text prepared as a book for a popular audience places the river trip in the context of Powell's later explorations of the region and closes with a chapter titled "The Grand Canyon." Leaving out the terse conclusive properties of the past-tense "was accomplished" keeps open the possibility of further "exploration"; concluding with "The Grand Canyon" leads, in a sense, to inconclusiveness.

Questions regarding the success of the scientific project of knowing the unknown multiply when we consider the curious "riddle" Powell poses in his *Outlines of the Philosophy of the North American Indians* (1877). The publication was based on a lecture, one from the many tours Powell embarked upon following the explorations that provided him with "considerable income." The lecture begins with a striking unconformity between the known and the unknown:

> I tell a riddle. There is an unknown known, and there is a known unknown; and I tell an answer. The unknown known is the philosophy of savagery; the known unknown is the philosophy of civilization. In those stages of culture that we call savagery and barbarism, all things are known—supposed to be known; but when at last something is known, understood, explained, then to those who have that knowledge in full comprehension, all other things become unknown. Then is ushered in the era of investigation and discovery; then science is born; then is the beginning of civilization. The philosophy of savagery is complete; the philosophy of civilization fragmentary. Ye men of science, ye wise fools, ye have discovered the law of gravity, but ye cannot tell what gravity is. But savagery has a cause and a method for all things; nothing is left unexplained.

Science, Powell goes on to suggest, though clearly his preferred system, is necessarily full of doubts. The scientific method and the underpinning philosophy of reason, representing the progress of "civilization," are all well and good, but such thinking does not render the unknown known; instead, it makes the known unknown. Coming to truth, Powell's riddle implies, includes elements of a process of "unknowing": "The verity of philosophy is questioned. The savage is a positive man; the scientist is a doubting man. And so we come back to our riddle; there is an unknown known, and there is a known unknown." According to Powell's scientific study of the philosophy of North American Indians, truth consists of layers of positive knowing and negative unknowing.

Powell's odd riddle relies on a double unconformity. In two adjective-noun incongruities based on the assumption that the known and the unknown should not be together, the adjective undoes the noun it modifies, so that the known (noun) is unknown (adjective) and the unknown is known. Their coming together in two different forms results in two different negations—in the case of "savage" philosophy, the known is not really known; in the case of Western science, we know only how little we know. In both cases the ability to know anything positively has the ground beneath it shift. The more Powell writes about the Colorado River, its canyons, and the people who inhabit the region, the less the layers conform. Readers who see Powell's story as either a factual or a fictional account of discovery, as an accurate or an inaccurate report of uncovering the truth, overlook the story's fundamental unconformity and thus miss an important element of its meaning.

While Powell's scientific beliefs and the search for knowledge played a prominent part in bringing him to the Colorado River and the Grand Canyon, in his own accounts of the adventures science mixes with literary concerns, knowing mixes with unknowing, and all this mixing creates an unconformity. The major's encounter with the river, his attempts to master it and render it meaningful, do not ultimately result in a completed mission. In the final chapter of the last and most popular version of the exploration, the writer's inability to comprehend and convey the sublimity and infinitude of the Grand Canyon leads to even greater respect for and more questions about the Colorado River. Grasping for help from music and painting, Powell finds that "the wonders of the Grand Canyon cannot be adequately represented in symbols of speech, nor by speech itself. . . . The elements that unite to make the Grand Canyon the most sublime spectacle in nature are multifarious and exceedingly diverse." In this latest and final conclusion, Powell's scientific "report"—a work in which fact and fiction were used to make the river and its canyons conform to a tale of making the unknown known—becomes clouded by persistent unknowing and teeters atop residual unconformity. In bringing his story to a close, Powell wrestles with the task of literarily compassing "the most sublime spectacle on earth," the grand result of "the work of waters." He observes, "We think of the mountains as forming clouds about their brows," but, counterintuitively, "the clouds have formed the mountains. Great continental blocks are upheaved from beneath the sea by internal geologic forces that fashion the earth. Then the wandering clouds, the tempest-bearing clouds, the rainbow-decked clouds, with mighty power and with wonderful skill, carve out valleys and canyons and fashion hills and cliffs and mountains.

The clouds are the artists sublime." The origin of the Grand Canyon—the "Sockdolager of the World"—is to be found in the clouds.

Placing the chapter "The Grand Canyon" at the conclusion of *The Exploration of the Colorado River and Its Canyons* has the effect of undermining the narrative of the 1869 river trip. On its own, the narrative relates an adventure that conforms to what we think we know about science, the natural history of the Colorado Plateau, the cultural history of American "Manifest Destiny," and the ongoing ecological history created by the coming together of the natural and cultural. But "The Grand Canyon" chapter is itself an embellishment, a device that makes the story complete—only this more complete story effectively and paradoxically renders the story *less* complete. In the last paragraph of the book Powell concludes that the Grand Canyon is not "a changeless spectacle." It cannot be seen "in one view" or known even after a year's study. "It can be seen only in parts from hour to hour and from day to day and from week to week and from month to month." By declaring that the Grand Canyon can only be known in parts, Powell tells us that the whole *cannot be known*. We can only keep trying to know something as well as we can, aware of its many parts, of unfolding time, of varying perspectives, and thus of constant change. The final paragraph returns to "change" and its cognates repeatedly, adding "infinite variety" and complexity to affirm the unlikelihood of exhausting our knowledge of the canyon. We can, however, come to know something of the sublime, as Powell suggests in the final words of the book: "By a year's toil a concept of sublimity can be obtained never again to be equaled on the hither side of paradise." That is, even if we can't really know the unknown, we can become aware of its presence.

Powell's story of exploration reveals unconformities between the world in which we live and the world we think we know, between West and East, water and rock, desert and river, plateau and chasm, biblical and geological time, orogeny and erosion, schist and sandstone, Creation and the perpetual formation of the world. The unconformity of the writer accounts in part for the unconformity of the story. He was raised by evangelists but drawn to earthly matters, could not even fit in at Oberlin College (a modern-day haven for nonconformists), which he attended briefly in the 1850s, presumably because of its emphasis at the time on theological rather than geological pursuits. Nor did the practices and goals of his work in the West conform to those of the standard western surveys of the era. Powell's West, Powell's earth do not agree at all with the West of Manifest Destiny or the world of Genesis.

The major used "embellishments" to supplement his barometer, chronometer, and sextant, rearranging the facts to tell a "truer" tale of the West. To read the book as a report runs the risk of seeing it as true or false in its particulars, and that, I think, is to miss the story. Such a reading makes the *Exploration* conform to preconceived notions of reports, science, history, nature writing, and so on and serves to partially bury the meanings of the text, the river, and the region under the dust and rubble of "the truth." Unconformity, covered by a layer of conformity, cannot readily pose its questions. A world thus formed is removed from our engagement with its richness. But to read the *Exploration* as river literature and to interpret its unconformities is to reopen the book and its revelations. An illustration of the Great Unconformity spreads out over the final two pages of the expanded, final version of the *Exploration*, and more than two kinds of rock unexpectedly smack into each other: Tapeats Sandstone–Vishnu Schist, to be sure, but also truth-fiction, conformity-unconformity, known-unknown, the intervening layers washed away down the river.

Out of the Sleep of Mild People, into the Wild Rippling Water: Deliverance

Telling stories about going down the river is a way of subduing its wildness, as if narrative were a kind of dam or diversion to channel the otherwise overwhelming onrush of energy into something we can understand if not fully grasp. Meaning, in the down-the-river stories I have been considering, is a function of force, and narrative operates as a device to control some of that force. That may explain the need for embellishments, even in nonfiction writing: they assist writers in drawing some sort of truth from the elemental power of moving water. Fictional downriver accounts extend such embellishments, attempting to capture the river's meaning to explore a more profound truth. James Dickey's *Deliverance* (1970), often ranked among the best novels of the twentieth century and made into one of the most successful river films of all time, has been compared to Conrad's *Heart of Darkness* for its treatment of nature and human savagery, though it is a tale of downriver rather than upriver adventure. It resembles Abbey's nonfiction essay in that it is a first-person, subjective narrative in which the river affords the characters a means of entry into the wilderness, an escape from middle-class ennui and emptiness, and it portrays a "last voyage" before damming changes the river forever. But it can also be likened to Cole's allegorical treatment of a down-the-river voyage and its pertinence to the search for meaning in life. As in Cole's series, the river at the center of Dickey's story is an idealized, fictional river, made up of the qualities of real waterways but altered into a special creation that forcefully carries human characters toward a moment of reckoning.

Dickey tells the story through a first-person narration even more radically subjective than Abbey's recounting. Narrator Ed Gentry ponders his innermost experiences and sensations as he describes how he and three other men from Atlanta floated down the Cahulawassee River in northeastern Georgia one mid-September weekend. Ed, vice president and graphics consultant for the firm Emerson-Gentry, is pulled into the getaway by his friend Lewis Medlock, whom Ed depicts as deeply concerned with fashioning a self capable of surviving the complexity of modernity by getting back to basics, vigorously strengthening his body and sharpening his mind to enhance a connection with nature, the wild, the "real." Both prone to and skeptical of Lewis's "enthusiasms," Ed embodies an ambivalence reflected in his approach to most matters, including work. He characterizes himself as part artist and part engineer, pursuing a mechanical approach to design problems in pursuit of "some kind of harmonious relationship" and always following a philosophy of "antifriction." Lewis lifts weights, practices archery, and canoes streams as he seeks a response to modern meaninglessness; Ed looks for the same but ambivalently and much less strenuously. He explains his philosophy of "sliding" to Lewis as they drive to the river put-in: "'Sliding is living antifriction. Or, no, sliding is living *by* antifriction. It is finding a modest thing you can do, and then greasing that thing. On both sides. It is grooving with comfort.'" Ed observes that their fellow two businessmen-voyageurs, Drew Ballinger and Bobby Trippe, "were not bored in the way Lewis and I were bored"; Drew is more earnest, Bobby is more cynical, and neither is as self-driven as Lewis nor as philosophically ambivalent as Ed.

Dickey frames the plot of *Deliverance* with "Before" and "After" chapters, unfolding the action in three chapters within the frame. (The interior chapters are titled with specific dates in the same manner as Powell's "diary.") The four men put in on the river deep in the backwoods, struggle at first with simply keeping the canoes afloat and moving forward, but eventually enjoy the downriver run and a peaceful camp that night. The next day, however, everything changes abruptly: "Two men stepped out of the woods, one of them trailing a shotgun by the barrel." These men, who seem to emerge from the wild as if part of it, drastically alter the course of the city men's recreational trip down the river. By day's end Bobby has been brutally raped, Drew has been killed, Lewis lies immobile in tatters (busted up by the river), and Ed has taken on the role of avenging assassin. The last day of the voyage Ed stalks and kills his prey, the remaining attacker, the other having been shot by Lewis and buried deep in the muck and trees. Ed then leads Lewis and Bobby down the river to the take-out and subsequently through the tense dealings with local law enforcement officials and medical professionals.

In the framing chapters and throughout the events of the trip, the river stands out as one of the book's most important characters, something more than just the scene of action. Readers initially encounter the river as an image, as part of a map unrolled on the first page. It appears to Ed almost like an element of a design problem; in manipulating the map, the men "laid the river out to run for us through the mountains 150 miles north." Ed's story thus begins with a representation of the river, something not quite real, a miniature version over which men (especially Lewis) have control. And the river runs unnamed for sixty pages, known to readers only by its proximity to certain towns and a blue line on the map. Gradually, however, the Cahulawassee grows from image to place to wild presence, an agent of change, finally. When Ed first sees it, he provides a mechanical, objective description—color, texture, width, depth—and calls it "pretty." As the canoes get under way and Ed is taken downstream by the Cahulawassee's "slow force," his two-dimensional picture of the river becomes more complex: "I felt the complicated urgency of current, like a thing made of many threads being pulled, and with this came the feeling I always had at the moment of losing consciousness at night, going toward something unknown that I could not avoid, but from which I would return." Being in or on the river introduces Ed, who is at first removed from the river and viewing it objectively, to a greater intimacy with its nature and an awareness of water's power.

Near the conclusion of the second day, his nerves increasingly frayed after the initial encounter with the backwoodsmen, Ed experiences the river differently. Saying that "something came to an edge in me," he begins to feel the river rather than merely view it objectively, and it becomes "pure energy." This signals a significant alteration in his relation to the river, from the objective to the subjective and beyond. Moments later, Drew is shot, overturning the canoe, and the river literally takes Ed in, tossing him about with such force that he feels himself "fading out," "joining" the river. Even his subjective understanding of the Cahulawassee is undone, rendering him less a self separate from the river and more a part of its wild nature. That process culminates in a moment of overlook, as Ed ascends a cliff face the morning of the final day in pursuit of their "redneck" assailant. One hundred and fifty feet above the Cahulawassee, Ed's vision and imagination merge. The outside and the inside intermingle, so that Ed is no longer himself and the river is no longer an "other"; viewer and viewed become one, and the river runs through it. "Let the river run," comments the narrator. From that standpoint, Ed beholds the river in all its glory: "The river was blank and mindless with beauty. It was the most glorious thing I have ever seen. But it was not seeing, really. For once it was not just seeing. It was beholding. I *beheld* the river in its icy pit of brightness, in its far-below sound and indifference, in its large coil and tiny points and flashes of the moon, in its long sinuous form, in its uncomprehending consequence."

Giving the word *beheld* special stress, Dickey distinguishes beholding as an active way of looking that connotes a special connection between the beheld and the beholder. It is no longer a subject looking out upon an object; the subject looks from a position within the world, a world that holds him, in which he belongs, an intimate "in-seeing" that transcends customary subject-object relations. Beholding is a sign of deliverance.

Numerous devices make clear that *Deliverance* involves more than just escape from the trials of the country or the wild river. The before-and-after frame, Ed's first-person narration with its meticulous study of his interior experience, two epigraphs at the very beginning of the novel, and its very title indicate that readers are faced with something more than an adventure story. In the final chapter of the book, Ed recounts the measures taken to escape any consequences of the action in the wild. Having become the leader, he arranges the men's story and rehearses it with Bobby and Lewis until his altered facts have replaced the reality left behind upriver: "My lies seemed better, more and more like truth." Later, Ed brings events into the present, remarking on the status of the surviving characters, including the Cahulawassee—the river no longer exists after damming, except inside of Ed. "In me it still is, and will be until I die, green, rocky, deep, fast, slow, and beautiful beyond reality." The river thus has itself been transformed by Ed's story, from unreal image on a map to the starkest and most deadly reality, then to a living form that transcends reality. Because of its presence within him Ed has been changed, utterly and forever; the river now informs all his thoughts, experiences, and actions in the world, improving his relations with others: "The river underlies, in one way or another, everything I do," providing Ed with a means of participating in the world more successfully and to measure up as a man more satisfactorily.

This measuring up at the end takes readers back to the beginning of the book, even before the story begins. Dickey launches *Deliverance* with two epigraphs, one from French writer Georges Bataille and the other from the Bible. The Bataille reference proposes that a "principle of insufficiency" lies at the base of human life. By the end of the book, Ed will have met the challenges of the wild through his special relation to the river, and that connection will have enabled him to surmount the insufficient existence he has described at the story's commencement. The second epigraph comes from Obadiah, the shortest book of the Bible, and at first seems to contain a warning to mountain men: "The pride of thine heart hath deceived thee, thou that dwelleth in the clefts of the rock, whose habitation is high; that saith in his heart, Who shall bring me down to the ground?" Dickey's use of verse 3 from Obadiah refers readers to a prophecy—"The vision of Obadiah"—that the people of God will be saved; their enemies, including those who stand by without assisting the "house of Jacob," will be destroyed. It is not the usual sort of biblical prophecy, in which the people of God are warned that they need to shape up or else. In Obadiah there is no "or else." Some will be delivered from the injustices of others: "But upon mount Zion shall be deliverance, and there shall be holiness; and the house of Jacob shall possess their possessions" (verse 17). Both epigraphs set the story in motion and support the theme of "deliverance" announced by the title.

"Deliverance" is truly a key word, one that unlocks several meanings of this down-the-river text. Beside the oblique reference to it by the Obadiah citation, the actual word or its root surfaces several times in the text. Lewis uses it to disparage a mutual acquaintance when expounding on his philosophical "self-system," saying the man "'doesn't deliver enough,'" whether "'on the river,'" at work, "'or, I'm fairly sure, in bed with his wife.'" "To deliver" here means to act responsibly, carry one's weight, have the right stuff, be able to do what needs to be done. In another instance Ed muses on the attractions of a young woman he encounters at work, seeing in her eye something that "promised other things, another life, deliverance." Sex presents the possibility of rescue from the mundane and routine and resonates with the sense of escape from grave danger implied by the title. Unpredictably, the self-admittedly unheroic and ambivalent Ed ultimately delivers himself and the surviving "city boys" from the evils of the country, from wild men and a "'wild goddamned river.'" But the main deliverance is from a state of meaninglessness, an existence in which images are disconnected from the real. The river plays a crucial role in Ed Gentry's deliverance from a life lived with sufficient middle-class trappings of success but without much meaning; but it is his very ambivalence, his ability to function in the world of representation and to transfer understanding from that world to the nonrepresentational, that enables him to survive the trials of the wild. Other members of his party either are intent on mastering brute nature or are mastered by it; Ed's ambivalent approach to life (even under great duress he frequently moves between reality and an imagined movie version of it) saves him by allowing him to bring together seemingly opposing attributes and values: outdoor (natural) and indoor (cultural) interests, physical and intellectual activity, imaginative and mechanical thought, self and other.

The trip down the wild Cahulawassee initiates Ed into more meaningful relations with the world, and that initiation serves as at least one aspect of Dickey's "deliverance." With its etymology of "setting free" and its connotation as a formal utterance or proclamation, the word could be applied to most down-the-river writings. Such works concern characters' relations with the flow and force of water as it moves ever down to the sea, whether that embodies some kind of steady state or a stage in some process or cycle. "Deliverance," in Dickey's novel, is associated with prophecy, and like many prophecies it is ambiguous, leaving much to interpretation. Does he use

Obadiah to condemn the mountain folk who dwelleth in the clefts of the rock or the people who dam rivers and lounge in beach chairs looking out over lakes created by dams? Does the prophet doom that "incompetent asshole," the "soft city country-club man," or the competent but toothless redneck from "the country of nine-fingered people"? The prophecy of *Deliverance* appears to be more ambiguous than Abbey's prophetic warning in "Down the River" that "industrial man" is becoming "an exile from the earth" bound for the "pain and agony of final loss." And Dickey's prophecy is certainly less hopeful than Cole's in *The Voyage of Life* paintings, with their promise of God waiting in the parting clouds above the dark but calm ocean.

Perhaps all downriver writings, pursuing some form of deliverance, have prophetic tendencies, revealing elements of the world if not foretelling inevitable outcomes. Such revelations do not necessarily issue from a discrete divine source, ushering us into a truth incorruptible. Stories that take us down the river often draw our attention to fundamental elements of the world that have been exposed by the stream's wearing away, delivering new pieces of knowledge to our view. And as much as we might wish for this to result in a solid, unquestionable, once-and-for-all known, going down the river is just as likely to deliver us unto the unknown. Dickey's deliverance may not differ all that much from Powell's, in which the exploration of the unknown concludes not with fixed, firm knowledge but with the never fully knowable Grand Canyon. Both writers question the seemingly unidirectional movement through previously unknown dangers to a stable outcome in which human beings triumph over river, come into knowledge, and stand on terra firma.

In the "Coda" to *Downcanyon*, Zwinger too undercuts a positivist, comprehensive view of the Colorado River: "There *is* something down there, and it cannot be explained in a listing of its parts." For her, the river is "so commanding" and the canyon it has cut "so huge and overpowering" that we must rely on a sense of "truth and beauty and love of this earth" in order to begin to understand the world. Considering the lesson of the Anasazi experience in Grand Canyon, she offers a passing conclusion, a kind of scientific prophecy: "All evidence verifies the hypothesis that environmental stress combined with over-population *does* trigger the kind of socioeconomic change and population dislocation that beset the Anasazi in the middle of the twelfth century." Zwinger uses the example to suggest that "when the climate turns bad," there's nothing humans can do about it. Going down rivers reminds us of what we know and what we do not, what we can and cannot do. Writers take readers down rivers to bring these matters to our attention, as we too head seemingly inexorably and incontrovertibly in one particular direction.

5 | *Crossing the River*

To go upstream or downstream entails moving in one particular direction, doing so with a particular goal in mind, and experiencing a particular length (though in some cases the entirety) of a river's course. Starting out at one end, one is driven, by one's own will or by the river itself, to the other. Crossing the river turns direction on its side; it is a transverse movement, only remotely connected to the waterway's beginning or conclusion. One crosses to get to the other side (and perhaps back again), the river's current both pushing and pulling one's attention into the present, at the junction of the past and the future. In this temporal regard crossing resembles being by the river, but crossing implies a more physically active mode of experiencing the stream than by-the-river meditation; and though the act of crossing can produce a meditative response, writers tend to use crossing not as an end in itself but as a means of creating possibilities. Because of this, crossing seems to churn up different ways of being in the present, at the very least, and creates different meanings for the river.

One key difference regards function. No longer a conduit, a river to be crossed operates more as an obstacle or marker, distinguishing one side from the other and sometimes deterring ready movement between the two. As my son Jack (nine or ten at the time) noted while reconnoitering the lower Rio Grande, both sides can appear quite similar—creosote, fox, ocotillo, great horned owl, prickly pear, rock wren, cottonwood, raven on both sides of the river, Sierra del Carmen rising on one side and Chisos Mountains on the other, wetlands giving way to dry lands all around. But though landforms, flora, and fauna may be the same on both banks, the river represents boundaries, borders demarcating differences due to economic and political conditions of the places separated, a line in the Tex-Mex sand.

Crossing over borders between states, whether political states or states of mind, can lead one into entirely new circumstances, and writings that deal with crossing rivers often have a transformative quality, even though the physical distance traversed may be minimal and the physical nature of there not much different from here. Writers use river crossing to explore other crosses, intermixes of the personal and political, historical and prospective, physical and spiritual.

All sorts of rivers are crossed for all sorts of reasons in any number of ways: over (by plane, bridge, kayak, or other craft or by a leap from a rope suspended from a branch), under (by tunnel—I tried this on foot once, beneath the Detroit River, and was accosted by border officials), through (swimming, wading, stepping-stones, all of which usually involve some swimming), or conceptually (by just looking, or imagining, or throwing a rock). Although reasons for crossing vary considerably, they share an essential quality, a condition in which crossing is the best (and sometimes only) option. Encountering the river as a separation between one side and the other, the crosser *must* cross, either because of where he or she is (this side) or because of where she or he is not (that side). Another fundamental trait of the crossing experience pertains to the number of transversals. In some cases, a river is crossed once and for all; one gets to the other side and just keeps going. Writings that center on such a cross typically involve a point of no return or the hope for a clean break from the point of departure and the past with which it is associated. Or a cross may have two parts, the crosser first exploring the other side or obtaining something of value, then returning home. This type of cross may be extended into multiple crossings, a situation made necessary by a commute, perhaps. All of these factors have bearing on the meaning of the rivers themselves, each providing different elements of significance, from the historical and political to the philosophical and psychological.

Less than a fortnight before the September 11 attacks, Akiko Busch swam across the Hudson River. Joined by a small group of friends, she crossed the river at a relatively narrow point some miles south of Poughkeepsie, half a mile from one bank to the other, then back again, the stream gentle because of the slack tide. The swimmers never left the state of New York; it was not a political or an economic crossing, and they were not making history. Busch remembers that it was very much a symbolic act, a purposeful crossing of the Hudson, formerly known to Algonquin speakers as Muhheakantuck, the "river that flows two ways." Her essay on crossing the Hudson, a chapter in her book *Nine Ways to Cross a River* (2007), treats the event as a form of "symbolic sport" or "metaphorical exercise." Having been confronted with a significant "series of divides" (middle age, familial disconnect, the death of friends), Busch situates the swim as the crossing of a physical divide that carries over into other conceptual or psychological divisions. Successfully crossing the river stands for crossing over other obstacles. It is a model for surmounting sundry difficulties, a "symbolic way of breaching the divide."

For Busch, the motivation for river crossing comes primarily from personal crises but leads to ways of addressing problems well beyond the private sphere. Crossing, she writes, is a small, ordinary act that nonetheless can restore a sense of wholeness, psychological well-being, "primal order and proportion." Personal renewal, however rewarding in itself, can also be part of river restoration; Busch links her experiences with a brief environmental history of the Hudson, from Hudson's voyage up the river (almost exactly four hundred years ago as I write this) as "savages" swam about his boat in the current, through the "growth of the American nation" along the "banks of its rivers," to the "industrial landscape" of the mid-nineteenth century and the "toll of contaminants" by the early twentieth, up to the Wild and Scenic Rivers Act (1968), the Clean Water Act (1972), and the modest but promising results of EPA efforts in the more recent past and the present. Swimming across rivers, Busch finds, connects her more intimately with rivers themselves and the human communities surrounding them, a greater understanding of a stream's environmental significance.

She further connects personal and environmental significance with larger historical conditions. Writing in retrospect about that "short swim across a wide river" completed some two weeks before the World Trade Center collapsed and "the world would change," Busch asserts that crossing provides "an image of possibilities realized" and suggests that this image can serve in the effort to restore order and proportion on a larger scale. An important element in those efforts involves finding a way onward, not succumbing to seemingly insurmountable troubles. Citing a tenet of environmental psychology that "perception is anticipatory," Busch proposes that crossing is not a limited, contained gesture but a way forward, "the possibility of getting there, somewhere, from here." The possibility of transformation—that's what crossing rivers is all about. Busch's is a story of "transformation and renewal," for the one who crosses, certainly, but also for the world in which crossing occurs and even for the rivers. While her book makes a claim for the activity of swimming itself as a kind of perpetual rebirth, the essays take part in "reclaiming [the river's] place in our popular imagination"; crossing becomes a metaphorical exercise to renew and reshape the significance of rivers. The history of that exercise goes back as far as Joshua leading the Israelites across the river, "until all the people were passed clean over Jordan"; back to Greeks ferried by Charon across the Styx; back to ritualistic Roman crossings of the Tiber. From those days to the present, the waters of the river provide the means of "transition from one state of being to another."

Sullen, Surging Waters That Lay between Her and Liberty: Crossing Once and for All

Like the Hudson, the Delaware is a tidal river, with the effects of the ocean felt as far up as Trenton, New Jersey, about 130 miles from the river's mouth in Delaware Bay. Perhaps no river has so secure a place in the popular imagination of the nation, its importance in American history unique and seemingly unquestionable: this is the river that Gen. George Washington crossed on an icy December morning in 1776. The supreme historical significance of the scene accounts for some of its familiarity, but no more so than does its depiction by a German-born painter. Emanuel Gottlieb Leutze's *George Washington Crossing the Delaware* (1851) is one of the most famous paintings in the world, some claiming that only the Mona Lisa's weird smile is as well known among artworks. Whether you have purposefully stridden the marble halls of the New York Metropolitan Museum of Art or idly flipped a New Jersey quarter in a Denver pool hall and come up tails, you have seen a version of Leutze's painting. In the late nineteenth century Mark Twain found a reproduction of it everywhere as he traveled along the lower Mississippi. Describing the interior of fine homes on the river between New Orleans and St. Louis, Twain mocked the work's popularity and the quality of some reproductions: "Over middle of mantel, engraving—Washington Crossing the Delaware; on the wall by the door, copy of it done in thunder-

and-lightning crewels by one of the young ladies—work of art which would have made Washington hesitate about crossing, if he could have foreseen what advantage was going to be taken of it."

In his massive painting Leutze sought to depict History in the making: jagged ice floes attack the teetering boat while the soldiers row desperately, fearful yet determined in their fight with the ice; the flag gleams in the new dawn, and the indomitable General Washington, his majestic saber seemingly hovering by his side, stands sternly erect just before amidships, his gaze fixed firmly on the future, left hand calmly across his midriff, right hand poised on his athletically bent right knee. Many have found historical inaccuracies in the representation, involving such details as the flag, the boats, the time of day, and even Washington's heroic stance. But as historian David Hackett Fischer has written in his comprehensive and readable study of the crossing, the inaccuracy of some of the details does not diminish the accuracy of the painting's themes: "liberty and freedom," the invention of new methods of social organization, and the creation of a unified whole out of "diversity" and "stubborn autonomy." The colossal canvas—twelve feet high, twenty feet wide—bears the grandest and best-known representation of an event that has been represented by more works of art than any other in American history. In many ways, Washington's crossing is *the* representative event of the American Revolution. The manipulation of detail, the scale of the painting, and the grandeur of its themes suggest that Leutze saw Washington as crossing more than the Delaware: traversing the river on Christmas night and marching into the teeth of a winter storm the next morning, the general and his army crossed from history into History, the action taking on the stature of myth.

"His Excellency" was leading his men to a victorious surprise attack on the Hessians, who, with some British light cavalry, were encamped east of the river while waiting for the Delaware to freeze entirely, then to make their own crossing and ultimately seize the rebel capital, Philadelphia. Washington's victory, although incomplete due to the inability of his troops stationed elsewhere on the river to negotiate the difficult mix of ice and flowing water, was indeed a turning point of the war. Leutze shows the general resolutely pursuing his course, as if his determination moved the boat as swiftly as the men at the oars, as if they were all going the only direction they could possibly go, as if the sum of their forces were but a part of a larger force and their vessel making an inevitable voyage from one set of conditions into another, with no looking back—truly History in the making. Time and life are more complicated, of course. Washington and his army actually crossed the Delaware more than once, first in retreat from the drubbings they had suffered in New York and New Jersey—a laborious crossing in early December that continued day and night for almost a week; then on the attack, driving the enemy away; then back to Pennsylvania to regroup and plan for the next step, crossing yet again as the campaign ensued in an operation far larger than the more famous crossing and in even worse conditions. But the Christmas crossing made possible one of the Continental army's first major victories in an otherwise seemingly lopsided war, and that victory "transformed attitudes toward the War of Independence on both sides of the Atlantic." Not only did Europeans begin to see the American undertaking in a different light, but Americans began to see themselves and their "Cause" differently—Washington's crossing and defeat of the Hessians at Trenton represented a "vindication of the Cause," with much of the American public interpreting it as "a Sign of God's Redeeming Providence, and proof that the Continental army was His instrument."

Leutze's painting portrays the epic quality of Washington's crossing, capturing the event's effect on the popular imagination. His subject is more than the historic transversal of the Delaware; it is the greatness of Washington, the justness of the cause, the glorious morning of revolution, and the prospects of America. His subject, in other words, is myth. The river separates the past (Old World empires, tyranny and aristocracy, dispossession of the people, lack of change and social movement) and the future (democracy, freedom, pluralism, possibility). It is a crossing of high drama, with everything on the line, the willful act of our first famous individual, the Father of Our Country in the act of fathering it. The mythical aspects of the crossing are so powerful that many Americans today understand Leutze's painting "more as a historical document of the American Revolution than a work of art," as the curator of American art at the Metropolitan Museum of Art has observed. So while Leutze's depiction may be a "theatrical" romanticization, a "melodramatic" exaggeration, or even a shoddy and heavy-handed fabrication, it is no less meaningful. Its significance, however, lies less in its inaccuracies than in the ways in which we have understood its meanings.

Certainly, the crossing came at a historically crucial moment. Several of Washington's own letters contain the general's dire description of the situation and his earnest entreaty to adjutants that they get their act together. Some letters make clear that Washington understood the fate of America, symbolized in the capital, Philadelphia, to hinge on the crossing. "When I reflect upon these things," he wrote to John Hancock on December 24, "they fill me with much concern, knowing that Genl Howe has a Number of Troops cantoned in the Towns bordering on & near the Delaware, his intentions to pass as soon as the ice is Sufficiently formed—to invade Pennsylvania, and to possess himself of Philadelphia, if Possible." In another letter to the president of Congress, dated December 27, 1776, Washington details the success of the Delaware crossing:

> [The troops were marshaled at McKonkey's Ferry so] that they might begin to pass as soon as it grew dark, imagining we should be able to throw them all over, with the necessary Artillery, by 12 OClock, and that we might easily arrive at Trenton by five in the Morning, the distance being about nine Miles. But the Quantity of Ice, made that Night, impeded the passage of the Boats so much, that it was three OClock before the Artillery could all be got over, and near four, before the Troops took up their lines of march.

He then records his worries prior to battle, the particulars of the combat, a list of prisoners and artillery taken, and his pride in his officers and men, whose "Behaviour upon this Occasion, reflects the highest honor upon them. The difficulty of passing the River in a very severe Night, and their march thro' a violent Storm of Snow and Hail, did not in the least abate their Ardour," he writes.

While Washington's letters underscored the strategic importance of the river crossing, and Leutze dramatized it as "the final stage in the progressive movement of world history," recent works have questioned the mythical status of the event. Taking up the subject in the 1950s, painter Larry Rivers approached Washington's crossing as "a national cliché," adding that Leutze's rendition treated the actual incident as "just another excuse for a general to assume a heroic, slightly tragic pose.... What I saw in the crossing was quite different. I saw the moment as nerve-wracking and uncomfortable. I couldn't picture anyone getting into a chilly river around Christmas time with anything resembling hand-on-chest heroics." Rivers's own *Washington Crossing the Delaware* (1953) does not use Washington's profile to suggest singleness of purpose and direction, instead situating the general as a much less distinct and triumphant figure; he faces the viewer, almost as if he were asking directions. This twentieth-century "'repainting' of a traditional American icon . . . undercuts the heroic Napoleonic stance" of the commander in chief, placing him as part of a ruddy and rustic ensemble, not so much crossing as floundering in the river.

Larry Rivers's recrossing of the Delaware set in motion literary reworkings of the momentous occasion and its wake. Frank O'Hara wrote "On Seeing Larry Rivers' *Washington Crossing the Delaware* at the Museum of Modern Art" a couple of years after viewing the painting. O'Hara's response is an example of ekphrasis, a poem written about another form of art, and it operates both as a commentary on the original painting and as an extrapolation of one or more of the original themes. River crossing is an apt topic for ekphrasis, which is itself a kind of crossing, from one genre into another. O'Hara's poem uses imagery from the painting and treats the subject "with similar irreverence and amused contempt." The poet's Washington crosses less into "the beautiful history" than into a nation of disconnected and discombobulated individuals, trepid and somewhat clueless in "the misty glare," beneath clouds of "the general fear." In both Rivers's painting and O'Hara's ekphrastic take on it, that long-ago moment seems now but "a crossing by water in winter to a shore / other than that the bridge reaches for."

In another example of literary crossing, Kenneth Koch wrote a version of *George Washington Crossing the Delaware* (1966) for the theater. A friend of O'Hara and Rivers, Koch had liked Rivers's painting's "mixture of romance, heroism and humor, the lightness about a historical event." The play, which was dedicated to Rivers, began as a favor to the painter, who had asked Koch to write something for the elementary school in Long Island that Rivers's son attended. Though eventually premiering in the New York theater scene instead of at a grade school, the play was nevertheless written to be performed by children and presents history from a childlike perspective, and, though seldom produced, it became an "underground classic." Koch's play, one in a series of crossings that began with Washington's several transversals and their subsequent interpretations, represents interpretation itself as a kind of crossing. Or is that crossing as a kind of interpretation? The Delaware, reduced to a cardboard prop in the play, serves as a kind of magical mirror that gives Americans the opportunity to study some of our foundational myths.

The play, for example, presents all of those fighting for the American cause as of one mind, as willing participants in a social experiment that entails throwing off the yoke of tyranny. In the first scene Washington tells his opponent, General Cornwallis, of "the philosophy we all have. It is bound to triumph over your own British authoritarian and colonial system. My men all see eye to eye on this point." In the mythical view of the American Revolution, "every man knows exactly why he is fighting," just as every man, "though he be the lowest in station in the entire Revolutionary Army," is kept fully informed by the general himself of everything the general sees and knows, and all of "his thoughts have been upon the subjects of his contemplation." This unity of belief and universally shared knowledge results in the perfect example of *e pluribus unum*—as one soldier remarks, "This is democracy in action, actually being practiced in a military situation." Leading the perfect democracy is the perfect commander in chief. A prominent aspect of American mythology, the saintly figure of Washington stands out in the play much like the figure of the general stands in Leutze's boat. Washington alone is the reason that an army "made up only of seedy criminals and starving bootblacks" could possibly have a chance against "the skilled and well-equipped troops" of the most formidable force in the world.

George Washington, Cornwallis tells the audience in a soliloquy, is "the greatest man who will ever live in America!" The British general is utterly bedazzled by his enemy, calling him "a perfect gentleman," a man of "perfect grace"—his "dress is perfect, his buttoning neat, and his shoes of a high polish." For Cornwallis, Washington embodies all of America, its people and the land itself: "There is nothing he could not accomplish, would he but set himself to it," he gushes and concludes his reverie of amazement with the observation that when Washington "reclines, one imagines one sees the stately bison taking its rest among the vast unexplored plains of this country, America." In this version of American mythology, the perfect man leads the perfect democracy (and the bison lies down untroubled by hunters). Where Leutze's painting crosses from history to myth, Koch crosses from myth not back into history but on into interpretation, raising questions of meaning. Absurdity in the play points to myths and makes them more vivid, but it does not debunk them. Koch does not set things straight; instead, his work sets things crooked, tilting Leutze's painting and other such pictures askew. And the play is unlike the works of Rivers and O'Hara in this regard; whereas these works can be seen as "undermin[ing] the heroism, masculinity and patriotism" of Leutze's myth, Koch uses "a witty approximation of reality for reality-subverting purposes." The result does not knock Washington off his heroic pedestal, as happens with Rivers's painting and O'Hara's poem. Koch nudges his audience to think again about the pedestal itself, the statue we put there, and the nation for which it stands.

Koch's *George Washington Crossing the Delaware* does not question the factual accuracy or historical value of the act of crossing. He leaves those issues alone, instead questioning the layers of meaning overlying the event, the gross reproductions of "Washington Crossing the Delaware," the seemingly unquestionable glory of the moment and its patriotic two-dimensional re-creations in crewel or on canvas. The playwright calls special attention to the act of crossing by placing it at the center of *George Washington Crossing the Delaware*, first as part of a dream sequence and then as a narrated offstage action at the play's conclusion. As scene 6 begins, the general sits on his bed a moment before proclaiming, "Good night, America." The stage directions then call for a placard to be displayed bearing the words "THE DREAM OF GEORGE WASHINGTON." In the dream Washington is played by a child while the adult Washington sleeps in bed, and the child chops down the cherry tree. But instead of perpetuating the myth of Washington's honesty, Koch uses this most familiar tale for an unusual purpose: to avoid the wrath of his father, the honest little woodchopper flees, shouting, "I cannot tell a lie, but I can run! I can flee from injustice! The tree was mine, to chop down as I pleased!" When his father returns from an unsuccessful chase, the audience learns that little Washington "swam across the river. It was the only way he could have done it. The ONLY WAY!" The general then awakes, recognizes the dream as the key to his strategy, and orders his men to "march at once for the Delaware River!"

While so clearly focused on the historical river crossing of the title, Koch's play also uses literary crossings to intensify and complicate an otherwise simple picture. With its childlike point of view, the play at times resembles a finger painting or a color-by-numbers version of a seminal moment in American history. In the speech directing the launch of the Continental army assault, Washington sounds more like Dr. Seuss than the Father of Our Country, as he calls for "Raids on the clothing tents, beautiful raids, / Raids on Cornwallis, and raids on his aides." (Koch attributed such speeches to the influence of the poem "The Night Before Christmas.") By the end of the play, however, that simplicity becomes clouded. In the final scene two old men watch and comment on the events that are occurring offstage. After first casting suspicion on the reliability of their vision and hearing, Koch has the "rapt" old men describe what little they can make out through the mist and darkness. When they can see no more, one says to the other, "What you saw was enough," and then artillery explodes to announce the concluding statement: "The American army has crossed the Delaware." Koch thus represents the Delaware crossing, unseen by the audience, as an event described by one poor-sighted character to another; the question-able reliability of these witnesses does not keep the event from becoming immediately storied, already a myth in the making.

What Koch has given the audience is not one but two river crossings, which he has concocted by crossing two American tales from the Washington mythology. This "double crossing" adds further complexity to the campy speeches of leading characters and makes crossing itself something to think about, a means of escape as well as a means of attack, a means of rethink-ing, maybe even a hybrid mixing of myth and countermyth. With its river crossing, crossing from one art medium to another, crossing history with myth and thus inverting the stories we live by, Koch's *George Washington Crossing the Delaware* playfully invites the audience to rethink basic ele-ments of the American story. It is not quite a crossing back over from myth to history but a movement toward clearing away the trappings of myth to reveal that things are much less clear. Koch's ekphrastic reworking of earlier paintings of the Delaware crossing obfuscates obfuscation in order to make possible interpretation (or reinterpretation) of the meaning of America. His interpretive crossing proposes an imaginatively engaged, critically reflective response to the fixity of American myths and the seemingly unidirectional trajectory of traditional versions of American history. The river, situated at the center of the X in Koch's various crossings, is that which must be crossed—a movement that helps us know where we have been and where we might be going.

Koch's play centers on a unique sort of crossing, a one-way movement across the river from one side to another and, in Washington's example, from the west to the east, from retreat to attack, and from the colonial past into the future of the republic. Although Washington's may be the most historically prominent river crossing, a more prevalent form of the one-way crossing of rivers occurred in the general south-to-north movement of escaping slaves. There are thousands and thousands of cases of fugitive slaves heading north to Canada, most of them undocumented except for advertisements posted by slave owners seeking return of their property. Not all of the escape routes featured the crossing of a river, though they always involved passing over a boundary, an arbitrary geopolitical line separating slavery from freedom, and the Ohio River especially signified such a line. Running almost a thousand miles from Pittsburgh to the confluence with the Mississippi, the Ohio served as an important boundary in the early republic. After Washington's historic crossing of the Delaware but before he was sworn in as president, Congress passed an Ordinance for the Government of the Territory of the United States North West of the River Ohio (1787). The Northwest Ordinance established that "there shall be neither Slavery nor involuntary Servitude in the said territory." The law ensured that the Ohio River would become a center of the historic movement of slaves out of bondage, and the physical crossing of the river serves as an apt symbol of that movement. The Ohio River "became a veritable River Jordan," as historian J. Blaine Hudson has noted, "the 'Dark Line' between slavery and nominal freedom."

Whereas Washington's crossing has been overrepresented, very few of the numerous slave crossings of the Ohio "have been immortalized in significant works of literature," the most famous exception being the case of Eliza Harris. There are slightly different versions of the actual crossing of the icy Ohio, but all accounts agree that it was "one of the most harrowing and memorable slave escapes in American history." Eliza Harris, with her two-year-old son held close to her in a shawl, barely eluded the grasp of slave catchers by fleeing over the frigid February waters of the river and up the bank into Ripley, Ohio, where she was helped from the shore by Chancey Shaw and sent on to the Reverend John Rankin and his family. Rankin's house, which he had built in 1828 on a bluff high above the river so that he could survey the scene on behalf of fugitive slaves, sheltered more than two thousand men, women, and children escaping from slave states; the house became "the single most famous landmark on the Underground Railroad" and was reputedly "immortalized in the African American spiritual *Swing Low, Sweet Chariot*." It was at the town of Ripley, according to some stories, that the Underground Railroad was given its name: Tice Davids swam across the Ohio River in the early 1830s, chased closely by his Kentucky master; as the slave owner watched his property clamber onshore and vanish down the narrow streets and alleys of Ripley, he reportedly "told everyone he knew that his slave 'must have disappeared on an underground road.'"

From Ripley, Eliza Harris and her son were conducted to Cincinnati, then Newport, Indiana, where they were sheltered and assisted by Levi and Catherine Coffin at their home, known by many as the "Grand Central Station of the Underground Railroad." (In his reminiscence Coffin wrote that his wife had given "Eliza Harris" her name during the stay, as the fugitive herself reminded them when they met again later.) Eliza Harris traveled up through Indiana to Sandusky, Ohio, and eventually to Canada, where she settled in Chatham. In any version her story is striking; but it is the fictional account in Harriet Beecher Stowe's *Uncle Tom's Cabin* (1852) that has had the profoundest effect. Stowe later wrote that her novel was spurred in part by reading an eyewitness account of Eliza's actual escape "with her child on the ice of the Ohio River from Kentucky." While Stowe gave differing reports of where she first heard the story of Eliza, questions of the source do not affect the scene's power in Stowe's novel, where it serves as a heroic liberation to balance the tragedy of the title character's death in slavery.

The story is told twice in the novel (as if to make up for the lack of information about such crossings), first by the narrator, then by Sam, a slave who saw the event while reluctantly accompanying Haley, the slave trader who has purchased Eliza's son, in pursuit of his property. The narrator explains that, having departed hastily with only the makings of a plan, Eliza headed to the river, which "lay, like Jordan, between her and the Canaan of liberty on the other side." "Great cakes of floating ice" nearly fill the "swollen and turbulent" river. Because no bridges spanned the river until after the Civil War, escaping slaves' options included only swimming, wading, or rowing a boat. Knowing that no ferry can pass through the ice yet also painfully aware that she has no alternative but to cross "the sullen, surging waters that lay between her and liberty," Eliza hesitates until suddenly capture is imminent: "Nerved with strength such as God gives only to the desperate, with one wild cry and flying leap, she vaulted sheer over the turbid current by the shore, on to the raft of ice beyond. It was a desperate leap—impossible to anything but madness and despair." She leaps, slips, stumbles, and springs over the ice, all the while clinging to her child, until she reaches the Ohio side and is helped up the bank by another Kentucky slave owner. Her escape so impresses Mr. Symmes that he assists her on her way, despite the fact that her rightful owner won't think his actions "'the most neighborly thing in the world.'" Later, when hearing an account of the "miracle" crossing, Eliza's mistress "sat perfectly silent, pale with excitement, while Sam told his story."

With the repetition of "despair" and its cognate in describing the crossing, Stowe brings out some of the salient qualities of all such traversals to freedom. Eliza's despair and miraculous strength result from the combination of "maternal love" and the frenzied response to "a fearful danger." Her successful escape across the river represents the movement of so many people, reduced to such horrifying conditions, out of imbruted bondage. The stories of that movement all involve some sort of crossing, whether of the actual Ohio River or of the figural Jordan, and are marked by desperation, courage, confidence, endurance, resourcefulness, trust, constant fear, lack of information, drive. John Parker, himself a former slave and later a Ripley Underground Railroad conductor who carried out river crossings for numberless fugitives, writes in his autobiography: "It was not the physical part of slavery that made it cruel and degrading, it was the taking away from a human being the initiative, of thinking, of doing his own ways." The "curse" of slavery, as Parker and others remembered, "was the making of a human being an animal without hope." Crossing the river was both a physical movement out of slavery and something else, an intellectual or spiritual movement into a state of hopefulness, of possibility, even a recovery of humanity.

Frederick Douglass made an observation similar to John Parker's regarding the unimaginably arduous process for undoing slavery's imbruting and dehumanizing effects. At the center of Douglass's autobiographical account is a different sort of crossing. He writes: "You have seen how a man was made a slave; you shall see how a slave was made a man." Douglass here uses a rhetorical figure known as chiasmus, a "crossing"; "chiasmus" means to shape something like the Greek letter chi, or X. His rhetorical crossing (which occurs in chapter "X" of the *Narrative*) moves from the past to the future, with a note of promise emerging in the second part of the phrase. Fugitive slaves' one-way river crossings, like Douglass's literary crisscross, emphasize the making of something new, the possibility of freedom and full humanity; these crossings all began on farms or in towns on one peculiar side of a figurative—and sometimes literal—river. Approaching the southern banks of the Ohio, perhaps with hounds and horsemen in pursuit, a fugitive looking over at Ripley would maybe see John Parker's house on Front Street, thick trees climbing a hillside that blocks any further view; in extreme desperation, someone like Eliza might have looked over the river and seen the Rankin home, sitting atop the crest in a clearing, a lantern in the upstairs window burning like a tiny North Star. Down to the river the figure runs, to cross once and for all.

And You That Shall Cross from Shore to Shore Years Hence: Endless Crossing

In crossings the river can function as a boundary, an obstacle, or the means to a new set of circumstances. The primary meaning of the river to emerge from single crossings is as a marker between two significantly different conditions. Multiple crossings, however, tell another story about rivers. Instead of leaving one world behind and crossing forever into a new state of existence, the multiple crosser turns around and comes back, returns and departs again. Demarcating different states, the river always remains, must always be crossed again, no matter which side of it one finds oneself occupying. Multiple crossings, centered as they are on the borderline constituted by the river, draw attention to the region in which they occur, the area surrounding the borderline; the two sides of the river often differ significantly from one another but also are connected to one another by the line and those who cross it. The Rio Grande is the most prominent example of such a line in contemporary North American culture. Flowing almost two thousand miles from where it rises in the San Juan Mountains of Colorado until it enters the Gulf of Mexico near Brownsville, Texas, the

Rio Grande ranks among the longest rivers in the United States. Such a length and the vastly varying bioregions through which it courses would be enough to make the Rio Grande complex, but a great deal of complexity stems from the stretch of 1,250 miles in which it serves as the boundary between the United States and Mexico.

The Rio Grande became the official border on February 2, 1848, with the signing of the Treaty of Guadalupe Hidalgo, ending the war between the two nations that had begun in 1846 after the U.S. Congress voted to annex Texas. Before the war the Rio Grande cut through the middle of Nuevo Santander, an "in-between" province of Mexico that suffered incursions by Texas cowboys coming down from the north and armies of the centralist Mexican government from the south. The treaty altered the cultural function of the river from "a focus of regional life" to a "symbol of separation," intensifying the region's occupants' "sense of being caught in the middle." By the end of the nineteenth century the borderline was crossed more and more for a variety of reasons, exacerbating cultural conflict due to economic disparity, ethnic differences, and an imbalance of power among the peoples along the river. In his study of the folklore of Texas-Mexico border peoples, the eminent scholar Américo Paredes observes a tendency among Mexican people of the region to idealize those who crossed the river, especially *tequileros*, smugglers, and *braceros* seeking work in Texas. They are "border-conflict heroes" resisting the laws imposed by a foreign power and enforced in a "heavy-handed and often brutal manner" by the Texas Rangers.

The work of Paredes centers on the *corridos* (ballads) that celebrated the heroes of "intercultural conflict," especially the brave man "with a pistol in his hand" who "defends his rights and those of other Mexicans against the *rinches* [Rangers]." To Paredes, the *corridos* reflect the beliefs and ideas of those people "living between two cultures" and thus enduring a "permanent crisis" of identity. Such people, he suggests, are caught up in metaphorically crossing the river endlessly, moving back and forth between "the pyramid and the skyscraper" while "searching for identity" as they negotiate between the press of their Indian and colonial past from one side and the encroachment of Anglo culture from the other. The Rio Grande—called Río Bravo on the Mexican side of the border—both cleaves and connects; it is a line one must ever traverse, for to cross only once means to reject or neglect a viable part of oneself. Physically moving back and forth across the river correlates with an internal psychical state of being unsettled, neither wholly here nor there but always seeking the other side, another part of the self. Poet and activist Gloria Anzaldúa, a native of the border region and scholar of its cultures, has called the Rio Grande a "1,950-mile-long wound" dividing the people who live along it—Chicanos and Chicanas—as well as each individual belonging to those groups. Although she describes the physical exertions of "*'mojados'* (wetbacks)" of both sexes as they "float on inflatable rafts across *el río Grande*, or wade or swim across naked, clutching their clothes over their heads" and then pulling themselves up the other side prayerfully, Anzaldúa's writing focuses on the emotional and intellectual experiences of women who must cross the river.

In *Borderlands/La Frontera: The New Mestiza,* Anzaldúa elaborates on the "ambivalence," "clash of voices," "mental and emotional states of per-plexity," and "internal strife" that plague women in the "cultural collision" occurring over and over on both sides of the Rio Grande. Noting the enor-mous physical risks facing *"la mojada, la mujer indocumentada"* (illegal or "undocumented" women), Anzaldúa develops a theory surrounding the effects of culture and river traversing on the consciousness of Chicanas. Crossing, despite its strife and danger, presents the possibility of coming into a new consciousness; not only does the crosser have the insights of the side from which she originates, but she has those to be found on the other side as well, and especially from the movement between both. Crossing rivers can inform cultural "cross-pollinations" that result in the creation of "a new *mestiza* consciousness"—a way of thinking that comes from the mixture or fusing of races and culture. Never fully at home on one side of the river or the other, "the new *mestiza* copes by developing a tolerance for contradictions, a tolerance for ambiguity." Anzaldúa attributes the inner resilience of border-crossing Mexican American women to three historical-mythical female figures, the *tres madres* of *la gente Chicana*: the Virgin of Guadalupe, La Malinche, and La Llorona.

These "three mothers" mediate between various parties: the Virgin "unites people of different races, religions, languages" as an intercessor between the human and the divine; La Malinche, first as a translator for Cortés and then giving birth to his child, both embodies and fosters cross-cultural connection, the Indian mother of the *mestizo* race; and La Llorona, "a combination of the other two," changes from period to period and region to region, becoming for some writers "a kind of cultural ambassador" who can bring together diverse groups to share and discuss experiences of a variety of issues. Though, as Anzaldúa observes, ambiguity surrounds all three figures, La Llorona is perhaps the most fluid of the three and in many ways symbolizes the border world of crossing. The fluidity of the legend of La Llorona comes not only from the traditional association of the Wailing or Weeping Woman with riverbanks and other forms of water; in her study of the figure as it evolves from folklore to contemporary media, Domino Renee Perez demonstrates that the Llorona legend is a dynamic mixture of fact and fiction whose meaning changes with each telling, depending upon the condition and concerns of storytellers and their audiences. The story "epitomizes transnational culture in the Mexican Americas—inhabiting both sides of the border"; La Llorona, as Perez observes, "does not recognize any border" and is thus an "ideal vehicle for creating intercultural dialogue."

The continuing importance of La Llorona to people on both sides of the border stems in part from the figure's history and from the story's adaptability. Perez has traced back versions of the story of La Llorona to at least the 1550s. Some of them depict the weeping mother as one of eight omens emerging before the arrival of Cortés and foretelling the coming conquest and subjugation of the indigenous people of Mexico, but she is most prevalent today in the border region. Marked by endless movement, a constant reminder of mortality and obligations, La Llorona haunts the border, frequently as a "figure of mourning" or warning and more recently as a "figure of revolt." In the poetry of Alicia Gaspar de Alba, one of many Chicana writers rethinking the meaning of their *tres madres*, La Llorona appears "as everything from ghost to guardian angel." Associating the figure with the act of writing, with bridges and river crossing, with her birthplace (El Paso, Texas), and with the border region in general, Gaspar de Alba "tracks" La Llorona as she wanders the Mexican American diaspora searching for her children and "their lost culture, their lost selves." Two volumes of Gaspar de Alba's poetry feature bridges in the title, signaling the writer's interest in the act of crossing rivers but also other borders, and La Llorona drifts in and out of the scenes of crossing.

El Paso, where Gaspar de Alba began writing poetry, is one of the most active crossing sites of the Rio Grande: over 8 million pedestrians and almost 14 million personal vehicles carrying almost 22 million passengers crossed the border there in 2008. The numbers represent those crossers who declared themselves to immigration officials, those with proper identification crossing from Mexico to Texas or Texas to Mexico for work or recreation, for visits, or returning to residences. Still uncounted others cross each day, from one side to the other, heading north or south in their traversals to make ends meet or to make a break for something else. The river runs out of energy and water by the time it reaches El Paso; concrete beds and canals keep it going and help maintain its borderline status until the Río Conchos rejuvenates it with ample flow near Ojinaga, Mexico (across from Presidio, Texas) a couple hundred miles downriver. Gaspar de Alba describes it as a land of shrieking winds and riparian lamentation, with ever-present threats from incorporeal beings. The winds blowing "without contrition," the scurrying dust-devils, and the harried human inhabitants all cross the border indefinitely, crossing into an indefinite world.

Around the structures that traverse the separating river—the Paso del Norte Bridge and the Bridge of the Americas, say—*la frontera* can resemble a sordid series of lines in the sand: chain-link fences lining multilane highways and sidewalks; lines of people and lines of cars stopping for ID checks; channeled river trickle beyond the fences through concrete banks emblazoned with mostly political graffiti (anticapitalist, pro–Che Guevara, antiwar, "Death to America"); the concrete bed of what's left of the Rio Grande overtopped in places by concrete roads running along and athwart railroad lines. On one such bridge Gaspar de Alba encounters a beggar from whom she might "learn to read / the crooked, brown palm / of the Río Grande," as if the act of crossing might enable one to make meaning out of the river, turning it into a source of wisdom, a key to understanding the border region and culture through which it runs. When she wrote the poem, Gaspar de Alba herself was crossing the Rio Grande daily, living and working in Ciudad Juárez during the day (teaching ESL in *maquiladoras*), taking a graduate poetry seminar at UTEP and serving cocktails in a swanky El Paso club at night. Her imaginative writing comes from the experience of crossing lines; but instead of offering her the opportunity of arriving at an endpoint, literature became a way of constantly crossing.

Calling herself a "Literary Wetback," the poet affirms that she is not from one side of the cultural divide or the other; rather, she is from the border—meaning both sides, which results in "cultural schizophrenia." Gaspar de Alba knows personally many ways of crossing: as a Chicana, as a lesbian, as a writer; her Llorona represents the sorrow of crossing, the pain, the loss but also the potential for making something new, a third way out of the crossing between two fixed states. To the literary wetback the river flows with bilingualism and biculturalism. Growing up in a strict Mexican family that resided in the United States, she remembers speaking only Spanish at home, where she was "*pura* Mejicana," and only speaking English at school, where she was an American citizen. In neither place was she Mexican American; that is, neither side recognized the other. Gaspar de Alba came to use writing as a means of cultivating an identity that rejected the separations imposed by either side of the divide. The river developed into more than a site of separation; it became a marker of connection, however fraught with suffering; it became the "point of all departures" and "the landscape of La Llorona." Influenced by the structures crossing the Rio Grande, Gaspar de Alba used writing as a method of bridging other divisions, "and at each bridge, I have seen La Llorona. She goes with me everywhere. . . . To me, La Llorona *is* the border. She is the voice and the soul and the grief of the border." The border, marked by the river and haunted by La Llorona, means crossing more than it means partition. *La frontera* is the place where the poet learns to negotiate the differences around and within her, to cross from one way of living, one language, one identity to the other and back again. La Llorona is transformed from a symbol of unrecoverable loss to a guide, a *coyote* assisting the literary wetback.

Although in much of the traditional folklore La Llorona is not expressly associated with the act of crossing, Gaspar de Alba's persistent use of the haunting figure affiliates La Llorona with all Chicanas who must cross. A poem from a section titled "La Frontera" in her first book ties the lamenting seeker of her lost children to La Malinche, the legendary translator and culture crosser: "Some say that the spirit of La Malinche is *La Llorona.*" The poem imagines La Malinche as having special powers (e.g., translation, powers of language) that awe the Aztec priests, and it continues with her rough usage by Cortés and the subsequent birth of their child, "the first mestizo," in Tenochtitlan. The scene changes abruptly in the final stanza, to a place hundreds of miles away and hundreds of years later:

The woman shrieking along the littered bank of the
Río Grande is not sorry. She is looking for revenge.
Centuries she has been blamed for the murder of her
child, the loss of her people, as if Tenochtitlan
would not have fallen without her sin. History
does not sing of the conquistador who prayed
to a white god as he pulled two ripe hearts
out of the land.

Here and in later poems Gaspar de Alba creates a new version of La Llorona by mixing the river-associated figure with the culture-crossing figure of La Malinche. This new mother still wails, mourning for what has been lost, but she is now more explicitly connected to the struggles of crossing; the poet thus transforms La Llorona into the "Patron saint of bus stops and turnstiles. / Virgin of the deported. / Mother of the dispossessed."

In Gaspar de Alba's poetry La Llorona gets mixed up in mestiza crossing activities in general and as an aide to the poet's literary crossing in particular. As such, La Llorona transforms from an embodiment of resigned lamentation into a figure of transformation; or, rather, her lamentations now participate in transformation and even transcendence. Perpetual crossing, instead of a movement of forced resignation or the passive desperation of the culturally, politically, and economically entrapped, becomes an active movement that engenders change; crossing, that is, makes possible new selves and even new worlds. La Llorona appears frequently throughout Gaspar de Alba's poetry, haunting rivers and coming to the support of those who must cross them, but she is most often associated with the liberating of a Chicana consciousness and voice. Learning the heritage of poems and stories about La Llorona enabled the writer to embrace her own cultural hybridity, and this led to her own experiments with "the mythic Weeping Woman of my own childhood fears." In those experiments the river crossing of border inhabitants functions as an emblem of the larger cultural crossing, and Gaspar de Alba suggests this crossing carries with it the possibility of transcending. Weaving together two languages, two cultures, two sides of the border, the Chicana writer creates a new tradition, emphasizing change, individuals' experience, and new ways of looking at the present.

Like La Malinche of another Chicana poet, Carmen Tafolla, La Llorona looks not only back in mourning but also forward to another world, another way of living beyond that available to either the Indian or the European: "I saw our world / And I saw yours / And I saw— / another," La Malinche says to Cortés. The revision of La Malinche–La Llorona in Chicana writing belongs to the creation of "a new *mestiza* consciousness" heralded in Anzaldúa's work and that of many others. It represents a new way of looking at the world and one's identity within it, a result of an endless crossing of the river that separates parts of history, parts of a people, and parts of the self. Crossing that river again and again, according to these border writers, can break down existing paradigms, transcending duality and dualistic thinking.

A couple thousand miles northeast of El Paso, the East River separates Manhattan from Brooklyn. The body of water is a far cry from the Rio Grande. A tidal strait connecting Upper New York Bay with Long Island Sound, the East River runs about sixteen miles, though "run" is not quite the right word. Its tidal nature makes it a give and take of water, the ocean's ebb and flow being its main source of current. The climate and terrain of the East River vary drastically from the aridity and chaparral of the lower Rio Grande; on a mid-March day I stood between the Brooklyn Bridge and Manhattan Bridge, wind driving a freezing rain against my face as I looked out on the storm-tossed black-gray water, wheeling gulls screeching a bleak weather report. The dark shapes of buildings rose on the island across the way; the slap of the river made by the pitch of the waves against the shore was nearly lost amid the dull roar of Brooklyn subway traffic, the beating sleet, and the road rumble of the two bridges. The chop of the water and dense mist made it difficult to think of crossing the river, even as a yellow water taxi hove into and then passed from view. Nonetheless, this is the site of another type of multiple traversal, the place where Walt Whitman leaned against the rail of the Fulton ferry as he crossed from shore to shore and imaginatively instigated an even greater commute.

Growing up in Brooklyn in the 1820s and 1830s, Whitman lived close to the East River and frequently rode the ferry back and forth, finding the experience "at once practical, enjoyable, and mystical." The distance between the two stations being about half a mile, the ferry run took about eight minutes on the steamboat, and Whitman enjoyed the trip immensely—

except when sharing the ride with tobacco users, those who chewed and spat but especially cigar smokers. On occasion, he would spontaneously "regale" fellow passengers with snatches of song. Though a rivalry between Manhattan and Brooklyn supporters marked the period, Whitman saw the river crossing as utterly connective, and this connectivity gave rise to one of his most successful poems. "Crossing Brooklyn Ferry," the poet's "greatest celebration of the transcendentalist unity of existence" and "essentially a poem of connection and camaraderie," originally appeared in the 1856 edition of *Leaves of Grass* under a different title and went through several revisions as he continued to expand and rework his magnum opus. (The version of the poem I cite below was published in 1881.) Throughout the nine sections of the poem, Whitman moves back and forth between images emanating from physically crossing the river and intimations of a profound oneness with others despite differences of place or time.

In the first section he acknowledges the flood tide below the ferryboat and the clouds and sun in the late-afternoon sky, and then he addresses the "Crowds of men and women attired in the usual costumes," "the hundreds and hundreds that cross, returning home" on the ferryboats; the section concludes with the poet turning his gaze far into the future, to "you that shall cross from shore to shore years hence." This inspired shift in time prepares the way for the grand connection the poet attempts to foster, and movement within the short first section resembles that of the poem as a whole: from the actual, physical, and sensorial crossing of the river to an imagined, intellectual, and textual crossing.

"Crossing Brooklyn Ferry" poses that the East River connects more than it separates, treating the ferry stops as two parts of a continuum. Both ends of the line, even if seemingly opposed to one another, are equally beautiful yet in different ways, Manhattan with its buildings and the tall masts of arriving vessels, Brooklyn with its picturesque heights. The poet suggests that he is capable of seeing the beauty of each as well as the continuum itself because of the special movement of shuttling-between. As such, crossing the river makes possible the larger movement and larger unity of the poem, providing a model, maybe even a map, for readers. In section 2 Whitman links the "glories strung like beads" that he experiences through his senses during "the passage over the river" to those that will most certainly be experienced by others "Fifty years hence . . . as they cross . . . , / A hundred years hence, or ever so many hundred years hence." Giving definite emphasis to "Others" (the word appears nine times in this section), Whitman projected "the ties between me and them" into the indefinite future. Those ties result from and reinforce the "simple, compact, well-join'd scheme" to which everything belongs. The palpable qualities of crossing the river thus allow the poet to affirm an impalpable connection between seemingly discrete individuals regardless of physical or temporal distinctions, as asserted in the opening of the next section and elsewhere: "It avails not, time nor place—distance avails not, / I am with you, you men and women of a generation, or ever so many generations hence." He crossed, he realized a kinship with others who cross, and he imagined a wonderful interpersonal crossing on the grandest scale.

Whitman devotes a good deal of attention to the stuff of actual river crossing, pointing out to readers the smallest details and celebrating the grandest vistas. Extensive lists of images convey a sense of the poet in motion, his eye ranging over the whole scene of ferry crossing. In section 3, for example, reporting that "I too many and many a time cross'd the river of old," he enumerates images from all seasons, from the play of winter light and shadow on the bodies of particular seagulls to the summer sky reflected in the water. His vision moves from that reflection to the wider environment: hazy hills, drifting vapor, arriving ships, laboring sailors, wake, waves, fire flickering from the foundry chimneys. Another list, comprising the sixth section, recounts the numerous missteps and transgressions that the poet himself has committed as he assures his readers that he "too knitted the old knot of contrariety" with lying, lust, frivolity, laziness. Though marking a turn away from the life of the river, this latter enumeration of "the dark patches" that fall on human experience contributes to the larger sense of motion in the poem, serving as a shadowy area that offsets all the many forms of light featured in the earlier list. Wide-ranging Whitman takes all of these things—those of the actual physical ferrying and those of the world environing the water, the minutiae of the moment and the "eternal float of solution" in which all is suspended—and groups them in a meaningful way, offering readers several ways of thinking about the range of material objects and sensory perceptions to be found while crossing the river. Even "contrariety," an opposing or pushing away, is taken in by the poetic embrace.

By associating an expanding spiritual dimension of existence with exist-ing objects that keep their places, Whitman advances the larger movement of the poem to which river crossing belongs. In other words, the actual crossing of the ferry between Manhattan and Brooklyn sets in motion a metaphorical crossing between the physical and the spiritual. The sights, sounds, and sensations of riding a steamferry between two locations are quite something on their own, but they are also indicators of something else. "Crossing Brooklyn Ferry" first sets the poet-speaker of the poem and his vision in motion, crossing from one place to another, then continually expands its scope to include others who cross the river, and eventually reaches well across the ages into the moment of the poem being read by any reader who at any time holds the book in hand and truly heeds the text it carries. Crossing begins as a physical movement over a stream, then grows in significance, ultimately functioning as a metaphor for another kind of movement, a textual crossing that permits reader and writer to connect on another plane, a dimension unaffected by either space or time. The poet presents the textual crossing as utterly dismantling the between-as-separation (section 5); textual crossing reveals a between-as-connection (section 8), a spiritual togetherness transmitted by the text itself and realized by the literary event of writing-and-reading. We who read the poem *now*, even years later, are perhaps somehow seen by the poet *then* (section 7); if we can read in an imaginative way, a kind of textual fusion can occur. This mystical connection, which "the study could not teach" and "the preaching could not accomplish," is only accomplished when readers acknowledge the poem itself as a means of crossing over.

Not only is the poem about crossing, but it also attempts to enact cross-ing. Just as the ferryboats connect two places by carrying passengers back and forth across the East River, Whitman poses the poem itself as a boat that connects the writer to readers, the self to others. Crossing—a move-ment that involves passing over a stretch between two states—overcomes both physical and philosophical "constraints." No difference or "distance," whether spatial or temporal, matters; perceived differences are only causes for celebration within the encompassing context of spiritual unity. Every-one is "struck from the float forever held in solution"; everything, "great or small," furnishes a part "toward the soul." Crossing, within the poem and beyond, becomes a way of unmooring the stationary, the self-contained, the disparate and discrete, loosing apparently individual things into the grand fluid mix and unity. With the merging of verb tenses and a shift in attention from "I" to "we," apparent boundaries between writer and reader are dissolved. Literature presents the possibility for thinking across perceived divides—the self, separated from others due to ways of perceiving, is urged by the poem to cross from one way of understanding space and time to another.

The river, with its eternal back-and-forthing, its embodiment of the all-encompassing solution in which everything is afloat, is integral to both movements, the palpable ferry floating between two waypoints and the impalpable spirit spanning time-space. Whitman concludes the poem with a long series of affirming imperatives—commands to sundry things essentially enjoining each simply to do what it does. The first among those charged is the river: "Flow on, river! flow with the flood-tide, and ebb with the ebb-tide!" He orders the waves to roll, the clouds to color the sky, the crossing passengers to cross on "from shore to shore," the "eternal float of solution" to hold together and buoy all things, and readers to entertain the possibility that the poet whom we now peruse may look, "in unknown ways," upon us. How could that possibly be? Only if we transcend customary notions of space and time, only if the reader too furnishes his or her part to the soul and, through an active interpretation of "Crossing Brooklyn Ferry," emerges from the poem endlessly crossing. While others have seen a "paradox of stasis in motion" as the basic symbolism and basis for transcendence in "Crossing Brooklyn Ferry," Whitman's version of transcendence comes from the imaginatively textual extension of the sense experience of crossing the river. Readers' imaginative participation in the movement of the poem makes good on the writer's overtures of connection. "We understand then do we not?"

6 | *Up and Down the River*

Time, blood, consciousness, cash, traffic, electricity, information, tears—all are often said to flow. And when we say such things flow, we are generally likening them to rivers and streams, to moving water. Rivers are the preeminent example of flow, and flow is one of the most (if not *the* most) characteristic features of rivers. Rivers are rivers, one might say, because they flow; flow is what rivers do. Fluvial geomorphologists such as Luna Leopold will tell you that flow plays an important role in the hydrologic cycle, which, of course, plays an important role in making life on Earth possible. Leopold describes the role succinctly: "The grand circle of movement of water from ocean to atmosphere to continent and back to ocean is the essential mechanism that allows organisms—including humans—to emerge, to develop, and to live on Earth." To understand rivers, then, to interpret their meaning in American life, necessarily involves coming to terms with flow. I conclude this primer with a consideration of flow, time, and reflection on the Concord River, especially thinking about how these things come together in Henry David Thoreau's first book, *A Week on the Concord and Merrimack Rivers* (1849).

If you are at all familiar with the Concord, you will wonder how it could possibly be linked with an inquiry into flow. In what must be deemed polite understatement, the United States Geological Survey explains that, because of its "relatively low stream gradient" (a "drop" of about five vertical feet for every horizontal mile), the Concord is "generally slow moving." Long known to residents for its mild current, the river, according to Nathaniel Hawthorne, "may well be called the Concord—the river of peace and quietness—for it is certainly the most unexcitable and sluggish stream that ever loitered, imperceptibly, towards its eternity, the sea. Positively, I had lived three weeks beside it, before it grew quite clear to my perception which way the current flowed." And more recently, in his informative guidebook to the stream and its feeders, Ron McAdow writes fondly of the lazy river's water that it "barely has the power to keep vegetation from its channel. It hasn't the energy to ripple its own surface."

Formed by the confluence of the Sudbury and Assabet rivers at Egg Rock in the town of Concord, the Concord River assumes the languor of the lower Sudbury, easing through meadow and marsh on its way to the Merrimack. But precisely because of its tranquility, its indolence in all seasons, the Concord River offers a lesson in flow. When a friend (Andrew Marcus) and I canoed a portion of the sixteen miles of its course on a warm June afternoon, we paused to eat apples, and, in the nonflow of the Concord, assisted by a slight breeze, we drifted back upstream, against the "current." Walking along with the river's flow in autumn, one is likely to pass maple leaves riding quietly on the water, regardless of how unhurried one's gait. And in winter the Concord, black with tannins and placid when the breeze dies, lies even more still next to the light dancing on frozen banks. As I stood watching from the Old Calf Pasture one February afternoon, a blue-and-yellow ball lost to the river revolved with greater speed than the speed with which it floated past. For Thoreau, a truly capable boater and a constant explorer of the local, the flow of his home stream provided the perfect opportunity for an experiment—a double experiment, really.

Part 1 of that experiment involves a two-week trip with his brother John in the late summer of 1839, boating on the Concord and Merrimack rivers, taking roads and trails into the White Mountains (the ultimate source of the Merrimack), and returning by more or less the same route to their hometown, all the while living "by their wits on the fish of the stream & the berries of the wood," as their neighbor Emerson recorded in his journal. The brothers Thoreau built their own boat for the trip and were trying out a different kind of relation to and movement through the world, and this intrigued their fellow Concordian. After hearing a lecture by the educational reformer Horace Mann, Emerson complained: "We are shut up in schools & college recitation rooms for ten or fifteen years & come out at last with a bellyfull of words & do not know a thing." Comparing himself unfavorably with the Thoreau brothers just after their return from the river trip, Emerson grumbled about "wordmen" like himself who "do not know an edible root in the woods" and "cannot tell our course by the stars nor the hour of the day by the sun." According to the great American Scholar himself, scholars—the learned, the thinkers, and the teachers—had to do more than just read books.

Part 2 of the experiment involves a literary adventure based on part 1, in which the writer travels back up the stream of time, guiding readers on literal and metaphorical rivers, going against the flow of experience and seeing anew various confluences: of place and history, writing and life, nature and culture. Thoreau's first book alters the time scheme of the actual river trip, leaves his brother unnamed, but otherwise retraces their journey, taking readers back into the past, through variegated scenery, and leading them into a series of reflections on a variety of topics: history, religion, Homer, time, friendship, literature, silence. These reflections, some of which had been previously published in the notoriously transcendental magazine called the *Dial*, are loosely connected to the brothers' fluid movement on the titular rivers and organized by chapters that follow the days of the week, from "Saturday" to "Friday." The literary changes Thoreau makes to the actual trip, including the reflective poems and essays that he weaves into the narrative, constitute the experimental nature of part 2: the creation of a book that connects everyday (if not necessarily run-of-the-mill) experiences to big ideas.

Critics and the reading public in general did not receive the experiment well. Few copies were purchased (the remainder famously and unceremoniously dumped on the author's front porch), and James Russell Lowell's contemporary critical witticism appears in many a later critique or apology: "We were bid to a river-party, not to be preached at." Lowell and others reacted most unhappily to the numerous and lengthy reflections, which they viewed as mere interruptions to an otherwise charming tale of an excursion. But Thoreau insists on connecting preaching and river party. That connection constitutes the "experiment in natural philosophy" of the book, which is at once an essay on the world we live in and a critique of the ways in which we live in it. Throughout the book the writer observes the land through which he and his partner travel and raises questions about what we commonly call "nature," urging readers, sometimes gently and sometimes not, to become mindful of something beyond our customary conception of the order of things, "a nature behind the common," in Thoreau's words, usually "unexplored by science or by literature." Going where science and literature commonly do not go, exploring unexplored nature in his book, Thoreau experiments with different ways of approaching, receiving, imagining, and communicating the world. His writing moves in a particularly peculiar fashion, asking readers to move with it—between science and literature and beyond—and perhaps be moved by it. He calls his compatriots to be at once more critical, more contemplative, and more creative; he invites and cajoles his readers to become both wilder and more worldly. Thoreau's Transcendental treatment of travel on New England waterways combines flow and reflection in an attempt to connect literature to life, the here and now to elsewhere and beyond.

This unique combination and the connections it fosters are accentuated by the form of the journey itself, which takes the shape of a palindrome. The brothers cast off from their hometown, float *down* the Concord, sail or row *up* the Merrimack, stow their craft for a time, and venture into the White Mountains; the outing eventually pivots on Agiocochook (Mount Washington), after which the Thoreaus retrieve the boat, float *down* the Merrimack, row or sail *up* the Concord, and finally "leap gladly on shore" in their hometown. The topical reflections occurring within the structurally reflective, a-b-c-b-a movement of the journey allow Thoreau to reconsider and extend his thinking on such things as memory and loss on a personal level (his brother having died of lockjaw three years after their river trip) while bringing personal experiences into contact with larger philosophical issues such as knowing, time, and being. Thoreau's palindrome provides a different set of approaches to understanding historical events and every-day occurrences, opening up fresh perspectives on place and creating an intriguing link betwixt reading and rivers. Though streams usually flow in one general direction (physically *down*, from a higher elevation to a lower, and, by metaphorical extension, *forth*, from the past to the future), Thoreau reminds readers that we can reverse our experience of flow by altering our own ways of moving and knowing. By taking us upstream as well as down, Thoreau draws attention to rivers' potential for improving our sense of place and time. If we only go with the flow of the river or course along with time, we leave a lot of land and history and experience and literature unconsidered, as he points out at the beginning of his book.

The book and the trip on which it is based begin and end on the Concord River, which, as I noted in chapter 2, has played a prominent part in the cultural history of the United States. Emerson's interest in the stream included its physical beauty and its rich history, but most important to his poetry was the Concord's function as an emblem of higher truths. Emerson—Thoreau's friend, mentor, and philosophical sparring partner—treated the physical, historical Concord as a point of departure for an ideal, transcendent river. Thoreau, however, uses the Concord as a point of departure and a point of return, which makes a significant difference in the river's meaning and in the writer's developing philosophy. For Thoreau, the river takes shape as the means by which one can access meaning in an uncommon manner. He attempts to show readers that going upstream and downstream can give us a better perspective on rivers, the structure of the journey reflecting the style of thinking advanced in Thoreau's writing. His river book involves an effort to rework the nature of literature, experimenting with its possible role in understanding the nature of things.

When They Flow by Our Doors: The River as Double Agent

One of the uses of literature for Thoreau (as for Whitman in "Crossing Brooklyn Ferry," which Thoreau admired) is as a tool for rethinking time and history. Where Emerson's poetry followed in the footsteps of his ancestors in establishing a hierarchy in which the Concord supersedes the Musketaquid and his spiritual river supersedes both the physical and the historical stream, Thoreau challenges the hierarchical pairings and keeps both members of sundry pairs in play throughout his book. Deliberately surveying the land around and between two rivers, Thoreau makes history present, connects the spiritual and the physical, and emphasizes flow as a quality of rivers that can inform our experience of nature and time. His literary experiment transports readers incessantly back and forth, between the familiar and the esoteric, the quixotic and the quotidian. His literary palindrome uses river doubles to highlight, entangle, and otherwise complicate pairs of apparent opposites: left bank and right bank; Indian and English; culture and nature; physical elements of the earth and elemental philosophical problems (time, knowledge, imagination, etc.). Flowing through his hometown, the Concord River gave him the opportunity to bring some of the loftier aspects of Transcendentalism down to earth while simultaneously freeing some portentous matters from the gravity of custom. Quoting Shakespeare's *As*

You Like It, Thoreau writes: "Verily there are 'sermons in stones, and books in the running streams.'" Although Thoreau's version differs slightly from the original, the point is that rivers and rocks and roots can serve to ground, in the fullest sense of the word, our thinking and experience, our awareness and understanding of the present.

Of course, one of the salient traits of rivers being their fluidity, they also "unground" people, putting us and our perspective in motion. While introducing the Concord at the outset of the brothers' journey, Thoreau considers rivers' capacity for moving humanity. He imagines that they were among our earliest guides as we began to explore our surroundings and asserts that they still "lure" us, "when they flow by our doors," to "distant enterprise and adventure," both downstream ("to the lowlands of the globe") and up (into "the interior of continents"). He portrays rivers' *motility*—their powers of physical motion—with a series of present participles: "leveling," "removing obstacles," "quenching," "bearing," and, most important, "conducting." Rivers shape the land and create the route by which the traveler goes, replenish the traveler's body and soul with water, and transport the traveler "through the most interesting scenery" to "the most populous portions of the globe" (places where "Culture" thrives) as well as to the regions "where the animal and vegetable kingdoms attain their greatest perfection" (places we usually deem "Nature"). By conducting us upstream and downstream, to natural places and cultural places, rivers bring these pairings and their conceived differences into relation with one another. The passage thus serves the introductory chapter of Thoreau's book by outlining the forthcoming movement of the brothers' journey, which visits historically significant spots and lands long cultivated but also wilderness and "Unappropriated Land," and it broaches one of the book's primary concerns: the conceptual area between nature and culture.

In addition to motility, Thoreau's introduction highlights the *motivity* of rivers, their ability to motivate humans, their powers to move us spiritually, psychically, or intellectually. Rivers can inspire in us or draw out of us the desire and the will to move. They beckon our settled selves to get up and go, operating in close proximity to our settlements ("flowing by our doors") and unsettling us by luring us to places far from home; they reach into our most civilized modes of existence and activate a "natural impulse" within us to travel beyond the customary; they call us hither, urge us yon, and bring us back. One of the marvelous qualities of rivers, Thoreau suggests, is their ability to connect here (culture, indoors, that which is inside us or to which we have become accustomed) and there (nature, the outdoors, that which is outside us or the unaccustomed). River flow moves humans, physically and intellectually, out of the mild and into the wild. Challenging accepted oppositions such as materialist and idealist, present and past rivers, physical river and literary river, Thoreau leads us to move between the elements of each pair and between pairs themselves, to flow in our thinking among the sundry relations that constitute rivers and their meaning. The Concord River's nature, with its slow current and reflective surface, invites up-and-downstream movement, in-between thinking, and thereby enables the traveler-writer to gain a different perspective.

Such is the goal of the literary experiment—to re-create or represent a different style of thinking and reveal a fresh perspective, as Thoreau makes clear on the going-forth leg of the journey, during which he claims, for example, that no one has ever really read the New Testament (because if we did, according to the mischievous writer, all hell would break loose). But after the pivotal climb of Agiocochook, heading now down the Merrimack on the return leg toward disembarkation, even Henry and John see differently: "Sitting with our faces now upstream, we studied the landscape by degrees, as one unrolls a map . . . , and there was variety enough for our entertainment in the metamorphoses of the simplest objects. Viewed from this side the scenery appeared new to us." More than just entertainment, the new perspective generated by the palindromic return provides the writer with the opportunity to "begin to discover where we are, and that nature is one and continuous every where." Such a discovery is necessary because common sense, the worldview that we tend to hold in common and in which we commonly function, bereaves the world in which and of which we think, leaving the thinkers bereft as well. In one of the many jokes to be found in *A Week*, Thoreau wryly observes: "Most people with whom I talk, men and women even of some originality and genius, have their scheme of the universe all cut and dried,—very *dry*, I assure you, to hear, dry enough to burn, dry-rotted and powder-post, methinks." Most people's thinking lacks moisture, lacks life. Thoreau uses the palindromic rivering of *A Week* to water our ways of knowing.

To achieve the goal of irrigating and revivifying his readers' methods of thinking, Thoreau experiments with the form of the pleasant river outing and the flow of reading to interrupt the business-as-usual way of perceiving things. Near the end of the book, almost back where he started, Thoreau regards "the common train" of thinking, by which one thought is connected to the next and our consciousness follows a seemingly "natural and uninterrupted sequence." To avoid a life of intellectual and spiritual desiccation, he proposes that readers open their minds to the possibility of a "steep," "sudden," otherwise "unaccountable transition . . . from a comparatively narrow and partial, what is called common sense view of things, to an infinitely expanded and liberating one." In doing so, he advises, we might learn to cultivate "a sense which is not common, but rare in the wisest man's experience; which is sensible or sentient of more than common." This "more than common" sense represents the end of Thoreau's project: to foster our own "unaccountable transitions," calling us forth out of narrow and partial views to more widely aware, more complex methods of attending to our senses and processing our experiences. Considering what can happen when rivers flow by our doors, he extrapolates from his own case, tracing the whole experiment back to his habit of standing "on the banks of the Concord, watching the lapse of the current," which imbues him with the resolve "to launch myself on its bosom, and float whither it would bear me." That he ends up, two weeks and almost four hundred pages later, where he started—back home on the Concord River—gives us a second look at the nature of flow as well as of the origin of his enterprise, underscoring its influence.

"Influence," of course, has to do with flow, "flowing in," from its Latin roots (*influere*), and we still use the word to indicate a kind of power that flows into us and moves us to think or do something. As he stood on the banks before launching himself on its bosom, Thoreau was influenced by the flow of the river, "following the same law with the system, with time, and all that is made." The river encourages him to give himself up to the flow of life, like the flotsam of logs and trees that "floated past, fulfilling their fate." And this particular river, "remarkable for the gentleness of its current, which is scarcely perceptible," influences inhabitants in less obvious ways. After questioning a "current" story about the river's current (or lack thereof), Thoreau writes that in certain circumstances the Concord actually lives up to the title of "river," though sometimes it is only "a deep, dark, and dead stream . . . a long woodland lake bordered with willows." The Concord is both a living stream and a dead stream, a river and a lake. Thoreau pursues this claim of opposing identities elsewhere in the book; while on the Merrimack near Chelmsford, for example, he looks back on the first part of the journey, remembering that "the Concord had rarely been a river or *rivus*, but barely *fluvius*, or between *fluvius* and *lacus*." Dusting off his Latin, Thoreau uses *fluvius* in its most general sense of "flowing water" and *rivus* to mean "river," the upshot being that the Concord is neither wholly a "stream" nor wholly a lake. Instead, the most significant characteristic of the river's physical nature is its betweenness. "Between *fluvius* and *lacus*," the Concord operates as one of nature's double agents, influencing humans doubly, leading us to launch ourselves on its riverine flow and also lulling us to linger in its lacustrine calm.

Thoreau also revisits the issue of the Concord-Musketaquid opposition, though with a result different from the one Emerson obtained. Asserting that the earlier people "properly named" it Musketaquid, which he glosses as "Grass-ground River," he questions the propriety of the English name, "which appears to have" something to do with "peace and harmony." The first name, he finds, will last, since it aptly characterizes the physical setting; the meaning of the second name is contingent upon those who reside along the physical river: "It will be Grass-ground River as long as grass grows and water runs here; it will be Concord River only while men lead peaceable lives on its banks." As long as it flows, that is, as long as it's a river, it will be Musketaquid; as long as people behave, it will be Concord too. By making a point of the opposing names and their connotations, Thoreau puts readers in motion between the two views of the river; both its physical nature and its plantation history are important to its current meaning.

As in the matter of the river-versus-lake nature of the Concord, Thoreau challenges the common opposition of the Indian versus English. In both cases he proposes that connection replace opposition. Part of the river's meaning comes from exploring its two natures (river and lake), the physical differences and the conceptual area between them; but part of the river's meaning also comes from exploring the historical differences of its two names and the conceptual area between them. One's experience of what is now known as the Concord will be enriched by awareness of its enduring

"Musketaquidity." For Thoreau, connecting the apparent opposites will afford us a better chance of determining our temporal and spatial coordinates, of understanding where we are. He devotes ample room to a critical history of the colonial project, pairing it with a description of Indian ways. The English are characterized as "that industrious tribe," coming from somewhere else to "pluck the wild flower" of the Native inhabitants "up by the root." Thoreau describes a peculiarly methodical intelligence at work in the colonial enterprise: "The white man comes, pale as the dawn, with a load of thought, with a slumbering intelligence as a fire raked up, knowing well what he knows, not guessing but calculating; strong in community, yielding obedience to authority; of experienced race; of wonderful common sense; dull but capable, slow but persevering." Thoreau's "white man" pays scant attention to other life-forms as he alters the land to suit his needs. He is forgetful of the past, remaking and renaming the land, attempting to place one world atop another.

After the description of the planting of "New Angle-land," Thoreau proposes that "there may be an excess of cultivation as well as of any thing else, until civilization becomes pathetic." Extolling the Indian's "rare and peculiar society with nature," he contrasts that relationship—one of respect and interdependence—with the Anglo tendency toward always "soothing and taming nature, breaking the horse and the ox," cultivation in the name of civilization. "The Indian," according to Thoreau, instead of having to endure Yankee "civilizing" and "improvement," "does well to continue Indian." We tend to see history as a movement from nature to culture. Progress and civilization are viewed as more or less irreversible processes, unidirectional flow related to the irrepressible flow of time. Thoreau's in-between, connective experience of the river allows him to question the view of history as the dead past and reconsider the relationship between nature and culture. By going upstream, Thoreau is enabled to think of history's influence on the present. The Concord River of the 1839 journey is full of and surrounded by the past, even as it flows on to the sea. The Musketaquid-Concord story informs the brothers' experience as they float down and later row up their home stream. As a literary experiment, the 1849 narrative of the journey recounts that experience and adds to it in a new present altered by ten years of events, including the death of Thoreau's fellow traveler. The journey comes forth now in a still newer present when we read it—but only if we read it in a way that allows us to move against the flow of time and narrative and history, neither negligent of the present nor forgetful of the past. Thoreau's Concord does not suggest that the past can be undone, that we can go back in time. The lesson, rather, is that our ways of thinking and living need not be bound to follow a certain direction or adhere to a particular account of history, reality, truth, nature, America, time. To learn the lesson, we need to study the nature of flow and be willing to move between the present and the past.

The treatment of Indian and English ways of dwelling in the land leads into a philosophical discussion of "a nature behind the common, unexplored by science or by literature." Thoreau claims to differ from historians, scientists, and poets (as well as preachers and other travelers) by inviting the river to influence his thinking. Under the influence of the Concord, he performs an experiment with flow that gives him new ways of experiencing the world to which he belongs. There are two types of intellectual movement regarding the concepts of nature and culture that Thoreau seeks to have readers make. One is to move out of the common view of nature, the view maintained by our culture (including our science and literature). The common cultural view of nature perpetuates a conceptual separation of people from place; the land, the planet, the cosmos all become a collection of objects and laws that we can admire, that we fear, and that we must attempt to control. Removed from the living system of rock, flora, soil, air, processes, water, and fauna that constitutes a bioregion, the common cultural view of nature tends to see these elements as mere resources for humans to tap and tyrannize. Such a view pits humans against the earth, fostering the illusion that we might be somehow above nature, a foolish and false superiority manifested for Thoreau in such phenomena as locks, dams, and factories. Taking a longer view, Thoreau posits that "if the fishes will be patient, and pass their summers elsewhere, meanwhile, nature will have levelled the Billerica dam, and the Lowell factories, and the Grassground River run clear again, to be explored by new migratory shoals." The Musketaquid will become clean again, free-flowing and full of life, from its mouth in the Merrimack near Lowell to the sources of its two main tributaries.

Thoreau also seeks to inspire readers to move between our ideas of culture and nature, which entails becoming willing to think of culture as a form of nature, an extension of natural forces and sources. One example of Thoreau's designs in this area comes in his account of the sound of dogs barking while the two brothers were camped on a small island near Billerica. The "barking of the house dogs," which he describes in detail, functions as both a sign of domestication and the soundtrack of a wilderness scene "in a retired and uninhabited district." Calling it an "instrument" and a "natural bugle," Thoreau links the howling and growling of dogs to other domestic tones such as "the clarion of the cock," "civil exhortations," and "war sermons." Rather than mere emblems of civilization or cultivation (or even pastoralism), "all these sounds, the crowing of cocks, the baying of dogs, and the hum of insects at noon, are the evidence of nature's health or *sound* state. Such is the never failing beauty and accuracy of language, the most perfect art in the world." As the conclusion of a list of night sounds (foxes in the dead leaves, a musquash rifling the brothers' goods, the river rippling, the song and cry of sparrow and owl, a fire alarm in far-off Lowell), Thoreau's summation surmises that nature's health unfolds audibly, the world articulating itself through myriad channels, including human language. Like the other sounds, human language is inextricable from nature, even though it is art at its most perfect.

In that sense, language belongs to the art-nature or culture-nature connection that Thoreau explores throughout the book. Like the boat in which the brothers float, the works of humans are not inherently "artificial" or "unnatural." The boat—which they built in a week and called *Musketaquid*—was "painted green below, with a border of blue, with reference to the two elements in which it was to spend its existence." When properly made, a boat could become "a sort of amphibious animal, a creature of two elements." Their craft is depicted as part of the elements, a natural extension of the boaters themselves, a connection between them and that through which they move. For Thoreau, the "artificial" is not simply "man-made." It is something made by humans who do not fully understand the nature of their work or that they themselves belong to nature. Artifice is still natural—of or pertaining to nature—even if its makers pretend otherwise. Culture and human activity are more intimately related to nature and natural phenomena than common sense usually allows. In discussions ranging from dams and animals to language and larceny, Thoreau continually entangles nature and culture, subtly insisting that, as the Concord itself is betwixt a *fluvius* and a *lacus*, our lives are situated somewhere in between. Human experience and the processing of that experience—the "making sense" of things—is always intermediate, connecting natural and cultural elements.

Its Water Was Fuller of Reflections: Thing, Image, Turning Point

While "flow" is of great importance to Thoreau's literary rivers experiment, his project places similar significance on the concept of "reflection." As the morning fog of the chapter "Sunday" dissipates, the brothers enjoy the calm waters of the Concord, and the narrator paints a scene that reflects the Thoreaus' own situation, providing another view of their experiences and his interpretation of them:

> Two men in a skiff, whom we passed hereabouts, floating buoyantly amid the reflections of the trees, like a feather in mid air, or a leaf which is wafted gently from its twig to the water without turning over, seemed still in their element, and to have very delicately availed themselves of the natural laws. Their floating there was a beautiful and successful experiment in natural philosophy, and it served to enoble [*sic*] in our eyes the art of navigation, for as birds fly and fishes swim, so these men sailed. It reminded us how much fairer and nobler all the actions of man might be, and that our life in its whole economy might be as beautiful as the fairest works of art or nature.

The two men in the skiff function as a figural reflection of the Thoreau brothers, one of four types of reflection at work in *A Week*, the other three being literal, conceptual, and structural. Here, he uses the figural reflection as an image to elucidate his theory of the nature-culture relation. These men—all four of them—and the two man-made objects in which they float represent "a beautiful and successful experiment in natural philosophy," the same experiment on which Thoreau has been working since his brother and he cast off at the beginning of *A Week*. Though boating may seem artificial or cultural, humans are nonetheless floating on nature's familiar waters. Boat making and boat floating are every bit as natural as the actions of fishes and birds, reflecting, to Thoreau's eye, what we all might aspire to: a way of life shaped by and never disconnected from nature, an artful economy of living modeled on natural systems, a mode of being in and experiencing the world that reflects the place and forces—the elements—that make us what we are.

The "two men in a skiff" scene of the "Sunday" chapter occurs on the last day of the Concord section of their going forth. Once the brothers enter the waters of the Merrimack, Thoreau will use the word "reflection" occasionally in reference to the philosophical ruminations included in his account of their voyage, but only on the Concord does the writer reproduce literal reflections, images in which something is seen twice. Reflection is a distinctive quality of the Concord River, one of its primary influences. That quality is related to flow, calmer waters permitting more distinct reflections, but Thoreau's attention to reflection intensifies, through extension and in some instances inversion, the effects of flow. Before they come across their mirror image floating in the skiff, Thoreau remembers that "the surface was so calm, and both air and water so transparent, that the flight of a kingfisher or robin over the river was as distinctly seen reflected in the water below as in the air above. The birds seemed to flit through submerged groves, alighting on the yielding sprays, and their clear notes to come up from below. We were uncertain whether the water floated the land, or the land held water in its bosom." The river provides an inverted view of the world, heightening the writer's awareness and unsettling the viewers' understanding of the nature of things. The type of uncertainty the Thoreaus experience is informed by a healthy, imaginative open-mindedness and leads to more thinking, to further reflection.

Just as he uses the doubling of the river's name to connect the past to the present and nature to culture, Thoreau uses the reflections of the river to connect thing and image and then directs our attention to related pairs. The paragraph of the kingfisher-robin, water-land reflection continues to explore changes in the world seen by the brothers: each actual oak, birch, elm, or willow, he writes, has an "ethereal and ideal tree making down from the roots," and "sometimes nature in high tides brings her mirror to its foot and makes it visible." Reflections that we can observe are connected to those we can imagine, the real tied to the ideal. In the intense stillness of what seemed "a natural Sabbath," Thoreau and his brother imagined that "the morning was the evening of a celestial day. The air was so elastic and crystalline that it had the same effect on the landscape that a glass has on a picture, to give it an ideal remoteness and perfection." Through a series of inversions, the natural and the cultural, the terrestrial and the celestial, world and representation are brought into relation, allowing Thoreau to move between actual landscape and conceptual fairyland.

Reflection thus gives us a new world to view or at least another aspect of the world to consider. In drawing our attention to the inverted scene in which morning is evening, up is down, and the ideal is real, Thoreau highlights nature's inversions as an opportunity for thinking about the world differently. Reflective inversion becomes a lesson learned from the river and is adopted as a method for fostering new ways of seeing. If literal reflections can affect *what* we see, conceptual reflection involves *how* we see. After a poetic interlude in which he remembers sailing "on this same stream" with "a maiden," Thoreau returns to reflection and connects it to improved vision. First, he treats reflection as a form of representation: recalling "the mirror-like surface of the water, in which every twig and blade of grass was so faithfully reflected," he describes the scene as an example of nature "exaggerating" certain objects, thereby magnifying reality. Nature's mirroring inversions deeply intensify the world through which we move, a method of representation that Thoreau's experiment employs when he structures the account as a palindrome, a reflective form of writing. He goes on to report that nature's reflections result not only in doubled scenes but in increased potential meaning, making it more difficult to get to the bottom of things. "The shallowest still water," he writes, "is unfathomable. Wherever the trees and skies are reflected there is more than Atlantic depth, and no danger of fancy running aground." Whenever the river's surface reflects the elements of its setting, nature represents itself as not readily measured or exhausted, multiplying the possible meanings of a scene and extending interpretation, perhaps endlessly. In such a setting, fancy or imagination will not reach a limit; it can easily be kept afloat, if one attends to it. To make good on the opportunity for meaning making afforded us by reflection, we must learn to look differently in a manner that acknowledges the multifaceted nature of all phenomena: "We noticed that it required a separate intention of the eye, a more free and abstracted vision, to see the reflected trees and the sky, than to see the river bottom merely; and so are there manifold visions in the direction of every object, and even the most opaque reflect the heavens from their surface. Some men have their eyes naturally intended to the one, and some to the other object." Thoreau promotes a method of perception that recognizes both the heavenly and the earthly aspects of "every object." Such seeing requires double intentions and the ability to move between those intentions. While some of us are realists, tending to see the thing, others are idealists, more interested in the reflection—a characterization that might explain why neither science nor literature helpfully explores a nature behind the common. Since we cannot quite manage to look at both sides of an object at the same time, we must try to gain different vantage points, see both sides in turn, and connect those two views in order to get more of the meanings that scenes and objects offer us.

Thoreau's thoughts on reflection belong to the "natural philosophy" being developed in *A Week* and are intimately connected to the larger reflection that structures the book. Most critics have emphasized either the cycle of seasons or the device of the week as the organizing motif, but it is important to keep in mind that the summer-passing-into-autumn and Saturday-to-Friday aspects occur within a structural palindrome; the narrator's movement and the narrative itself are neither simply circular nor linear. The travelers go out and come back by roughly the same path, pivoting but by no means culminating in "Thursday" on "the summit of AGIOCO-CHOOK." As the turning point, Agiocochook plays a significant role in the palindrome, though a fair number of readers have interpreted Thoreau's terse account of the summiting as "flat," "inadequate," and "perfunctory." Thoreau's narrative of the event is indeed terse, even in the journal he kept at the time, and the travelers' experience of the peak is understated, but to characterize it as flat or insignificant is to neglect both the physical and the reflective traits of the turning-point ascension of Agiocochook.

The route the brothers followed is anything but uninteresting. Mount Washington, Thoreau's Agiocochook, is situated east of the Pemigewasset Valley. After stashing the boat at Hooksett, the brothers walked to Concord, New Hampshire, took the stage to Plymouth, walked north up the Pemigewasset through Thornton, Lincoln, and Franconia (where they visited the Old Man of the Mountain, may he rest in peace), then headed east to Crawford Notch, where they arrived on September 9. They "ascended the mountain" the next day, which is all the journal says on the matter, descended, and then rode to Conway, Concord, and finally Hooksett. Andrew Marcus and I retraced the route in a borrowed Oldsmobile we named the "Deliberator," parking and then trekking up the Ammonoosuc Ravine until it meets

Crawford Path at the Lake of the Clouds and on up to Agiocochook's top (a short but steep ascent, vertically about 3,700 feet) in weather most foul. As we found, the approach from the west takes climbers through perhaps the worst of the mountain's fabled weather (called by many the worst in North America, by others simply the worst in the world), offers perilous hiking conditions (with slick rock and hard scrambles), provides some of the finest views in the White Mountains (which we did not learn until the clouds broke during our descent), and leads to "the highest peak east of the Mississippi River and north of the Carolinas"—an altitude of 6,288 feet. It is difficult to imagine the ascent of Agiocochook, under any conditions, being either flat or insignificant.

From Crawford Notch, where they likely began on September 10, to Agiocochook's summit, the brothers climbed approximately 4,300 feet in roughly 8 miles, about half of the route being above the tree line. The final ascent via Crawford Path requires less exertion than the Ammonoosuc section but is a good, tough hike nonetheless, even for such fit lads as the Thoreau brothers, the path becoming particularly "steep and boulder-strewn" in the last mile. Andrew and I, groping along a totally befogged Crawford Path toward the peak above Lake of the Clouds, chilled to the bone by the mist and stories of those who have perished on Mount Washington, discussed Thoreau's taciturn write-up, in both journal and published account, of the mountaintop part of his trip. Maybe he was too worn out by the climb to write (our first but not best thought). Perhaps he could not express the sublimity of the experience. Maybe he did not want to take away from the riparian by making the mountainous too momentous, turning the account into a "Journey to Agiocochook" instead of an excursion up and down two rivers.

Thinking back on the episode and its role in the literary experiment, I have come to see that the summit of Agiocochook works reflectively in the book—not as a mirror that gives back an image of a scene but as the place where scene and image, reflection and reflected, material and ideal, spiritual and physical come together. The peak experience serves as a fold or hinge that highlights the relationship between the two parts it connects. Thoreau's experiment—the trip, the text, the palindrome—hinges on Agiocochook. The peak, in this way of reading, is neither climactic nor anticlimactic, for climax isn't really the point. As the hinge of the palindrome, summiting Agiocochook is not the focus of the story but rather enables the story by structuring the reflective, going-out-and-coming-back nature of the trip. Enlightenment, in *A Week*, is not to be found on top of the mountain. Instead, the return and the overall structure to which it belongs is the enlightenment. The silence that follows "AGIOCOCHOOK" in the text—the physical space of a portentous section break—emphasizes the *process of enlightenment*, underlining the fact that enlightenment is an on-going, back-and-forth process, not a once-and-for-all attainment, thereby transferring its significance from physical object or place, however freighted with mythological value, into that of experiential, imaginative reflection. As a geographical source of headwaters, the mountain makes rivers possible; as a narrative hinge, it makes their meaning possible.

Thoreau's story begins and ends on the Grass-ground River, and, as he "said before, the Concord is a dead stream, but its scenery is the more suggestive to the contemplative voyager, . . . its water was fuller of reflections than our pages even." Other accounts of travel on the Concord—for example, Henry Parker Fellows's nineteenth-century *Boating Trips on New England Rivers*; Ron McAdow's twentieth-century guide to the Concord, Sudbury, and Assabet rivers; and John McPhee's more recent excursion—usually go only one way. Thoreau presents his structurally reflective journey (the palindrome) and its interior reflections (on nature, culture, place, history, etc.) as the means by which readers might make an "unaccountable transition" to new ways of seeing. His own adventure and, even more important, his literary rendering of that adventure go downstream and upstream on waterways, producing a meaningful connection between the physical Concord and the conceptual Concord. The river itself is the source of reflections and a living lesson in flow. Thoreau's going-forth-and-coming-back movement on the river allows him to cover more territory (at least twice as much) as most travelers, to deepen experience by dealing with two sides of the world we experience, and to highlight reflection. The actual journey's peculiar form of movement makes possible the literary experiment not only by providing the basic story but also by opening up a different view of rivers and flow.

And All Things Seemed with Us to Flow: Rivers, Literature, Meaning

Having pivoted and headed back the way they came, having reclaimed their boat and now fleetly coursing downstream on the Merrimack, the brothers, still in the hinge chapter "Thursday," experience an epiphany of flow. Thoreau reflects on a series of topics: on the nature-culture connection, positing that "Art is not tame, and Nature is not wild, in the ordinary sense"; on American history (the Hannah Duston captivity-and-escape episode); on literary heroes (Goethe); and, finally, on flow:

> Thus we "sayled by thought and pleasaunce," as Chaucer says, and all things seemed with us to flow; the shore itself, and the distant cliffs, were dissolved by the undiluted air. The hardest material seemed to obey the same law with the most fluid, and so indeed in the long run it does. Trees were but rivers of sap and woody fibre, flowing from the atmosphere, and emptying into the earth by their trunks, as their roots flowed upward to the surface. And in the heavens there were rivers of stars, and milky-ways, already beginning to gleam and ripple over our heads. There were rivers of rock on the surface of the earth, and rivers of ore in its bowels, and our thoughts flowed and circulated, and this portion of time was but the current hour.

River travel leads to reflection; reflection reveals flow; flow connects all elements of nature, from thing to thought. Rivers, in Thoreau's book, become cosmic microcosms; picking up on their meanings can enable us to understand the workings of the cosmos in its earthly (matter, rock, flora) and celestial (stars, galaxies) forms. Human consciousness and the meanings we create also take on the qualities of rivers, ideas pouring into matter, matter pouring into ideas. Because of the fluidity and circulation of our thoughts and their relations to the earthly and celestial, we have the capacity to connect these diverse rivers to one another, understand the relations better, and communicate the meaning of those connections. Literature becomes a special opportunity for us to come to terms with flow and learn its lessons.

In recent years physicists have said that time does not flow. Time just *is*, its apparent flow resulting from consciousness, and "talk of the river or flux of time is founded on a misconception." One lesson from *A Week* is that life, if not time, flows, and life's flow teaches us something about connectivity. Introducing the Concord and its tributaries, Ron McAdow writes, "It is our craving for connection with the great flow of nature that takes us onto the water. The river has a kind of life to it." Thoreau's "all things seemed with us to flow" does not necessarily mean that "all things flowed"; rather, it means that, in the brothers' experience, all things assumed the quality of the river on which the brothers moved, all things became connected by the brothers' new way of seeing. And that way of seeing springs from participation—conscious, reflective, imaginative participation—in the flow of things. We should not forget, however, that Thoreau's way of seeing also involves careful observation of the world through which one passes as well as paying attention to the methods and conditions of that passing-through. Studying the river's fundamental property of fluency, one discerns that flow creates the river itself, from bed to bend and beyond; flow largely determines what types of life-forms live in or near rivers and how they will live. If indeed the river is "the carpenter of its own edifice," then flow serves as architectural principle, design technique, and builder's tool.

The physical world provides numerous examples of flow's lessons, many of which Thoreau observes as the brothers follow the rivers' ways. And yet Thoreau's developing natural philosophy does not confine itself to biotic or geological questions. While engineers might measure flow in terms of acre-feet and geographers in cubic feet per second or inches of runoff, the natural philosopher reckons those but also the less quantifiable aspects of flow. Fluvial processes, natural laws such as gravity, and down-to-earth material movement meet and mingle with philosophical fluidity, intellectual movement, and spiritual onwardness. When all things seem to flow, the natural philosopher registers both the perception of the workings of geomorphology and what psychologist Mihaly Csikszentmihalyi calls "optimal experience," the condition in which "the contents of consciousness are in harmony with each other." One experiences a sense of deep connection between self and situation, person and place. Actor, action, scene, and setting all come together. Flow, in this sense, is a way for humans to participate more fully in moments and events and thus become more deeply involved in life. Cultural anthropologist Victor Turner speculates that, when experiencing flow, one reaches out to nature and to others. Flow entails origins, destinations, and especially moving between; for Turner, it is a lesson in liminality. Thoreau uses his travel experiment as a basis from which he can literarily experiment with a kind of liminal writing that will lead to optimizing the experiences of his readers, a means of introducing us to flow.

Thoreau's story of flow traces a cultural drift from an intimate relation with nature and life, to a loss of spontaneity and naturalness, and then to a potential pivot from which we can reverse the trajectory. The river falls and flows to the sea, culture lapses and flows from nature; but with imaginative reflection we can understand flow and maybe turn things around. Reflecting, in *A Week*, belongs to that "uncommon sense" that allows us to recognize, consider, and learn to live in the flow of a "nature behind the ordinary"— that is, beyond the "nature" that neither science nor literature customarily allows us. To common sense and cut-and-dried schemes, the Concord may not appear to be much of a river, and rivers in general may not mean much. With reflection and uncommon sense, however, we might be able to irrigate and invigorate cut-and-dried schemes. We might become apprised of the fact that meaning flows and that the Concord's flow means many different things, historically, presently, and potentially. From its terrestrial origins in tectonic shift, in glaciers and their meltwater, the Musketaquid-Concord follows a relatively short and staid course over bedrock of Dedham granite, between drumlins and ponds; but as Thoreau demonstrates, its reflective waters, however slow or shallow, are unfathomable, and so is its ultimate meaning. Its lessons in flow require more thought, more creative reflection, on our part.

By "our part" I mean that which is to be played by readers in Thoreau's literary experiment in natural philosophy. In *Thoreau's Complex Weave*, an important critical study of *A Week*, Lynck Johnson argues that the writer attempted to create a new kind of American literature, one "rooted in nature" that could reverse centuries of decline and perhaps undo the concomitant "destruction of the wilderness." This is one of the important outcomes of Thoreau's experiment: a new kind of writing that bears hope for a different sort of transcendence, one that is both a "rising above" and a "rooting in"—transcendence as affirmation of nature rather than escape from nature. But that kind of writing cannot be realized without a new kind of reading, a reflective way of reading that does not follow the traditional party lines of science and literature. The structural palindrome of *A Week* serves as a revitalizing, naturalizing artifice involving a necessary inversion that leads to reversal and renewal. Thoreau shows us how to read the Concord and Merrimack, how to read "rivers from end to end," how to think about nature backward and forward through attention to reflective doubles and especially to recognition of flow. In doing so he makes a case for writing and reading as a peculiarly connective mode of experience and communication. Thoreau's writing, his "complex weave," associates seemingly disparate parts of life and presents a vivid description of complexity. It practices precisely what it preaches, arguing for a style of thinking that faces up to complexity, that embraces intricacy, and that endeavors to interpret life's textual richness. Necessarily, Thoreau's natural philosophy revises literature itself. Reconfigured as "writing and reading based on and returning to flow and reflection," literature then becomes a special opportunity for turning, reversing, revolving, revolutionizing. Literature in these terms becomes a boat, a bridge, waders, a PFD, anything that deepens our experiential connection to flow. Or, to put it another way, literature is a channel through which meaning flows between us and the river.

Notes

Introduction

"plays a part" to "live on Earth": Leopold 1.

U.S. river statistics: Palmer 10.

"nature and culture . . . in modern thought": Goodwin 145.

"our grim Philosophers" to "Radical Moisture": Erasmus 112.

"Embosomed for a season . . . dry bones of the past": Emerson, *Nature*, *Works* 1: 9.

Subsystems of the river in geomorphology: Charlton 10–20.

Rivers of America series: See Fitzgerald. The idea for the series belonged to Constance Lindsay Skinner (1877–1939), and the works were published first by Farrar & Rinehart (later Rinehart & Co. and eventually Holt, Rinehart and Winston).

Emerson references: From "The American Scholar" essay, Emerson, *Works* 1: 101.

"have acquiesced . . . form and process": Leopold ix.

1. Overlooking the River

"Zits" comic strip: Scott and Borgman.

"from its earliest" to "rivers and streams": Thomann 99.

"but little conscious" to "any day thoughtlessly": Thoreau, *Writings* 317.

"the preeminent city . . . great genetrix": Heat-Moon 226.

Information on the Transitional or Terminal Archaic peoples of the Delaware: Cotter, Roberts, and Parrington 9.

Lenape and "Manayunk": Cotter, Roberts, and Parrington 32.

"practically all . . . they could get": Cotter, Roberts, and Parrington 39.

Brady's Bluff: The bluffs near Trempealeau, rising to 1,160 feet above sea level at Brady's, are composed of Jordan Sandstone with a covering in some areas of Oneonta Dolomite (Fremling 36–39).

"Lay low . . . turn myself loose": 53. Page numbers that are unaccompanied by author and title refer to Mark Twain, *Life on the Mississippi*.

Clemens had become "Mark Twain": Lawrence Howe understands the Clemens-into-Twain remaking as the attempt to invent a representative American self through writing. Ron Powers emphasizes that the chosen name linked the writer with "dangerous water" (*Dangerous* 252), while Richard S. Lowry examines the making of the "Littery Man" through the Foucauldian notion of the "author-complex" (10).

Life on the Mississippi: Dewey Ganzel describes the composing process of *Life on the Mississippi* as marked by "diligence and despair," which Twain had tried to alleviate by revisiting the river in 1882 (55). While for Ganzel the return fizzles, a recent biographer suggests that it caused Twain to alter the original goals of his book and renewed his fierce love for the river (Powers, *Mark Twain*).

"the Mississippi is well worth reading about": 39.

"historical history," "physical history": 41.

"the first white man" to "paint a picture": 41.

"alter its locality" to "always moving bodily *sidewise*": 40–41.

"cut-offs" to "man of him": 40.

"Apparently nobody happened . . . notice of it": 43.

"La Salle the Frenchman" to "make it useful": 43–44.

"Louis the Putrid": 48.

"Apparently the river" to "apparently": 50–51.

"great barges" to "five or six more": 50–51.

"adventure" to "the marvellous science of piloting": 63.

"brings together" to "pleasant surprises and contrasts": Twain, *Autobiography* 1: 328.

"a man that drunk . . . if he wanted to": 56. Mud, in fact, is one of the key traits of the Mississippi. "Every day," according to John M. Barry, "the river deposits between several hundred thousand and several million *tons* of earth in the Gulf of Mexico. At least some geologists put this figure even higher historically, at an average of more than 2 million tons a day" (39). Like Twain before him, Barry delights in the Mississippi's mud, reporting that the river has deposited almost 1,300 cubic miles of sediment in the Gulf of Mexico (39) and is "the only river in the world" that has mud lumps—little volcanoes on the river bottom "spewing gasses and liquid mud" (69).

"learning the river": 72.

"the great Mississippi . . . shining in the sun": 64.

"Boy after boy" to "come in glory": 67.

"desire to be a steamboatman": 66.

"comforting day-dreams of the future": 67.

"I never was great in matters of detail": 68.

"incredible adventures" to "void of art": 70.

"speechless" to "half-witted humbug": 71.

"science of piloting," "learning the river": 63.

"cub" to "change the subject": 73.

"to fear that . . . phase of it": 74.

"I was gratified" to "'I—I—nothing, for certain'": 75.

"'You're the stupidest'" to "disturb your mother with": 76.

"the gentlest way" to "just like A B C": 76.

"uneducated passenger": 94.

"fairly bristled" to "river set down": 77.

"had got to learn this troublesome river *both ways*": 79.

"'I have not . . . never thought of it'": 80–81.

"note-booking" to "confusion of meaningless names": 81.

"at the end" to "it was, too": 85.

"'My boy . . . very dark night'": 85.

"stoop-shouldered" to "'*No!*' . . . different ways": 86. Twain here is learning about one of the more maddening but wondrous traits of the great river: its ability to remake itself constantly. Most rivers shape and reshape their channels through erosion and deposition, but because of scale the Mississippi does so in a particularly complex way. In his fascinating study of the 1927 flood, Barry writes that "the complexity of the Mississippi exceeds that of nearly all other rivers" and lists "sediment load"—mud—among the ingredients of that complexity, along with size, depth, variations in the bottom, sideways sliding, and tidal influences (39).

"a man . . . twenty-four hours": 87.

"in all . . . and 'thort-ships'": 89.

"I went to work . . . was the chief": 88.

"'I have n't got brains'" to "'or kill him'": 90. For a description of Bixby's evaluation of his cub's success, see Hutcherson.

"to read it as if it were a book": 91.

"It turned out . . . reading-matter": 94–95.

"mastered the language" to "the majestic river!": 95. Brian McCammack detects something of this larger lesson in what he sees as Twain's ability to enjoy the river's beauty even after he has become a pilot, though David H. Malone gives more weight to Twain's sense of loss, which he attributes to the economic function of piloting (89). In that reading Twain remains ever after a self divided (Malone 80), a conclusion shared with other critics (cf. Brazil 112). For Henry Nash Smith, Twain only "professes" to have lost the poetic vision, for in the act of that professing Twain writes with noticeable poetry of the scene, even though the poetry is part of a familiar pattern in which "exalted rhetoric" is "followed by a deliberate deflation" (80). The opposition between poet-artist and engineer-scientist still impresses writers: Andrei Codrescu, who remembers reading *Life on the Mississippi* while growing up in Romania before immigrating to the United States, visited Hannibal during the flood of 1993. The experience and his reading of Twain's book prompted him to remark: "We are a nation of engineers, not poets, and are baffled when nature mocks our engineering" (Codrescu 117).

"The glories" to "out like that": 95, emphasis added.

"No, the romance . . . steamboat": 96.

"sometimes wonder . . . learning his trade?": 96. Further complicating the problem of meaning in Twain's account, Marion Montgomery finds conflicting romanticisms in *Life* that result in an unresolved dilemma between a romantic belief in the nation's progress and nostalgia for a lost childhood.

"returns to his muttons": The title of chapter 22 (167–74).

"scribbler of books": 166.

"Our Christianity . . . to such things": Twain, *Autobiography* 2: 292.

"was oppressed" to "fight": Twain, *Autobiography* 2: 37.

"they vanish . . . nothing": Twain, *Autobiography* 2: 38.

By keeping things muddy: Some readers hold that the river is the one "constant in the book," a symbol of "some eternal force in Nature that might unite man with his moral origins" (Malone 88–89)—a symbol, in other words, that would underpin our search for meaning. Richard Bridgman provides a darker view of the river, believing that it "carried fundamental feelings of despair for Mark Twain" (109). These feelings run throughout the book, according to Bridgman, which should have been called "Death on the Mississippi" (107).

"It is discouraging . . . not have petrified": Twain, *Autobiography* 1: 182.

"a thing" to "nature mixed them": 170. Twain exaggerates (slightly), though the mud at the bottom of the river is more than a thousand feet thick in the lower valley (Eifert 186). Regarding the makeup of the 230 million tons of sediment that the river dumps in the delta each year, I do not wish to suggest that the mud is problem free or that it is at all drinkable at present. Daniel Spurr provides a scary update on Mississippi muck in his account of a 1995 trip down the river with his son Steve and daughter Adriana. Health concerns surface when they reach New Orleans, causing them to take a closer look at the ingredients of river and mud alike, which are found to contain high levels of "alachlor, a chemical that controls weeds among the fields of soybean, corn, and cotton, and atrazine, used on corn, sorghum, and sugarcane, both classified by the Environmental Protection Agency as 'probable' and 'possible' carcinogens," along with DDT and PCBs, which "have an affinity for the muck, clinging to it, surfacing when churned up by flood or propellers" (Spurr 223–24).

2. By the River

"We step . . . and are not": Heraclitus 35.

"As they step . . . flow upon them": Heraclitus 17.

"In rivers the water . . . time present": Quoted in Rzóska (title page). For introductions to rivers in Western cultural history, see Herendeen 21–114 and Jones 3–47.

Writings of Anne Bradstreet: For Bradstreet's experiences along the Merrimack River in New England, see Stanford 127.

"living so little" to "where once he's laid": 209. Page numbers that are unaccompanied by author and title refer to the Harvard edition of Anne Bradstreet's works edited by Jeannine Hensley.

"man was made for endless immortality": 210.

"Under the cooling shadow . . . there would I dwell": 210.

"Which to the longed-for ocean" to "I count best": 211.

"the fatal wrack . . . curtains over kings": 213.

"shall last and shine": 214.

"the nature of the human condition in time and eternity": Laughlin 11.

"The Flesh and the Spirit": 215.

"the struggle between the visible and the invisible worlds": Stanford i.

"masterpiece": For example, McElrath and Robb xxi.

"process of meditation for the benefits of the reader": Stanford 103.

"glimpse redemption": Gordon 268.

Modes of Bradstreet's thinking: Stanford 93.

"But Ah, and Ah, again, my imbecility!": 206.

"a causeway of American history": Bartlett 191.

Information on the area before the founding of Concord town: McAdow
    105–10.

"an old village" to "with which our river abounded": Emerson, *Works* 11: 39–40.

Devastation of Native peoples: Shattuck 2. Shattuck explains that "about the
    year 1612" the first peoples of New England "were visited with a pestilential
    disease, whose horrible ravages reduced their number to about 1800 [from
    well over 18,000]. Some of their villages were entirely depopulated" (2).

Act of Incorporation: Citations from Shattuck 4–5. Derivations of "Musket-
    aquid" and "Concord" found in Shattuck 5n.

"Concord Hymn": Emerson, *Works* 9: 139.

"Musketaquid": Emerson, *Works* 9: 124–27.

"Two Rivers": Emerson, *Works* 9: 213.

"It came about" to "on the offspring": Hughes, *Autobiography* 65.

"looked out the window" to "in our past": Hughes, *Autobiography* 65–66.

"The Negro Speaks of Rivers": Hughes, *Autobiography* 66.

"suggesting the whole of the people and their history": Oktenberg 95.

"a mystic union . . . every age": Wagner 394.

"with the accumulated" to "in the future": Oktenberg 96.

"the cradle . . . Garden of Eden": G. Hutchinson 415.

"referred to . . . in Genesis": Herendeen 32.

Link between "The Negro Speaks of Rivers" and spirituals: For example,
    Mullen, introduction 5. See also Rampersad; Duplessis; and G. Hutchinson.
    James de Jongh understands Hughes to be "claim[ing] his legacy-vocabulary
    of place" from his forerunners in African American literature, bringing to-
    gether different meanings of rivers (65).

"As the rivers . . . even this America": Jemie 103.

"burned off the ground": 133. Page numbers that are unaccompanied by author and title refer to Ernest Hemingway, *In Our Time*.

"Nick lay down . . . and went to sleep": 142.

"The sun . . . of the river": 145.

"It was a good camp": 147.

Structure of the work: Constance Cappel Montgomery points out that "nowhere in the content of the story is the name of the river given" and that Hemingway cited the Fox as the river by which the story takes place (142). William Adair, noting that Nick himself is a writer, calls the location of the story "to a great extent invented." That reading puts the story's emphasis on imagination and creation rather than recollection and experience (Adair 587n); similarly, Mark Browning suggests that, rather than describing an actual fishing trip, Nick may be expressing a dream or mental exercise while lying in a hospital, making the river "a creation of Nick's mind, combined out of memories of the Fox and the name of the Two-Hearted" (87).

"It was a long time" to "all the old feeling": 134.

"where he was from the position of the river": 135.

"a very serious coffee drinker": 141–42.

Reminders of the devastating fire: 134, 136.

"It was too heavy. It was much too heavy": 134 (cf. Hannum 105).

"felt he had left . . . back of him": 134.

Tainted grasshoppers: 136 (cf. Hannum 107).

"He looked back . . . fish the swamp": 156.

Nick wounded in battle: 63.

"the live feeling": 154.

"unsteadily" to "was only tired": 149.

Critics on the swamp and dread: See Hannum; Adair. Hannum equates the swamp with "the challenge of the female" (110). More recently, Sarah Mary O'Brien reads the swamp as unsettling the distinctions between such opposites as nature and culture.

"It could not all be burned. He knew that": 135.

Nick's process of renewal: Lisa Narbeshuber attributes Nick's newly forged relation to time to his refusal "to move at the speed of the machine"—that is, a rejection of some of the cultural tendencies of modernity (25).

Hughes as "cultural ambassador" and "forerunner": Wright, "Forerunner" 67.

"swirling black water": 90. Page numbers that are unaccompanied by author and title refer to Richard Wright, "Down by the Riverside," in the Harper and Row edition of *Uncle Tom's Children*.

"'Stop em from killin black folks!'": 101 (cf. McCarthy 734).

Publication information for "Down by the Riverside": Ward and Butler 103.

New York Times review: VanGelder.

Summary of the parts of *Uncle Tom's Children*: Tuttleton 266.

The song "Down by the Riverside": 63.

Biblical instances of baptism and rebirth "down by the riverside": Herendeen 33; Ward and Butler 104; Graves 283.

The river "everywhere": 56.

"producing a situation . . . 'down by the riverside'": JanMohamed 53.

"waste of desolate and tumbling waters": 70.

"'flowin strong n tricky'": 60.

"over the darkening flood" to "glistening blackly": 64.

"fear flowed under everything" to "losing all sense of direction": 65.

"the past would tell him nothing": 67.

"as though by gravity of the earth itself": 92.

"the terrible devastation of the great flood of 1927": Kinnamon 56.

"undergoes his ordeal with courage, intelligence, and resourcefulness": Kinnamon 92.

"coping with white oppression": Kinnamon 93.

"South End": 72.

"wild waters": 86.

Flood as the symbol of fate: Walker 192.

"unrelieved bleakness" to "racial relations": Howard 50.

Mann cheered and dehumanized by white soldiers: 72.

Rate of river rising: 84.

"droning": 56, 64, 88.

"a wild commotion" to "roar of loosened waters": 82.

"deep brown" to "tide of liquid tar": 54–55.

"one black palm . . . the brown current . . .": 102, final ellipsis points in the original.

"the darkness" to "blurred dawn": 94.

"life of the mind" to "its mountain-bed": xv. Page numbers that are unaccompanied by author and title refer to Kathleen Dean Moore, *Riverwalking: Reflections on Moving Water.*

"essential value was clarity": 142.

"professional lives" to "in that land": xi–xii.

"'Philosophy . . . not the same'": 141.

"art of poking around": 27.

The discipline of philosophy: 142–44.

"wonder and hoping": 28.

"So I poke . . . the farther bank": 31.

"an avocation for the dissolute": 30.

"Everything . . . look for it there": 31.

"life everlasting" and other biblical passages for her father's funeral: 126–27.

"times of a river" and spawning salmon: 130.

"was born" to "go back home": 3–4.

"because it had clean, cold rivers": 5.

"the homing instinct" to "children back home?": 6–7.

"walk out into a world" to "your own decisions and memories": 9.

"Scientists say" to "the Willamette River": 10.

"'an Episcopalian and a bait fisherman'": 5. Page numbers that are unaccompanied by author and title refer to Norman Maclean, *A River Runs Through It.*

"great trout rivers" to "religion and fly fishing": 1.

"is the river we knew best" to "part of us": 13.

"painted on one side . . . Missoula, Montana": 7.

"LO|VE" and "with a hash-mark between": 69.

"down the length of the Big Blackfoot River": 102.

"at the height of his power": 21.

"big-fish fisherman, looking with contempt": 12.

"If he studied" to "world turned to water": 20.

"studied the situation" to "my other shortcomings": 17.

"eventually the watcher . . . was the river": 61.

Becoming the river: 62.

"studying the situation": 17.

"all that existed of me were thoughts": 40.

"looking for answers to questions": 42.

"to find something" to "haunting": 27, 29.

"I still do not understand my brother": 47.

"'I don't know, that's my trouble'": 82.

"'All there is . . . isn't even visible'": 92.

"with each step" to "a world perfect and apart": 37.

"As the heat . . . deposit, and quietness": 63.

"reading the New Testament" to "'underneath the water'": 94–95.

"'if you listen'" to "'the same thing'": 96.

"one big cast for one last fish": 97.

"the last fish we were ever to see Paul catch": 100.

"We sat on the bank . . . what a river was saying": 101.

"A river, though . . . to each of us": 102.

"'You like' . . . 'what happened and why'": 104.

"too old to be much of a fisherman": 104.

"Eventually, all things" to "I am haunted by waters": 104.

"loved and did not understand": 104.

3. Up the River

"without comparison . . . ever been seen": 38. Page numbers that are unaccompanied by author and title refer to Jacques Cartier, *The Voyages of Jacques Cartier.*

"the land God gave to Cain": 10.

"fish in appearance like horses": 46.

"warm and in good health" to "it is so hot": 69–70.

"to make our way up the river as far as we possibly could": 59.

"frozen up in the ice": 79.

Description of Donnacona's "harangue": 50.

"as far as possible": 53.

"much astonished" to "emptied itself there": 54.

Lane's report: The scholar John Seelye notes that Lane's report, "though occasionally obscure, emphasizes the dramatic nature of a river voyage into the unknown interior" and thus can be read as "a continuation of the genre established by Cartier" (*Prophetic Waters* 38).

"attempted to understand . . . rather than differences": Cook xvii.

"the particularities" to "things necessary": Lane 255. Page numbers that are unaccompanied by author and title refer to Ralph Lane, "Discourse on the First Colony."

"a man impotent" to "vp his Riuer of Choanoke": 259.

"a most notable Riuer . . . the Riuer of Morotico": 263.

"This Riuer of Morotico" to "the head of that Riuer": 263–64.

"There is a Prouince . . . most strange Minerall": 268.

"Wassador" at Chaunis Temoatan: 268.

"tooke a resolution . . . into that Riuer": 264.

"voyage vp the Riuer" to "two dayes victuall left": 266.

"whether we should aduenture . . . back againe": 267.

"resolution" to "contrary opinion": 268.

"the riuers mouth . . . against the same": 272.

"not without both payne, and perill": 275.

"God was pleased not utterly to suffer vs to be lost": 272.

"some people could not tel whether to thinke vs gods or men": Hariot 378.

"set downe this voyage" to "least amongst vs": 272.

"this riuer of Moratico promiseth great things": 273.

"a good mine": 273.

"the most sweete . . . manured in the world": 273.

"diverted attention . . . North America": Kuppermann 376.

"spent our victuall" to "fiftie in this time we buried": 2: 143. Volume and page numbers that are unaccompanied by author and title refer to John Smith's *A True Relation* (1608), in *Complete Works*, vol. 1, and *The Generall Historie of Virginia, New-England, and the Summer Isles* (1624), in *Complete Works*, vol. 2.

"muttered against Captaine Smith . . . the Chickahamania river": 2: 146.

"up the river . . . many high lands": 1: 43.

"put our selves . . . wilde wildernes": 1: 45.

"to refresh": 1: 45.

"quagmire" to "beset with 200. Salvages": 2: 146.

"barricado," "bogmire," "the Captaine": 1: 45.

"executed": 1: 47.

"Emperour": 1: 53.

"discourse," "much delighted," "forsake," "upon his River": 1: 47, 53, 57.

"Corne, Venison" to "accompanie me": 1: 57.

"many strange triumphes" to "estimation": 2: 146.

"the King of Pamaunkee" to "were to them Antipodes": 2: 147.

"strangely painted" to "hellish notes and screeches": 2: 147–48.

"he could either divine" to "devils," "fiends," "ugly": 2: 149.

"Here more then ... beene a monster": 2: 150.

"rescue," "esteeme," "Powhatan disguised himselfe" to "one death or other": 2: 151.

"grim attendants": 2: 259.

"she hazarded the beating out of her own brains to save": 2: 259.

"Famous Chickahominy Voyage": Warner 100.

"the conclusion was ... occupations as themselves": 2: 151.

"a child of twelve or thirteen years of age": 2: 258.

"paper speake": 2: 149.

"What really happened ... seemingly contradictory accounts": 1: lxx. In his brief biography of Smith accompanying the three volumes of collected writings, Philip Barbour provides a pithy summary of what happened: Powhatan, impressed by Smith's self-confidence and gadgetry, inducted the captain "into his tribe as a subordinate werowance." Pocahontas, in this account, played a part in the ceremony. "After that, Smith was subjected to further inquiry and finally returned to Jamestown on January 2, 1608, escorted by a squad to guide, help, and protect him. The episode was the source of the Pocahontas legend" (1: lix). For an example of scholarly defenses of Smith, see Lemay.

"unsolvable contradiction": Seelye, *Prophetic Waters* 55.

"based on actual historical events and public records": From the credits of *The New World*.

"the only truth": *The New World*.

"historical point of origin": Tilton 5.

"Art and Nature would seldom work in tandem in America": Seelye, *Prophetic Waters* 63.

"the ur-myth of American literature" and "the accommodating savage": Seelye, *Prophetic Waters* 66.

"The river the higher grew worse and worse": Quoted in Warner 110.

"muddles ... the wild, wet woods": Seelye, *Prophetic Waters* 66.

"abstract men" to "next door to starvation": 3. Page numbers that are unaccompanied by author and title refer to Henry Marie Brackenridge, *Views of Louisiana*.

"mere gratification" and "an idle curiosity": 200.

"the last settlement of whites" to "habitations of Americans": 219.

"The current ... great impetuosity": 205.

"beauty of the scenery" to "animated beings": 234.

"1640 miles" to "civilized life": 262.

"the savage state ... at a distance": 257.

"and thus by perseverance became conquerors": 215.

"Fellow of the Linnean Society": 4.

"the face of nature" to "loaded with sluggish prejudice": 6.

"ignorant and savage man . . . means of fear": 230.

"lesson" and "in such a manner . . . peregrinations": 230, 200.

"mournful gloom" and "wait for the turn of the tide": 193. Page numbers that are unaccompanied by author and title refer to Joseph Conrad, "The Heart of Darkness," serialized in *Blackwood's Edinburgh Magazine*. John Batchelor claimed that Conrad's novella itself turned the tide of literary history, marking the invention of the "modern novel" (232). Conrad himself said that he was reading Twain's *Life on the Mississippi* while voyaging on the Congo (Higdon 355).

"'The conquest of the earth . . . into it too much'": 196.

"a flabby, pretending" to "gloomy circle of some Inferno": 206.

"'All Europe contributed'" to "nerves [going] wrong": 497. William Atkinson, however, reads Conrad's text "as an attack on foreign imperialism & a defense of the British variety" (379). In any case, many critics, including Clement Abiaziem Okafor, hold that Conrad merely used Africa as a background for his Eurocentric views, portraying the continent "as a land of savages who do not have any worthwhile culture or civilization" (20). Okafor follows Chinua Achebe, whose work he contrasts with Conrad's. Achebe wrote that Conrad expressed the European desire to set up Africa as "a foil to Europe, a place of negations" (2).

"'Going up that river . . . earliest beginnings of the world'": 481.

"'penetrated deeper and deeper into the heart of darkness'": 483.

"'the farthest point . . . kind of light'": 197.

"seemed to lead into the heart of an immense darkness": 657.

"the hollow men" to "Not with a bang but a whimper": Eliot 77, 80.

"terminate" to "straight into Kurtz": *Apocalypse Now*.

The Wagnerian-scored attack on the Viet Cong at the mouth of the river: Walter Benn Michaels has characterized the scene as the true end of the film: the depiction of the Vietnam War as "an attempt to make the world safe for surfing." For Michaels, the attack nullifies the need to proceed any farther up the Nung, for nothing "we could find at the river's source could be as horrible as what we have already found at its mouth" (1173).

"fucking savages" to "all the way": *Apocalypse Now*.

4. Down the River

The Voyage of Life: "The most important series of Thomas Cole's professional career" (Parry 226) was originally commissioned by Samuel Ward and exhibited in New York City in 1840. The paintings I saw in the National Gallery were a second set, with some slight differences from the first, completed by Cole in Italy in 1842 (Parry 265).

"Ocean of Eternity" to "tragic consequences for both man and nature": National Gallery of Art's on-line guide to the collection.

"Mr. Mark Twain" to "told the truth": Twain, *Adventures* 32.

"some stretchers" to "sivilized": Twain, *Adventures* 32, 265.

Colorado River statistics: Palmer 193; Blinn and Poff 488, 495.

"complete physical" to "complex plumbing system": Carothers and Brown 6, 15.

"the Colorado River . . . countless diversions": Blinn and Poff 487.

"the river no longer can clear its throat": Lucchitta 31. See Philip Fradkin's *A River No More* for a book-length study of the effects of human activity on the Colorado River.

"1000 tons . . . skipping by every second": Stevens, "The 67 Elephant Theory" 25.

Ann Zwinger: Zwinger won the John Burroughs Medal for natural history writing in 1976 for an earlier work about the Green River, *Run, River, Run*, which earned her "a distinguished reputation as a meticulous researcher and reliable guide to the natural history" of the American Southwest (Anderson and Edwards 241).

"a book" to "year-round picture": 6. Page numbers that are unaccompanied by author and title refer to Ann Zwinger, *Downcanyon*.

Details of the river: 119–30.

Whitewater as underwear: 120.

"like a cinnamon roll" to "tamarisk thickets": 126–27.

"Sitting high . . . my future being": 125. Thomas J. Lyon holds that Zwinger's subtle use of "I" in her writing demonstrates that her "self is tied up with landscapes" (*Incomparable Land* 128). Peter Wild places her among "old-fashioned naturalists who would prefer to keep their private lives in the background" (165).

"impressions of the natural scene" to "in simple fact": x. Page numbers that are unaccompanied by author and title refer to Edward Abbey, *Desert Solitaire*.

"enormous silt trap" to "real estate speculators": 173. "Down the River" is the longest chapter of *Desert Solitaire*, the "dominant concerns" of which are the "integrity, stability, and beauty" of the desert through which the Colorado flows (Scheese 308). For an overview of the book and brief description of each chapter, see Bryant. Don Scheese observes that though "Abbey's ego loom[s] large" throughout the book, the perspective is nevertheless more "*eco-* than *ego-*centered" (307)—or, as Ann Ronald puts it, an examination "of selfhood" but also "of wilderness, of progress, of desecration" (605). To Lawrence Buell, Abbey depicts the "nature seeker's psyche" as rife with "splits and self-deceptions" (74). The shift in attention from place to person may belong to Abbey's attempt to move readers closer to both "the wildness of the nonhuman world" and "the wild side of our own humanity" (Slovic 114). Paul Bryant situates "Down the River" as one of several chapters in the book addressing a paradoxical desire to merge with one's surroundings and the will to establish one's autonomy (9).

"the new dam already under construction": 174.

"very intimate relation with the river": 176.

"renew our affection for": 177.

"ignorance and carelessness" and "deliberate": 179.

"multinefarious delights of what Ralph calls syphilization": 183.

"incredible *shit* we put up with" to "all their rotten institutions": 177–78.

"deep in the wild . . . men and women": 189.

"Under the desert sun" to "Therefore, sublime": 219.

"screen" to "the river and reality": 209. To be fair, Zwinger's "factual natural history" is offset by "relevant personal response," as Thomas Lyon has noted ("Western Nature Essay" 1248). This, however, differs considerably from Abbey's *Desert Solitaire*, which Peter Wild characterizes not as an explanation of nature but as an effort to represent "the overwhelming exhilaration of living with nature" (160).

"living river" to "coherence and significance": 206.

"The beavers . . . on the Colorado": 173.

"last voyage" to "wild and free": 219–20.

"deeper into Eden": 183.

"rebirth backward in time and into primeval liberty": 177.

"the only home . . . we ever need": 190.

"memorial," "tombstone": xii.

"leave [the] river" to "meant for us": 220.

"*Floating down the river*" as the fulfillment of a dream: 176.

"the splendid river" to "insouciant Colorado": 205.

"Probably there is . . . such impressive surroundings": Dutton 207. Although I've seen the Great Unconformity up close, I still find it difficult to get my head around what it represents. Geologist K. E. Karlstrom observes: "Details are difficult to unravel because erosion has removed most of the record, and we do not know where the eroded sediment was deposited" (Karlstrom et al. 37). Other geologists demonstrate that the Great Unconformity results from the erosion of rock layers approximately ten kilometers thick (Timmons et al. 79). Stephen Pyne, noting that the Great Unconformity was "first seen by Powell," describes it as a "long break in the stratigraphic record, during which two ranges of mountains rose and wasted away to a nearly horizontal plain" (35). See Edwin D. McKee for a more complete discussion of various unconformities in the Grand Canyon (26–47). Wallace Stegner examines some of the poetic potential of the "enigmatic unconformity" in *Beyond the Hundredth Meridian* (119–23).

Putting the major and the river on the map: Dolnick 13. For a thorough treatment of Powell and mapping, see Van Noy (100–41). Saying that "the Colorado River is the river of John Wesley Powell," geologist Charles B. Hunt notes that the major was the first to explore, chart, and explain the formation of the canyons of the river (61). Pyne reminds readers that Powell's book opened "the floodgates of tourism," making the river and especially the Grand Canyon "internationally renowned" (27).

"Let us understand . . . this is the Grand Canyon": 89–90. Page numbers that are unaccompanied by author and title refer to John Wesley Powell, *The Exploration of the Colorado River and Its Canyons*.

"breaks away . . . is lost": 161.

"the last great exploration within the continental United States": Stegner, introduction vii.

"Chief" to "by that stream": *Deseret Evening News*, September 11, 1869, reprinted in *Utah Historical Quarterly* 15 (1947): 142.

"one of the most perilous journeys ever attempted by man": The movie *Ten Who Dared* credits the screenplay to Lawrence Edward Watkin and Powell's "journal," which is cited at the beginning of the movie as the story's source.

"surely one of the great" to "later age, for astronauts": Pyne 22–23. In the same vein, Donald Worster likens Powell to "a conquering hero come home from the front" (196–97). Karl Hess Jr. writes that the major's exploits, along with his career as a scientific bureaucrat, made him "the first truly modern western hero" (15), although those heroics were informed by a spirit that ultimately ruined the West (24).

"the thought grew ... read the book": Bell 559. James Aton, who reads the trope as part of a larger "Nature-as-Book metaphor," suggests that Powell thought of his mission "in near messianic terms" and considered himself "the high priest of that sacred text" (38–39).

"add a mite to the great sum of human knowledge": Powell, "Letters" 74.

The major's crew: Goodman left after three weeks and too much excitement. Dunn and the Howlands, in a remarkable event still the source of dispute, walked away from the expedition and out of the canyon to be killed before reaching any town or outpost. The Disney version depicts the latter three as turning their backs on science and the search for knowledge, driven by greed or hunger and guided by astrology.

"Country worthless to anybody or anything": Sumner 117.

"The exploration of the Great Cañon of the Colorado was accomplished": 537 (March 1875). Compare Powell's earlier, brief account: "Here ended the 'Great Unknown,' no longer thus to be designated" (Bell 563). And so the story is still told: historian and biographer Donald Worster states that Powell's expedition "removed the phrase 'unknown' from the last large area of the coterminous United States" (201).

"omissions, inaccuracies, and errors": Stanton 106–07. Claiming that Powell crew member Sumner said that "'there's lots in that book besides the truth'" (Stanton 104), Stanton castigates Powell for maintaining that the report on the exploration really was his "'diary written on the spot'" (111). See also Ghiglieri 4–11; Aton 32–33; Worster 256; Dolnick 32–33; and Stegner, *Beyond* 149–52.

"landmark river of the West": Palmer 177.

"The distance ... through a canyon": 131.

"One must not ... carved by the waters": 133.

"The river is running" to "name it Flaming Gorge": 128–29. Rick Van Noy, observing that "names are essential to the process that brings space into place," adds that in writing his account, Powell was "becoming conscious of how his names and his narrative would create the story of the place" (114). Robert Brewster Stanton claims that most names bestowed on the canyon region by the Powell parties actually came from the second expedition (124–25).

"little flag" to "the swift current": 119.

Early wrinkles in navigating the river: 124.

Geological and literary patterns: In her study of the hydraulics of Colorado River rapids in the Grand Canyon, geologist Susan Werner Kieffer discusses the alternation pattern in terms of "kinetic and potential energy" (299). Literary scholar Murray G. Murphey calls Powell's use of the river's rhythmic alternation the "perfect vehicle around which to structure his account" (197–98).

"He can tell . . . a story complete": 123. See Murphey: "The *Exploration* cannot be regarded as a purely factual account: it is rather a literary work and must be interpreted as such" (197). Regarding the different versions of the voyage, Worster writes that "each embellishment of Powell's narrative strengthened the impression that there was a vast unknown part of America that was at last being revealed as unified and coherent" (162).

Oramel Howland likened to King Lear: 123. Regarding the illustrations, Hal Stephens and Eugene Shoemaker note that artists took "some liberties" in making line drawings from the photographs; for example, "in composing the pictures of the canyons, they often exaggerated the height and steepness of canyon walls" (4).

"the canyon opens" to "What shall we find?": 148.

"the excitement of the day" to "name is adopted": 152.

"Very slowly we make our way" to "the brink": 152–54. Murphey has pointed out that, "by presenting his account in the form of a journal, Powell is able to build the suspense day by day as the party moves on through the ever-deepening canyons" (198).

"the narrow, angry channel below" to "open compartment with water": 154.

"This seems a long time" to "on which life depends": 154.

"set up a shout" to "were shouting about": 157. Stegner notes that the actual size of the keg varies in different accounts, from three to ten gallons (*Beyond* 65). Dolnick says ten, based on Sumner's assessment (68). Compare Worster 167.

Events of "June 18": 168–69. A melodramatic etching by R. A. Muller titled *The Rescue* accompanies the account, embellishing the scene even more. Muller depicts Bradley stretched on a narrow protuberance, seemingly still wearing pants but clutching the end of something trouserlike, the other end of which is clutched by Powell's left hand as the rest of him dangles in space against the face of the precipice. The etching is considerably longer than it is wide, and the effect of it on the page forces the narrowed prose it accompanies to descend like a cataract.

"In one place . . . got up safe": G. Bradley 46. According to George Bradley's entry for June 18, they had just named Lodore (40). No other account confirms Powell's dating of the trouser rescue, including his letters to newspapers. Michael P. Ghiglieri also observes that Powell changed the setting of the action, placing the event "many miles upstream on the Yampa while climbing a cliff on that river, which the 1869 crew did not do" (159). Worster uses the episode to exemplify Powell's embellishing "to the point of fictive invention" (170).

"We are now ready" to "among the boulders": 247. Today most Grand Canyon floats begin some sixty miles upriver, at Lees Ferry, fifteen miles below Glen Canyon Dam. Lees Ferry, near the confluence with the Paria River, marks the division between the upper and lower basins of the Colorado (Blinn and Poff 483). The Little Colorado is the primary tributary of the Colorado in the Grand Canyon, joining the river about sixty miles below the Paria (Stevens, *Colorado River* 71).

"a lothesome [*sic*] little stream, so filthy and muddy that it fairly stinks": G. Bradley 61.

"as disgusting a stream as there is on the continent": Sumner 119.

"If Major does not do something soon I fear the consequences": G. Bradley 62.

"We have an unknown . . . we know not": 247. Stressing the mythical nature of Powell's description, James Aton sees the unknown as an "underworld," equating the major with "Odysseus and Aeneas" (36).

"Sockdolager of the World": The name was recorded by Frederick Dellenbaugh, artist and assistant topographer on the second expedition (222–23).

"widespread geologic upheaval": Stevens, *Colorado River* 9–10.

"a perfect hell of waves": Sumner 119. George Bradley refers to Sockdolager as "the worst one we had seen on the river and the walls being vertical or rather coming to the water on both sides we had to run it" (63). Jack Hillers, photographer on the second expedition, wrote this in his diary of the trip: "Came to a hell of a looking place. Here the granite comes up, two gulches having emptied their debris, forming the biggest fall we have seen" (Fowler 136). Powell biographer Edward Dolnick comments that the name "Sockdolager" was applied to the rapid on the 1871 trip (328).

"about eleven o'clock . . . mad, white foam": 249–50.

For recent measurements of Sockdolager's fall, compare Ghiglieri 207 and
Stevens, *Colorado River* 74. Ghiglieri calls Powell's manipulation of the
numbers an act of "literary excess" that "made his 'history' . . . even more
fictional" (6).

"our arrival here is very opportune": 286–87 (cf. Powell, *Exploration of the Colorado River of the West* 104). Despite the questions I am pointing out, most
readers prefer to consider the mission accomplished. The Disney rendition
of the Powell expedition, for example, trumpets a tale of the triumph of reason and science: the major, played by John Beal, becomes a prophet of a new
religion, proclaiming a new Genesis (the history of Earth's formation) and
new Revelation (of the future of America in the West). Disney's treatment,
although terrifically corny, is not exceptional; other readings by historians,
biographers, scientists, and some literature scholars are less comical but no
less intent on making the Powell story, its river, and its canyon conform to
a particular version of human (and especially western) relations to nature
(and especially the wilderness). What matters most in such approaches to
the expedition is the extent to which it proves that human beings, equipped
with reason and determination, can overcome nature and uncover truths
that lie concealed in the land. Powell's account becomes material proof of
the supposedly objective truth of a dramatic American story about heroics,
wilderness, progress, and science.

"considerable income": Stephens and Shoemaker 4.

"I tell a riddle . . . is left unexplained": Powell, *Outlines* 3.

"The verity of philosophy . . . known unknown": Powell, *Outlines* 3. Powell
makes a related claim in "The Larger Import of Scientific Education," an
1885 article for *Popular Science Monthly*: "The history of the world is replete
with illustrations to the effect that the greater the ignorance, the greater the
abomination of *unconforming* opinion, and the greater the knowledge, the
greater the charity of dissenting opinions" (qtd. in Rabbitt 20, emphasis
added). Some of these ideas receive greater treatment in his later work *Truth
and Error* (1898).

"the wonders . . . exceedingly diverse": 394.

"the most sublime" to "work of waters": 390.

"We think of the mountains" to "the artists sublime": 393. Van Noy reads
Powell's version of a "decentered" (37) sublime as more "ecological" than
"Romantic" (116).

"a changeless spectacle" to "hither side of paradise": 397.

Dickey's Cahulawassee River: Based on the Chattooga River, the location for much footage of the Boorman film, "though the most dramatic scenes featured the waterfalls in the gorge of the nearby Tallulah River" (Lane 4).

"some kind of harmonious relationship": 18. Page numbers that are unaccompanied by author and title refer to James Dickey, *Deliverance*.

"'Sliding is living . . . grooving with comfort'": 41.

"were not bored in the way Lewis and I were bored": 8.

"Two men stepped . . . by the barrel": 107.

"laid the river . . . 150 miles north": 3.

Ed's first view of the "pretty" Cahulawassee: 70.

"I felt . . . I would return": 73.

"something came to an edge in me" to "pure energy": 139.

"fading out," "joining" the river: 144.

"Let the river run": 170.

"The river was blank . . . its uncomprehending consequence": 171.

"My lies seemed better, more and more like truth": 253.

"In me" to "everything I do": 275–76.

"'Doesn't deliver enough'" to "'with his wife'": 48.

"promised other things, another life, deliverance": 28.

"'wild goddamned river'": 151.

"incompetent asshole," the "soft city country-club man": 201.

"the country of nine-fingered people": 56.

"industrial man" to "agony of final loss": Abbey 192.

"There *is* something . . . of its parts": Zwinger, *Downcanyon* 237.

"so commanding" to "love of this earth": Zwinger, *Downcanyon* 237.

"All evidence verifies" to "when the climate turns bad": 234.

5. Crossing the River

"river that flows two ways": 3. Page numbers that are unaccompanied by author and title refer to Akiko Busch, *Nine Ways to Cross a River*.

"symbolic way of breaching the divide": 2.

"primal order and proportion": 17–18.

Brief environmental history of the Hudson: 9–13.

"short swim" to "possibilities realized": 9.

"perception is anticipatory": 8. A. K. Saran writes: "The overall function of environment perception . . . is not to reveal present reality nor to recall past reality; rather it is to predict the future. Perception is anticipatory" (111).

"the possibility of getting there, somewhere, from here": 2.

"transformation and renewal": 13.

Swimming as perpetual rebirth: 19.

"reclaiming [the river's] place in our popular imagination": 14.

"until all the people were passed clean over Jordan": Joshua 3: 17; for information of classical Greek and Roman crossings, see Jones 19–20.

"transition from one state of being to another": Jones 35.

"Over middle . . . taken of it": Twain, *Life* 276.

"liberty and freedom" to "stubborn autonomy": Fischer 4–6.

Details about Washington's first crossing: Fischer 132; for a description of the later, larger crossing, see 267.

"transformed attitudes . . . of the Atlantic": Fischer 262.

"vindication of the Cause" to "was His instrument": Fischer 259.

"more . . . work of art": Quoted in Jaffe.

"theatrical" romanticization, a "melodramatic" exaggeration: See Wierich.

"When I reflect" to "Philadelphia, if Possible": Washington 430. Other letters, written the same day to his "Brothers of Passamaquoddy" and to his "Brothers of the St. John's Tribe," describe a different kind of crossing. Washington sent letters to these parties as devices to reach across cultural divides and maintain connections with needed allies. Informing his correspondents that "in token of my Friendship I send you this from my Army on the Banks of the great River Delaware," he urges them to keep "the Chain of Friendship, which I sent you in February last from Cambridge bright & unbroken" (433–34).

"that they might . . . lines of march": Washington 454.

"Behaviour . . . abate their Ardour": Washington 456.

"the final stage in the progressive movement of world history": Wierich 55.

"a national cliché" to "hand-on-chest heroics": Larry Rivers, quoted in Davidson 74.

"'repainting' . . . Napoleonic stance": H. Smith 185.

"with similar irreverence and amused contempt": Perloff 84.

"the beautiful history" to "bridge reaches for": O'Hara 94.

"mixture of romance . . . a historical event": Kenneth Koch, quoted in R. Bradley.

"underground classic": R. Bradley.

"the philosophy . . . on this point": 44. Page numbers that are unaccompanied by author and title refer to Kenneth Koch, *Bertha and Other Plays.*

"every man" to "military situation": 47.

"made up" to "well-equipped troops": 50.

"the greatest man" to "this country, America": 45.

"undermin[ing] the heroism, masculinity and patriotism": H. Smith 185.

"a witty approximation of reality for reality-subverting purposes": Benedikt 159.

"Good night, America" to "GEORGE WASHINGTON": 59.

"I cannot tell" to "the Delaware River!": 63.

"Raids . . . his aides": 49.

Influence of "The Night Before Christmas": R. Bradley.

"rapt" to "crossed the Delaware": 65–66.

"there shall be . . . in the said territory": Ford 343.

"became a veritable River Jordan" to "nominal freedom": Hudson 5.

"have been immortalized in significant works of literature": Hudson 129.

"one . . . American history": Hudson 130.

Eliza Harris's escape described: Hagedorn 135–37. For a discussion of different sources of Stowe's story of the crossing, some of which move the scene farther downriver near Cincinnati, see Nye 98–101 and Kirkham 104–09.

"the single most" to "*Swing Low, Sweet Chariot*": Griffler 61.

Ripley and the naming of the Underground Railroad: Hagedorn 12.

"Grand Central Station of the Underground Railroad": Blockson 203 (cf. Hagedorn 138–39).

Naming of "Eliza Harris": Hendrick and Hendrick 64. E. Bruce Kirkham reports that one witness remembered the escaping woman's real name was "Mary" (106).

"with her child . . . Kentucky": xix. Page numbers that are unaccompanied by author and title refer to Harriet Beecher Stowe, *Uncle Tom's Cabin.* For the importance of the crossing scene to Stowe's novel, see Hedrick 212. Many commentators describe the crossing as "the most famous scene in the novel" (Gates and Robbins 68), though some suggest that it only became so after theatrical versions added hounds in hot pursuit of the fugitives and other dramatic flourishes (e.g., Gossett 268).

"lay, like Jordan" to "swollen and turbulent": 54.

Available means of crossing: Hudson 12.

"the sullen, surging waters that lay between her and liberty": 56.

"Nerved with strength . . . madness and despair": 62.

"'the most neighborly thing in the world'": 63.

"sat perfectly silent . . . told his story": 75.

"maternal love" and "a fearful danger": 52.

"It was not . . . his own ways": Parker 25.

"was the making of a human being an animal without hope": Parker 26.

"You have seen . . . made a man": Douglass 75.

"a focus of regional life" to "caught in the middle": Paredes 25.

"border-conflict heroes" to "brutal manner": Paredes 28.

"intercultural conflict" to "against the *rinches*": Paredes 27.

"living between two cultures" to "searching for identity": Paredes 47.

"1,950 mile-long wound": 24. Page numbers that are unaccompanied by author and title refer to Gloria Anzaldúa, *Borderlands/La Frontera: The New Mestiza*.

"'*mojados*' (wetbacks)" to "over their heads": 33.

"ambivalence" to "cultural collision": 100.

"*la mojada, la mujer indocumentada*": 34.

"cross-pollinations" and "a new *mestiza* consciousness": 99.

"the new *mestiza* . . . tolerance for ambiguity": 101.

"three mothers" to "a combination of the other two": 52.

"a kind of cultural ambassador": Perez 9.

La Llorona as symbol of the border world of crossing: Rebolledo and Rivero 194.

The legend of La Llorona as dynamic mixture: Perez 12.

"epitomizes . . . of the border": León 7.

"does not recognize" to "intercultural dialogue": Perez 9.

Early versions of La Llorona: Perez 16–19.

Reminder of mortality and obligations: Rebolledo 78.

"figure of mourning" and "figure of revolt": Perez 35.

"as everything from ghost to guardian angel": vii. Page numbers that are unaccompanied by author and title refer to Alicia Gaspar de Alba, *La Llorona on the Longfellow Bridge: Poetry y otras movidas 1985–2001*.

"their lost culture, their lost selves": Rebolledo and Rivero 194.

El Paso crossing statistics: Bureau of Transportation Statistics Web site (http://www.transtats.bts.gov/bordercrossing.aspx).

Description of border region and winds blowing "without contrition": Gaspar de Alba, *Beggar* 9–10.

"learn to read . . . Río Grande": Gaspar de Alba, *Beggar* 13.

"Literary Wetback" and "cultural schizophrenia": 40.

Growing up Mexican American: 40–43.

"point of all departures" and "the landscape of La Llorona": viii–ix.

"and at each bridge . . . of the border": x.

"Some say that the spirit of La Malinche is *La Llorona*": Gaspar de Alba, *Beggar* 16.

"The woman shrieking . . . out of the land": From the poem "Malinchista, a Myth Revised" (Gaspar de Alba, *Beggar* 16–17).

"Patron saint . . . the dispossessed": 106–08.

"the mythic Weeping Woman of my own childhood fears": 42.

Creating a new tradition: 43.

"I saw our world . . . another": Carmen Tafolla, "La Malinche," in Rebolledo and Rivero 198.

"at once practical, enjoyable, and mystical": Folsom and Price 3. Ezra Greenspan writes that Whitman rode the ferry on a daily basis as an adult (168).

Statistics of the ferry trip: Oliver 287.

Whitman's disdain for tobacco: Oliver 289.

Whitman's singing: Reynolds, *Walt Whitman* 52.

Manhattan-Brooklyn rivalry: Reynolds, *Walt Whitman* 32.

"greatest celebration of the transcendentalist unity of existence": Loving 219.

"essentially a poem of connection and camaraderie": Greenspan 168.

"Crossing Brooklyn Ferry": All citations to the poem throughout the text are from Walt Whitman, *Leaves of Grass* 159–65.

Overcoming "constraints": Killingsworth, *Cambridge* 49. On poet or poem as boat, see the commentary of Gay Wilson Allen and Charles T. Davis in Whitman, *Walt Whitman's Poems* 157, 158.

Dissolution of boundaries between writer and reader: Oliver 65.

"paradox of stasis in motion": Allen, *Reader's Guide* 187. In *The New Walt Whitman Handbook* Allen attributes the idea to V. K. Chari's *Walt Whitman in the Light of Vedantic Mysticism*. M. Jimmie Killingsworth suggests that rather than transcendence, "Crossing Brooklyn Ferry" represents a "rejection of temporal limits" and promotes a "spatially situated view of experience" (*Walt Whitman* 129).

6. Up and Down the River

"The grand circle . . . live on Earth": Leopold 1.

"relatively low stream gradient" to "generally slow moving": United States Geological Survey, "Concord."

"may well be . . . the current flowed": Hawthorne, *Mosses* 6.

"barely has the power . . . its own surface": McAdow 2.

"by their wits . . . by the sun": Emerson, *Journals* 7: 238.

"We were bid to a river-party, not to be preached at": Lowell.

"experiment in natural philosophy": 49. Page numbers that are unaccompanied by author and title refer to the Princeton edition of Henry David Thoreau, *A Week on the Concord and Merrimack Rivers*.

"a nature behind the common" and "unexplored by science or by literature": 56.

Palindrome: Etymologically, "running back again" (*Oxford English Dictionary*). In the most literal sense, a palindrome is "writing that reads the same from left to right and from right to left" (Holman and Harmon 340). I'm using the term somewhat metaphorically to suggest a structure in which a traveler returns via the same route she or he went, as opposed to a circle (a more roundabout way of going and coming back) or a ray (a line going in one direction, a voyage of no return). Palindromes usually assume a structure of a-b-c-b-a (or a-b-c-c-b-a, wherein the pivot is doubled), which gives them a reflective or mirrorlike quality.

"leap gladly on shore": 393.

Leaving too much unconsidered by not going upstream: 7.

"Verily there are 'sermons in stones, and books in the running streams'": 248. Compare *As You Like It* (act 2, scene 1): "Tongues in trees, books in the running brooks, / Sermons in stones and good in every thing."

"lure" to "their greatest perfection": 12.

"Unappropriated Land": 314.

"Sitting with our faces" to "continuous every where": 349. Whereas I emphasize the effect of reversing direction, H. Daniel Peck adds speed and wind to the variables altering the travelers' new perspective (23–24).

"Most people . . . powder-post, methinks": 69.

"the common train" to "more than common": 386.

"on the banks" to "would bear me": 12–13.

"following the same law" to "fulfilling their fate": 12–13.

"remarkable . . . scarcely perceptible": 9.

"a deep, dark . . . bordered with willows": 44.

"the Concord . . . *fluvius* and *lacus*": 110.

"properly named": 9.

"Grass-ground River" to "on its banks": 5. Lynck C. Johnson, in his essay on *A Week* in *The Cambridge Companion to Henry David Thoreau*, points out that the title for an early version of the book was "Merrimack & Musketaquid" (42).

"that industrious tribe" to "slow but persevering": 53.

"there may be" to "continue Indian": 55–56.

The Concord section of the journey and Thoreau's use of the past: The Merrimack legs of the journey also provided ample opportunities for Thoreau to develop his approach to history, a key example being his treatment of the Hannah Duston (or Dustan, as Thoreau writes it) captivity-and-escape story, which he retells in the present tense (320–24). Peck has written that in the shift to present-tense narration "the historical time of Henry Thoreau and Hannah Duston suddenly conflate" (19–20). Peck uses the Duston treatment to exemplify Thoreau's approach to history as "creative reconstruction" or "creative remembering" (19). Similarly, Alfred I. Tauber cites the episode as an example of Thoreau's use of the river "both as a conduit into [the] past and as the vehicle of bringing history into his present" (48). For more on Thoreau's "uses of the past," see the chapter by that name in Johnson, *Thoreau's Complex Weave* 122–62; see also Carafiol 121–46; Burbick 15–34; and J. Hutchinson.

"if the fishes . . . new migratory shoals": 34.

"barking" "in the world": 41–42.

"painted green below . . . spend its existence": 15.

"a sort of amphibious animal, a creature of two elements": 16. The boat lasted a long time as *Musketaquid*, until Nathaniel Hawthorne bought it from Henry in 1842 and renamed it *Pond-Lily*. The purchaser speculated in his journal that "it is not very likely that I shall make such long voyages in her as Mr. Thorow has" (Hawthorne, *American Notebooks* 356–57). When he moved to Salem in 1846, Hawthorne gave the boat to Thoreau's friend Ellery Channing, "who in turn used it for many years until it finally rotted to pieces" (Harding 139).

"Two men . . . art or nature": 48–49.

"the surface . . . in its bosom": 45.

"ethereal and ideal" to "remoteness and perfection": 45–46.

"on this same stream" to "a maiden": 46.

"the mirror-like surface" to "the other object": 48.

"the summit of AGIOCOCHOOK": 314.

"flat," "inadequate," and "perfunctory": Peck 28, 31; Garber 336.

"ascended the mountain" and departed for Hooksett: Thoreau, *Journal* 136–37.
Harding describes this section of the journey (92); for a more detailed reconstruction, see McKee. As William Howarth shows, the actual trip's pivot
was more of a loop than an abrupt reversal and retracing. In the literary version, however, the palindromic device obtains. See also Kilbourne.

"the highest peak . . . the Carolinas": Daniell and Smith 9.

"steep and boulder-strewn": Howarth 222.

"said before . . . our pages even": 61.

"Art is not tame . . . the ordinary sense": 316.

"Thus we 'sayled' . . . the current hour": 331.

"talk of the river . . . misconception": Davies 40.

"It is our craving . . . life to it": McAdow 3. On flow as creator of rivers and habitats, see stream ecologist H. B. N. Hynes: "The way in which water flows
and the fact that it actually forms the patterns of rivers and streams and their
beds are fundamental to most of the properties of biotic habitats in running
water" (3).

"the carpenter of its own edifice": Leopold 281.

"optimal experience" to "with each other": Csikszentmihalyi and Selega
Csikszentmihalyi 24.

Flow and liminality: Turner 57.

"rooted in nature" to "wilderness": Johnson, *Thoreau's Complex Weave* 164.

"rivers from end to end": 211.

Works Cited

Abbey, Edward. *Desert Solitaire: A Season in the Wilderness*. New York: Ballantine, 1968.

Achebe, Chinua. "An Image of Africa." *Research in African Literatures* 9.1 (1978): 1–15.

Adair, William. "'Big Two-Hearted River': Why the Swamp Is Tragic." *Journal of Modern Literature* 17.4 (1991): 584–88.

Allen, Gay Wilson. *The New Walt Whitman Handbook*. 1975. New York: New York UP, 1986.

———. *A Reader's Guide to Walt Whitman*. 1970. Syracuse: Syracuse UP, 1997.

America's River. Spec. issue of *Audubon* May–June 2006.

Anderson, Lorraine, and Thomas S. Edwards. *At Home on This Earth: Two Centuries of U.S. Women's Nature Writing*. Hanover, NH: UP of New England, 2002.

Anzaldúa, Gloria. *Borderlands/La Frontera: The New Mestiza*. 1987. 3rd ed. San Francisco: Aunt Lute Books, 2007.

Apocalypse Now. Dir. Francis Ford Coppola. Omni Zoetrope, 1979.

Atkinson, William. "Bound in *Blackwood's*: The Imperialism of 'The Heart of Darkness' in Its Immediate Context." *Twentieth Century Literature* 50.4 (2004): 368–93.

Aton, James M. *John Wesley Powell*. Boise: Boise State UP, 1994.

Barry, John M. *Rising Tide: The Great Mississippi Flood of 1927 and How It Changed America*. New York: Simon and Schuster, 1997.

Bartlett, George B. *Concord: Historic, Literary and Picturesque*. 1885. 16th rev. ed. Boston: Lothrop, 1895.

Batchelor, John. "'Heart of Darkness,' Source of Light." *Review of English Studies* ns 43.170 (1992): 227–42.

Bell, William. *New Tracks in North America: a journal of travel and adventure whilst engaged in the survey for a southern railroad to the Pacific Ocean during 1867–8*. London: Chapman and Hall, 1869.

Benedikt, Michael, ed. *Theatre Experiment: An Anthology of American Plays*. Garden City, NY: Anchor Books, 1968.

Beus, Stanley S., and Michael Morales, eds. *Grand Canyon Geology*. 2nd ed. New York: Oxford UP, 2003.

Blinn, Dean W., and N. Leroy Poff. "Colorado River Basin." *Rivers of North America*. Ed. Arthur C. Benke and Colbert E. Cushing. Amsterdam: Elsevier Academic, 2005. 482–538.

Blockson, Charles L. *The Underground Railroad*. New York: Prentice Hall, 1987.

Brackenridge, Henry Marie. *Views of Louisiana; Together with a Journal of a Voyage Up the Missouri River, in 1811*. 1814. Chicago: Quadrangle Books, 1962.

Bradley, George. "George Y. Bradley's Journal, May 24–August 30, 1869." Ed. William Culp Darrah. *Utah Historical Quarterly* 15 (1947): 31–72.

Bradley, Robin. "Kenneth Koch Stages Two New Plays." *New York Times* Jan. 12, 1979.

Bradstreet, Anne. *The Complete Works of Anne Bradstreet*. Ed. Joseph R. McElrath Jr. and Allan P. Robb. Boston: Twayne Publishers, 1981.

———. *The Works of Anne Bradstreet*. Ed. Jeannine Hensley. Cambridge, MA: Belknap P of Harvard UP, 1967.

Brazil, John R. "Perception and Structure in Mark Twain's Art and Mind: *Life on the Mississippi*." *Mississippi Quarterly: The Journal of Southern Culture* 34.2 (1981): 91–112.

Bridgman, Richard. *Traveling in Mark Twain*. Berkeley: U of California P, 1987.

Browning, Mark. *Haunted by Waters: Fly Fishing in North American Literature*. Athens: Ohio UP, 1998.

Bryant, Paul T. "The Structure and Unity of *Desert Solitaire*." *Western American Literature* 28.1 (1993): 3–19.

Buell, Lawrence. *The Environmental Imagination: Thoreau, Nature Writing, and the Formation of American Culture*. Cambridge, MA: Belknap P of Harvard UP, 1995.

Burbick, Joan. *Thoreau's Alternative History: Changing Perspectives on Nature, Culture, and Language*. Philadelphia: U of Pennsylvania P, 1987.

Busch, Akiko. *Nine Ways to Cross a River: Midstream Reflections on Swimming and Getting There from Here*. New York: Bloomsbury, 2007.

Carafiol, Peter. *The American Ideal: Literary History as a Worldly Activity.* New York: Oxford UP, 1991.

Carothers, Steven W., and Bryan T. Brown. *The Colorado River Through Grand Canyon: Natural History and Human Change.* Tucson: U of Arizona P, 1991.

Cartier, Jacques. *The Voyages of Jacques Cartier.* Ed. Ramsay Cook. Toronto: U of Toronto P, 1993.

Charlton, Ro. *Fundamentals of Fluvial Geomorphology.* London: Routledge, 2008.

Codrescu, Andrei. *New Orleans, Mon Amour: Twenty Years of Writings from the City.* Chapel Hill, NC: Algonquin Books, 2006.

Conrad, Joseph. "The Heart of Darkness." *Blackwood's Edinburgh Magazine* Feb. 1899: 193–220; Mar. 1899: 479–502; Apr. 1899: 634–57.

Cook, Ramsay. "Donnacona Discovers Europe: Rereading Jacques Cartier's *Voyages.*" Introduction. *The Voyages of Jacques Cartier.* By Jacques Cartier. Toronto: U of Toronto P, 1993. ix–xli.

Cotter, John L., Daniel G. Roberts, and Michael Parrington. *The Buried Past: An Archaeological History of Philadelphia.* Philadelphia: U of Pennsylvania P, 1992.

Cox, James M. Introduction. *Life on the Mississippi.* By Mark Twain. New York: Penguin, 1984. 9–24.

Csikszentmihalyi, Mihaly, and Isabella Selega Csikszentmihalyi, eds. *Optimal Experience: Psychological Studies of Flow in Consciousness.* Cambridge: Cambridge UP, 1988.

Daniell, Greg, and Steven D. Smith, eds. *White Mountain Guide.* 27th ed. Boston: Appalachian Mountain Club Books, 2003.

Davidson, Michael. "Ekphrasis and the Postmodern Painter Poem." *Journal of Aesthetics and Art Criticism* 42.1 (1983): 69–79.

Davies, Paul. "That Mysterious Flow." *Scientific American* Sept. 2002: 40–47.

Deliverance. Dir. John Boorman. Warner Bros., 1972.

Dellenbaugh, Frederick S. *A Canyon Voyage: The Narrative of the Second Powell Expedition down the Green-Colorado River from Wyoming, and the Explorations on Land, in the Years 1871 and 1872.* New York: G. P. Putnam's Sons, 1908.

Dickey, James. *Deliverance.* New York: Delta, 1970.

Dolnick, Edward. *Down the Great Unknown: John Wesley Powell's 1869 Journey of Discovery and Tragedy Through the Grand Canyon.* New York: Harper Collins, 2001.

Douglass, Frederick. *Narrative of the Life of Frederick Douglass, an American Slave, Written by Himself.* 1845. Ed. David W. Blight. Boston: Bedford Books, 1993.

Duplessis, Rachel Blau. *Genders, Races, and Religious Cultures in Modern American Poetry, 1908–1934.* Cambridge: Cambridge UP, 2001.

Dutton, Clarence E. *Tertiary History of the Grand Cañon District.* 1882. Introduction by Wallace Stegner and a new foreword by Stephen J. Pyne. Tucson: U of Arizona P, 2001.

Eifert, Virginia S. *River World: Wildlife of the Mississippi.* New York: Dodd, Mead, 1959.

Eliot, T. S. "The Hollow Men." *Selected Poems.* New York: Harcourt Brace Jovanovich, 1936.

Emerson, Ralph Waldo. *Journals and Miscellaneous Notebooks of Ralph Waldo Emerson.* Ed. William Gilman et al. 16 vols. Cambridge, MA: Harvard UP, 1960–84.

———. *The Works of Ralph Waldo Emerson.* Ed. James Elliot Cabot. 14 vols. Boston: Houghton Mifflin, 1883.

Erasmus. *In Praise of Folly.* Ed. Hendrik Willem van Loon. Trans. John Wilson. Roslyn, NY: Walter Black, 1942.

Fellows, Henry Parker. *Boating Trips on New England Rivers.* Boston: Cupples, Upham, 1884.

Fischer, David Hackett. *Washington's Crossing.* New York: Oxford UP, 2004.

Fitzgerald, Carol. *The Rivers of America: A Descriptive Bibliography.* 2 vols. New Castle, DE: Oak Knoll P; Washington, DC: Center for the Book in the Library of Congress, 2001.

Folsom, Ed, and Kenneth M. Price. *Re-scripting Walt Whitman: An Introduction to His Life and Work.* Malden, MA: Blackwell, 2005.

Ford, Worthington Chauncey, et al., eds. *Journals of the Continental Congress, 1774–1789.* Washington, DC: Government Printing Office, 1904–37. http://lccn.loc.gov/05000009.

Fowler, Don D., ed. *"Photographed All the Best Scenery": Jack Hillers's Diary of the Powell Expeditions, 1871–1875.* Salt Lake City: U of Utah P, 1972.

Fradkin, Philip L. *A River No More: The Colorado River and the West.* New York: Knopf, 1981.

Fremling, Calvin R. *Immortal River: The Upper Mississippi in Ancient and Modern Times.* Madison: U of Wisconsin P, 2005.

Ganzel, Dewey. "Twain, Travel Books, and *Life on the Mississippi.*" *American Literature* 34.1 (1962): 40–55.

Garber, Frederick. "A Space for Saddleback: Thoreau's *A Week on the Concord and Merrimack Rivers.*" *Centennial Review* 24 (1980): 322–37.

Gaspar de Alba, Alicia. *Beggar on the Córdoba Bridge. Three Times a Woman: Chicana Poetry.* Ed. Gary Keller. Tempe: Bilingual, 1989. 1–50.

———. *La Llorona on the Longfellow Bridge: Poetry y otras movidas 1985–2001.* Houston: Arte Público, 2003.

Gates, Henry Louis, Jr., and Hollis Robbins, eds. *The Annotated "Uncle Tom's Cabin."* New York: Norton, 2007.

Ghiglieri, Michael P. *First Through Grand Canyon.* Flagstaff: Puma, 2003.

Goodwin, Brian. "Bateson: Biology with Meaning." *A Legacy for Living Systems: Gregory Bateson as Precursor to Biosemiotics.* Ed. Jesper Hoffmeyer. New York: Springer, 2008. 145–52.

Gordon, Charlotte. *Mistress Bradstreet: The Untold Life of America's First Poet.* New York: Little, Brown, 2005.

Gossett, Thomas F. *"Uncle Tom's Cabin" and American Culture.* Dallas: Southern Methodist UP, 1985.

Graves, Neil. "Richard Wright's Unheard Melodies: The Songs of Uncle Tom's Children." *Phylon* 40.3 (1979): 278–90.

Greenspan, Ezra. *Walt Whitman and the American Reader.* Cambridge: Cambridge UP, 1990.

Griffler, Keith P. *Front Line of Freedom: African Americans and the Forging of the Underground Railroad in the Ohio Valley.* Lexington: UP of Kentucky, 2004.

Hagedorn, Ann. *Beyond the River: The Untold Story of the Heroes of the Underground Railroad.* New York: Simon and Schuster, 2002.

Hannum, Howard L. "'Scared Sick Looking at It': A Reading of Nick Adams in the Published Stories." *Twentieth Century Literature* 47.1 (2001): 92–113.

Harding, Walter. *The Days of Henry Thoreau: A Biography.* 1962. Princeton, NJ: Princeton UP, 1992.

Hariot, Thomas. "A briefe and true report of the new found land of Virginia." Quinn 1: 317–87.

Hawthorne, Nathaniel. *The American Notebooks.* Centenary Edition of the Works of Nathaniel Hawthorne. Vol. 8. Ed. Claude M. Simpson. Columbus: Ohio State UP, 1972.

———. *Mosses from an Old Manse.* 1846. Centenary Edition of the Works of

Nathaniel Hawthorne. Vol. 10. Ed. J. Donald Crowley. Columbus: Ohio State UP, 1974.

Heat-Moon, William Least. *River-Horse: The Logbook of a Boat Across America.* Boston: Houghton Mifflin, 1999.

Hedrick, Joan D. *Harriet Beecher Stowe: A Life.* New York: Oxford UP, 1994.

Hemingway, Ernest. *In Our Time.* 1925. New York: Charles Scribner's Sons, 1958.

Hendrick, George, and Willene Hendrick. *Fleeing for Freedom: Stories of the Underground Railroad as Told by Levi Coffin and William Still.* Chicago: Ivan R. Dee, 2004.

Heraclitus. *Fragments.* Trans. T. M. Robinson. Toronto: U of Toronto P, 1987.

Herendeen, Wyman H. *From Landscape to Literature: The River and the Myth of Geography.* Pittsburgh: Duquesne UP, 1986.

Hess, Karl, Jr. "John Wesley Powell and the Unmaking of the West." *Environmental History* 2.1 (1997): 7–28.

Higdon, David Leon. "Conrad and Mark Twain: A Newly Discovered Essay." *Journal of Modern Literature* 12.2 (1985): 354–61.

Holman, C. Hugh, and William Harmon. *A Handbook to Literature.* 6th ed. New York: Macmillan, 1992.

Howard, William. "Richard Wright's Flood Stories and the Great Mississippi Flood of 1927: Social and Historical Backgrounds." *Southern Literary Journal* 16.2 (1984): 44–62.

Howarth, William. *Thoreau in the Mountains.* New York: Farrar, Straus and Giroux, 1982.

Howe, Lawrence. "Transcending the Limits of Experience: Mark Twain's *Life on the Mississippi.*" *American Literature: A Journal of Literary History, Criticism, and Bibliography* 63.3 (1991): 420–39.

Hudson, J. Blaine. *Fugitive Slaves and the Underground Railroad in the Kentucky Borderland.* Jefferson, NC: McFarland, 2002.

Hughes, Langston. *Autobiography: The Big Sea.* The Collected Works of Langston Hughes. Vol. 13. Ed. Joseph McLaren. Columbia: U of Missouri P, 2002.

———. *The Poems: 1921–1940.* The Collected Works of Langston Hughes. Vol. 1. Ed. Arnold Rampersad. Columbia: U of Missouri P, 2001.

Hunt, Charles B. "Geologic History of the Colorado River." United States Geological Survey, *The Colorado River Region* 59–130.

Hutcherson, Dudley R. "Mark Twain as a Pilot." *American Literature* 12 (1940): 353–55.

Hutchinson, George. *The Harlem Renaissance in Black and White*. Cambridge, MA: Belknap P of Harvard UP, 1995.

Hutchinson, Jamie. "'The Lapse of the Current': Thoreau's Historical Vision in *A Week on the Concord and Merrimack Rivers*." *ESQ* 25.4 (1979): 211–23.

Hynes, H. B. N. *The Ecology of Running Waters*. Toronto: U of Toronto P, 1970.

Jaffe, Ina. "George Washington Crossing the Delaware." Natl. Public Radio. Feb. 18, 2002. http://www.npr.org/programs/morning/features/patc/georgewashington/.

JanMohamed, Abdul R. *The Death-Bound-Subject: Richard Wright's Archaeology of Death*. Durham, NC: Duke UP, 2005.

Jemie, Onwuchekwa. *Langston Hughes: An Introduction to the Poetry*. New York: Columbia UP, 1976.

Johnson, Lynck C. "*A Week on the Concord and Merrimack Rivers*." *The Cambridge Companion to Henry David Thoreau*. Ed. Joel Myerson. Cambridge: Cambridge UP, 1995. 40–56.

———. *Thoreau's Complex Weave: The Writing of "A Week on the Concord and Merrimack Rivers."* Charlottesville: UP of Virginia, 1986.

Jones, Prudence J. *Reading Rivers in Roman Literature and Culture*. Lanham, MD: Lexington Books, 2005.

Jongh, James de. "The Poet Speaks of Places: A Close Reading of Langston Hughes's Literary Use of Place." *A Historical Guide to Langston Hughes*. Ed. Stephen C. Tracy. Oxford: Oxford UP, 2004. 65–84.

Karlstrom, K. E., et al. "Paleoproterozoic Rocks of the Granite Gorges." Beus and Morales 9–38.

Kieffer, Susan Werner. "Hydraulics and Geomorphology of the Colorado River in the Grand Canyon." Beus and Morales 275–312.

Kilbourne, Frederick. "Thoreau and the White Mountains." *Appalachia* 14 (1919): 355–67.

Killingsworth, M. Jimmie. *The Cambridge Introduction to Walt Whitman*. Cambridge: Cambridge UP, 2007.

———. *Walt Whitman and the Earth: A Study in Ecopoetics*. Iowa City: U of Iowa P, 2004.

Kinnamon, Kenneth. *The Emergence of Richard Wright: A Study in Literature and Society*. Urbana: U of Illinois P, 1972.

Kirkham, E. Bruce. *The Building of "Uncle Tom's Cabin."* Knoxville: U of Tennessee P, 1977.

Koch, Kenneth. *Bertha and Other Plays.* New York: Grove, 1966.

Kuppermann, Karen Ordahl. "A Continent Revealed: Assimilations of the Shape & Possibilities of North America's East Coast, 1524–1610." *North American Exploration.* Ed. John Logan Allen. Lincoln: U of Nebraska P, 1997. 1: 344–99.

Lane, John. *Chattooga: Descending into the Myth of Deliverance River.* Athens: U of Georgia P, 2004.

Lane, Ralph. "Discourse on the First Colony." Quinn 1: 255–94.

Laughlin, Rosemary M. "Anne Bradstreet: Poet in Search of Form." *American Literature* 42.1 (1970): 1–17.

Lemay, J. A. Leo. *The American Dream of Captain John Smith.* Charlottesville: UP of Virginia, 1991.

León, Luis D. *La Llorona's Children: Religion, Life, and Death in the U.S.-Mexican Borderlands.* Berkeley: U of California P, 2004.

Leopold, Luna B. *A View of the River.* Cambridge, MA: Harvard UP, 1994.

Leutze, Emanuel Gottlieb. *George Washington Crossing the Delaware.* 1851. Oil on canvas. Metropolitan Museum of Art, New York.

Lewis, Meriwether, and William Clark. *The Journals of Lewis and Clark.* Ed. Bernard De Voto. New York: Houghton Mifflin, 1953.

Loving, Jerome. *Walt Whitman: The Song of Himself.* Berkeley: U of California P, 1999.

Lowell, James Russell. "A Week on the Concord and Merrimack Rivers." *Massachusetts Quarterly Review* Dec. 1849. Rpt. in *Pertaining to Thoreau: A Gathering of Ten Significant Nineteenth-Century Opinions.* Ed. Samuel Arthur Jones. Hartford, CT: Transcendental Books, 1970. 16.

Lowry, Richard S. *"Littery Man": Mark Twain and Modern Authorship.* New York: Oxford UP, 1996.

Lucchitta, Ivo. *Canyon Maker: A Geological History of the Colorado River.* Flagstaff: Museum of Northern Arizona, 1988.

Lyon, Thomas J. *This Incomparable Land: A Guide to American Nature Writing.* Minneapolis: Milkweed, 2001.

———. "The Western Nature Essay since 1970." Taylor et al., 1246–53.

Maclean, Norman. *A River Runs Through It and Other Stories.* Chicago: U of Chicago P, 1976.

Malone, David H. "Analysis of Mark Twain's Novel *Life on the Mississippi.*" *The Frontier in American History and Literature.* Ed. Hans Galinski. Frankfurt:

Verlag Moritz Deisterweg, 1960. 80–93.

McAdow, Ron. *The Concord, Sudbury, and Assabet Rivers: A Guide to Canoeing, Wildlife, and History*. 1990. 2nd ed. Marlborough, MA: Bliss Publishing, 2000.

McCammack, Brian. "Competence, Power, and the Nostalgic Romance of Piloting in Mark Twain's *Life on the Mississippi*." *Southern Literary Journal* 38.2 (2006): 1–18.

McCarthy, B. Eugene. "Models of History in Richard Wright's *Uncle Tom's Children*." *Black American Literature Forum* 25.4 (1991): 729–43.

McElrath, Joseph R., Jr., and Allan P. Robb, eds. Introduction. *The Complete Works of Anne Bradstreet*. Boston: Twayne Publishers, 1981.

McKee, Christopher. "Thoreau's First Visit to the White Mountains." *Appalachia* 31 (1956): 199–209.

McKee, Edwin D. "Stratified Rocks of the Grand Canyon." United States Geological Survey, *The Colorado River Region* 23–58.

McPhee, John. Introduction. *A Week on the Concord and Merrimack Rivers*. By Henry David Thoreau. Ed. Carl F. Hovde, William L. Howarth, and Elizabeth Hall Witherell. Princeton, NJ: Princeton UP, 1980. ix–xlvi.

Michaels, Walter Benn. "The Road to Vietnam." *MLN* 94.5 (1979): 1173–75.

Montgomery, Constance Cappel. *Hemingway in Michigan*. New York: Fleet, 1966.

Montgomery, Marion. "The New Romantic vs. the Old: Mark Twain's Dilemma in *Life on the Mississippi*." *Mississippi Quarterly: The Journal of Southern Culture* 11 (1958): 79–82.

Moore, Kathleen Dean. *Riverwalking: Reflections on Moving Water*. New York: Lyons and Burford, 1995.

Mullen, Edward J., ed. *Critical Essays of Langston Hughes*. Boston: G. K. Hall, 1986.

———. Introduction. Mullen 1–35.

Murphey, Murray G. "John Wesley Powell: *Exploration of the Colorado River*." *Landmarks of American Writing*. Ed. Hennig Cohen. New York: Basic Books, 1969. 194–206.

Narbeshuber, Lisa. "Hemingway's *In Our Time*: Cubism, Conservation, and the Suspension of Identification." *Hemingway Review* 25.2 (2006): 9–28.

National Gallery of Art. "The Collection." http://www.nga.gov.

The New World. Dir. Terrence Malick. New Line Cinema, 2005.

Nye, Russell B. "Eliza Crossing the Ice—A Reappraisal of Sources." *Critical Essays on Harriet Beecher Stowe*. Ed. Elizabeth Ammons. Boston: G. K. Hall, 1980. 98–101.

O'Brien, Sarah Mary. "'I, Also, Am in Michigan': Pastoralism of Mind in Hemingway's 'Big Two-Hearted River.'" *Hemingway Review* 28.2 (2009): 66–86.

O'Hara, Frank. *Selected Poems*. Ed. Mark Ford. New York: Knopf, 2008.

Okafor, Clement Abiaziem. "Joseph Conrad and Chinua Achebe: Two Antipodal Portraits of Africa." *Journal of Black Studies* 19.1 (1988): 17–28.

Oktenberg, Adrian. "From the Bottom Up: Three Radicals of the Thirties." *A Gift of Tongues: Critical Challenges in Contemporary American Poetry*. Ed. Marie Harris and Kathleen Aguero. Athens: U of Georgia P, 1987. 83–111.

Oliver, Charles M. *Critical Companion to Walt Whitman*. New York: Facts on File, 2006.

Palmer, Tim. *America by Rivers*. 1996. Washington, DC: Island, 1998.

Paredes, Américo. *Folklore and Culture on the Texas-Mexican Border*. Ed. Richard Bauman. Austin: U of Texas P, 1993.

Parker, John P. *His Promised Land*. Ed. Stuart Seely Sprague. New York: W. W. Norton, 1996.

Parry, Elwood C., III. *The Art of Thomas Cole: Ambition and Imagination*. Newark: U of Delaware P, 1988.

Peck, H. Daniel. *Thoreau's Morning Work: Memory and Perception in "A Week on the Concord and Merrimack Rivers," the Journal, and "Walden."* New Haven, CT: Yale UP, 1990.

Perez, Domino Renee. *There Was a Woman: La Llorona from Folklore to Popular Culture*. Austin: U of Texas P, 2008.

Perloff, Marjorie. *Frank O'Hara: Poet among Painters*. 1977. Chicago: U of Chicago P, 1998.

Pocahontas. Dir. Mike Gabriel and Eric Goldberg. Walt Disney Pictures, 1995.

Powell, John Wesley. "The Cañons of the Colorado" (third paper). *Scribner's Monthly, an Illustrated Magazine for the People* Mar. 1875: 523–37. This series ran in the Jan., Feb., and Mar. issues of 1875. Later articles were titled "An Overland Trip to the Grand Cañon" (Oct.) and "The Ancient Province of Tusayan" (Dec.).

———. *The Exploration of the Colorado River and Its Canyons*. 1895. New York: Penguin Nature Library, 1987.

———. *Exploration of the Colorado River of the West and Its Tributaries, Explored in 1869, 1870, 1871, and 1872, Under the Direction of the Secretary of the Smithsonian Institution.* Washington, DC: Government Printing Office, 1875.

———. "The Larger Import of Scientific Education." *Popular Science Monthly* 26.4 (1885): 456.

———. "Letters of Major J. W. Powell to the Chicago Tribune." Ed. William Culp Darrah. *Utah Historical Quarterly* 15 (1947): 73–88.

———. *Outlines of the Philosophy of the North American Indians.* New York: Douglas Taylor, 1877.

———. *Truth and Error; or, The Science of Intellection.* Chicago: Open Court, 1898.

Powers, Ron. *Dangerous Water.* New York: Basic Books, 1999.

———. *Mark Twain: A Life.* New York: Free, 2005.

Pyne, Stephen J. *Dutton's Point: An Intellectual History of the Grand Canyon.* Grand Canyon Historical Association, 1982.

Quinn, David Beers. *The Roanoke Voyages 1584–1590: Documents to Illustrate the English Voyages to North America under the Patent Granted to Walter Raleigh in 1584.* 2 vols. New York: Dover, 1991.

Rabbitt, Mary C. "John Wesley Powell: Pioneer Statesman of Federal Science." United States Geological Survey, *The Colorado River Region* 1–22.

Rampersad, Arnold. *The Life of Langston Hughes.* Vol. 1. Oxford: Oxford UP, 1988.

Rebolledo, Tey Diana. *Women Singing in the Snow: A Cultural Analysis of Chicana Literature.* Tucson: U of Arizona P, 1995.

Rebolledo, Tey Diana, and Eliana S. Rivero, eds. *Infinite Divisions: An Anthology of Chicana Literature.* Tucson: U of Arizona P, 1993.

Reynolds, David S. *Walt Whitman.* Oxford: Oxford UP, 2005.

———. *Walt Whitman's America: A Cultural Biography.* New York: Knopf, 1995.

Ronald, Ann. "Edward Abbey." Taylor et al. 604–09.

Rzóska, Julian. *On the Nature of Rivers, with Case Stories of Nile, Zaire & Amazon.* The Hague: Junk, 1978.

Saran, A. K. *Environmental Psychology.* New Delhi: Anmol, 2005.

Scheese, Don. "*Desert Solitaire:* Counter-Friction to the Machine in the Garden." *The Ecocriticism Reader: Landmarks in Literary Ecology.* Ed. Cheryll Glotfelty and Harold Fromm. Athens: U of Georgia P, 1996. 303–22.

Scott, Jerry, and Jim Borgman. "Zits." Comic strip. King Features, Aug. 15, 2006.

Seelye, John. *Beautiful Machine: Rivers and the Republican Plan, 1755–1825.* New

York: Oxford UP, 1991.

———. *Prophetic Waters: The River in Early American Life and Literature.* New York: Oxford UP, 1977.

Shattuck, Lemuel. *A History of the Town of Concord; Middlesex County, Massachusetts, from Its Earliest Settlement to 1832.* Boston: Russell, Odiorne, 1835.

Slovic, Scott. *Seeking Awareness in American Nature Writing.* Salt Lake City: U of Utah P, 1992.

Smith, Hazel. *Hyperscapes in the Poetry of Frank O'Hara: Difference, Homosexuality, Topography.* Liverpool: Liverpool UP, 2000.

Smith, Henry Nash. *Mark Twain: The Development of a Writer.* Cambridge, MA: Belknap P of Harvard UP, 1962.

Smith, John. *The Complete Works of Captain John Smith.* 3 vols. Ed. Philip L. Barbour. Chapel Hill: U of North Carolina P, 1986.

Spurr, Daniel. *River of Forgotten Days: A Journey Down the Mississippi in Search of La Salle.* New York: Henry Holt, 1998.

Stanford, Ann. *Anne Bradstreet, the Worldly Puritan: An Introduction to Her Poetry.* New York: B. Franklin, 1975.

Stanton, Robert Brewster. *Colorado River Controversies.* Ed. James M. Chalfant. New York: Dodd, Mead, 1932.

Stegner, Wallace. *Beyond the Hundredth Meridian: John Wesley Powell and the Second Opening of the West.* 1954. New York: Penguin, 1992.

———. Introduction. Powell, *The Exploration of the Colorado River and Its Canyons* vii–xii.

Stephens, Hal G., and Eugene M. Shoemaker. *In the Footsteps of John Wesley Powell: An Album of Comparative Photographs of the Green and Colorado Rivers, 1871–72 and 1968.* Denver: Powell Society, 1987.

Stevens, Larry. *The Colorado River in Grand Canyon: A Comprehensive Guide to Its Natural and Human History.* Flagstaff: Red Lake Books, 1983.

———. "The 67 Elephant Theory or Learning to Boat Big Water Hydraulics." *River Runner* 5.1 (1985): 24–25.

Stowe, Harriet Beecher. *Uncle Tom's Cabin; or, Life Among the Lowly.* 1852. New York: Harper and Row, 1965.

Sumner, John C. "J. C. Sumner's Journal, July 6–August 31, 1869." Ed. William Culp Darrah. *Utah Historical Quarterly* 15 (1947): 113–24.

Tauber, Alfred I. *Henry David Thoreau and the Moral Agency of Knowing.* Berkeley: U of California P, 2001.

Taylor, J. Golden, et al., eds. *A Literary History of the American West*. Fort Worth: Texas Christian UP, 1987.

Ten Who Dared. Dir. William Beaudine. Walt Disney Pictures, 1960.

Thomann, Robert V. "The Delaware River—A Study in Water Quality Management." *River Ecology and Man*. Ed. Ray T. Oglesby, Clarence A. Carlson, and James A. McCann. New York: Academic, 1972.

Thoreau, Henry D. *Journal*. Vol. 1. Ed. Elizabeth Hall Witherell et al. Princeton, NJ: Princeton UP, 1981.

———. *A Week on the Concord and Merrimack Rivers*. 1849. Ed. Carl F. Hovde, William L. Howarth, and Elizabeth Hall Witherell. Princeton, NJ: Princeton UP, 1980.

———. *The Writings of Henry D. Thoreau: Journal*. Ed. J. C. Broderick. Vol. 3. Princeton, NJ: Princeton UP, 1990.

Tilton, Robert S. *Pocahontas: The Evolution of an American Narrative*. Cambridge: Cambridge UP, 1994.

Timmons, J. Michael, et al. "Geologic Structure of the Grand Canyon Supergroup." Beus and Morales 76–89.

Turner, Victor. *From Ritual to Theatre: The Human Seriousness of Play*. New York: Performing Arts Journal, 1982.

Tuttleton, James W. "The Problematic Texts of Richard Wright." *Hudson Review* 45.2 (1992): 261–71.

Twain, Mark. *Adventures of Huckleberry Finn*. 1885. Ed. Gerald Graff and James Phelan. Boston: Bedford Books, 1995.

———. *Life on the Mississippi*. 1883. New York: Penguin, 1984.

———. *Mark Twain's Autobiography*. Ed. Albert Bigelow Paine. 2 vols. New York: Harper, 1924.

———. "Old Times on the Mississippi." *Atlantic Monthly* Jan.–Aug. 1875.

United States Dept. of Transportation. Research and Innovative Technology Administration, Bureau of Transportation Statistics. http://www.transtats.bts.gov/bordercrossing.aspx.

United States Geological Survey. *The Colorado River Region and John Wesley Powell*. Washington, DC: Government Printing Office, 1969.

———. "Concord River Drainage Basin—Surface Water." ma.water.usgs.gov/basins/concordsfw.htm.

VanGelder, Robert. "Four Tragic Tales." *New York Times Book Review* Apr. 3, 1938: 7, 16. Rpt. in *Richard Wright: The Critical Reception*. Ed. John M. Reilly.

New York: Burt Franklin, 1978. 11.

Van Noy, Rick. *Surveying the Interior: Literary Cartographies and the Sense of Place*. Reno: U of Nevada P, 2003.

Wagner, Jean. *Black Poets of the United States: From Paul Laurance Dunbar to Langston Hughes*. Trans. Kenneth Douglas. Urbana: U of Illinois P, 1973.

Walker, Margaret. *Richard Wright: Daemonic Genius*. New York: Warner, 1988.

Walt Disney's Ten Who Dared. New York: Dell, 1960.

Ward, Jerry W., and Robert J. Butler. *The Richard Wright Encyclopedia*. Westport, CT: Greenwood, 2008.

Warner, Charles Dudley. *Captain John Smith: A Study of His Life and Writings*. New York: Henry Holt, 1881.

Washington, George. *The Papers of George Washington*. Revolutionary War Series. Vol. 7. Ed. Philander D. Chase et al. Charlottesville: UP of Virginia, 1983–95.

Whitman, Walt. *Leaves of Grass*. Ed. Harold W. Blodgett and Sculley Bradley. New York: New York UP, 1965.

———. *Walt Whitman's Poems*. Ed. Gay Wilson Allen and Charles T. Davis. New York: New York UP, 1955.

Wierich, Jochen. "Struggling through History: Emanuel Leutze, Hegel, and Empire." *American Art* 15.2 (2001): 53–71.

Wild, Peter. *The Opal Desert: Explorations of Fantasy and Reality in the American Southwest*. Austin: U of Texas P, 1999.

Worster, Donald. *A River Running West: The Life of John Wesley Powell*. New York: Oxford UP, 2001.

Wright, Richard. "Down by the Riverside." 1936. *Uncle Tom's Children*. New York: Harper and Row, 1965. 54–102.

———. "Forerunner and Ambassador." *New Republic* July–Dec. 1940: 600–01. Rpt. in Mullen 67–68.

Zwinger, Ann. *Downcanyon: A Naturalist Explores the Colorado River through the Grand Canyon*. Tucson: U of Arizona P, 1995.

———. *Run, River, Run: A Naturalist's Journey Down One of the Great Rivers of the West*. New York: Harper and Row, 1975.

Index of Rivers, Writers, and Artists

AMERICAN LAND
AND LIFE SERIES